Uniforms

OF THE

British Army

a PRIVATE, 1742.

b 38TH FOOT. GRENADIER, 1751.

c 38TH GRENADIER, 1768.

d 38TH 1ST STAFFORDSHIRE REGT. OFFICER, 1792.

e 38TH SERJEANT, 1812.

f 38TH OFFICER, LEVEE DRESS, 1826.

g THE SOUTH STAFFORDSHIRE REGIMENT.

h 80TH STAFFORDSHIRE VOLUNTEERS. PRIVATE, 1793.

i 80TH OFFICER, 1840.

j 80TH PRIVATE, 1852.

k 80TH OFFICER, 1860

l 80TH PRIVATE, 1864.

m 80TH OFFICER, 1875.

P. Simnin.

17.

Plate 42

RICHARD SIMKIN'S

Uniforms
OF THE
British Army

Infantry, Royal Artillery, Royal Engineers
and other corps

W. Y. CARMAN

From the collection of Captain K. J. Douglas-Morris, RN

Webb & Bower
EXETER, ENGLAND

Frontispiece:
42.
**The South Staffordshire Regiment
(late 38th and 80th)**
a   1742, private 38th
b   1751, grenadier 38th
c   1768, grenadier 38th
d   1792, officer 38th
e   1812, sergeant 38th
f   1826, officer levée dress 38th
g   (c.1905) officer in frock coat,
    officer full dress mounted
h   1793, private 80th
i   1840, officer 80th
j   1852, private 80th
k   1860, officer 80th
l   1864, private marching order
    80th
m   1875, officer 80th

Page 6:
21.
10th Foot, 1685, officer

First published in Great Britain 1985 by

Webb and Bower (Publishers) Limited
9 Colleton Crescent, Exeter, Devon EX2 4BY

Designed by Malcolm Couch
Plates photographed by Stephen Angeloni

British Library Cataloguing in Publication Data

Carman, W.Y.
    Richard Simkin's uniforms of the British
    Army: the infantry regiments.
    1. Great Britain, *Army* ——Infantry——
    Uniforms——History
    I. Title   II. Simkin, Richard
    356'.186   UC485.G7

ISBN 0-86350-031-5

Colour origination by Peninsular Repro Services Limited, Exeter
Typeset in Great Britain by August Filmsetting Limited,
Haydock, Merseyside

Printed and bound in Hong Kong by Mandarin Offset Ltd

Contents

10th REGIMENT OF FOOT.
(The only British Infantry Regiment that wore a Blue Uniform.)
1685.

Plate 21

Plates

INTRODUCTION

The aim of this book is to cover the uniforms depicted in the water-colours painted by Richard Simkin from the Douglas-Morris Collection less, of course, those of the Cavalry and the Royal Horse Artillery, which appeared in *Uniforms of the British Army: the Cavalry Regiments* (Exeter, 1982).

This book begins with two august bodies – the Gentlemen-at-Arms and the Royal Company of Archers – which have remained ever since as the personal guards of the Sovereign on special occasions in England and Scotland respectively.

Better known are the men of the Household Brigade. The Life Guards and the Blues and Royals (Royal Horse Guards and 1st Dragoons) are the mounted part of this Brigade, and the Foot Guards carry out the dismounted duties on ceremonial occasions. The Grenadier Guards, the Coldstream Guards, the Scots Guards and the Irish Guards all existed in the period which Simkin depicted but the Welsh Guards who were raised during the First World War are not included.

As in the case of the previous book, the water-colours available do not cover every regiment then in existence. In the case of Infantry of the Line there had been 109 regiments of Foot, and this selection has thus been made from the large group paintings and the small single or limited-group pictures in order to cover as many regiments as possible and at the same time to depict the evolution of uniform distinctions throughout the centuries. To compensate for the many missing regiments, a brief history and outline of all the 109 pre-1881 regiments has been given. Each entry includes the title from the raising of the regiment and takes in the changes, not only up to Simkin's time but also up to the Army of today, with the amalgamations and reductions so that a serving soldier may be able to trace his 'ancestors' and their uniforms.

The largest part of the British Army had been the Infantry of the Line which increased in battalions and regiments throughout the years, frequently to suffer reduction and disbandment when peace was achieved. The newest and younger regiments were the first to go but the overall numbers gradually increased, rising to 109 regiments in 1880, after which many were combined and reduced to 69, and were even more drastically reduced in modern times.

The many special and individual differences that appeared for cavalry regiments were not to be seen in normal infantry regiments who originally dressed in a similar style, differing by colour distinctions and fighting equipment. Therefore one regiment frequently looked like another, which means that if each regiment was described individually and fully here there would be much monotonous and repetitive reading. So the infantry section begins with the general development of units and dress and each major variation is then treated in a separate section.

Thus the introduction of grenadiers and fusiliers merits a special subject as does light infantry, both as companies and as regiments. The employment of Highlanders in the eighteenth century wearing their own Scottish dress has little relation to the dress of line infantry as was also the case for the later Lowland regiments, and so they have sections on their own variation of a Scottish dress. The introduction of green-clad riflemen in the eighteenth century brought a new type of uniform to the British Army and they remain today as the Royal Green Jackets with their own story to be told.

With the gradual acceptance that a red coat might not be the best fighting garment came the introduction of service drab or khaki which eventually took over in all units and it thus needs a special chapter. But these groupings do not exhaust the variations of infantry dress and there are special aspects such as those of drummers, buglers, fifers, bandsmen and pioneers, all of which demand their own treatment, as do the distinctions of rank, not only of the officers but also of the other ranks. So these and other aspects are dealt with in detail even though they may have general application.

The Royal Horse Artillery which operated with the Cavalry was illustrated and described in the first volume, but the more ancient and much larger part of the Royal Artillery which operated with the Infantry in garrison defence and siege work is to be considered here, their dress being somewhat similar to that of the Infantry (even though in the Army List the Royal Artillery takes precedence), whereas the uniform of the Royal Horse Artillery tended towards that of the light cavalry.

The Board of Ordnance (for many years a military force not part of the regular Army) included among its men not only artillery but also engineers, and was at first only an officer body. To perform the actual hard work controlled by the engineers were artificers and Sappers and Miners (whose story is told up to the time when all was combined into the large Corps of Royal Engineers).

To convey the bulky material needed by an army in the field were such units as the Corps of Waggoners, the Military Train and later the Army Service Corps, whose story and uniforms are described. There are other corps but as no water-colours by R. Simkin are in this collection, they are not mentioned.

It is unfortunate that no collection of Simkin's working material has come to light, whether sketches or water-colours obviously 'taken from life', although he must have made hundreds of roughs and original studies. The repetition of poses and of uniforms suggests that many tracings were used for the basic figures, and were altered or amended to depict a special regiment not only by himself but by his helpers, like his daughters. Some modern collectors criticize the vast quantity of his work which appears in print or in water-colours, but were it not for this prolific and cheap method of reproduction, much information would not be available today. It seems that photographic outlines were used in some cases and the story is that his helpers coloured these basic types and that when they were finished to Richard Simkin's standard and approval it was only then that he signed them, perhaps adding his own touches. It is to be regretted that the date of execution is often omitted but it may be reasoned that if his work was being retailed in galleries then a picture that appeared to be 'out of date' might not have sold.

Simkin was willing to turn his hand to any request. Apart from direct sales to the public, he executed commissions from regiments, either for display in the mess or elsewhere or to illustrate a historical record. His work appeared in periodicals and some recruiting posters seem to be his, although the workers on the lithographic stones may have lost some of his characteristic features. He was obviously a diligent worker and created his own sphere of uniform production, though he lacked the artistic ability of some of his military contemporaries. He admired the work of Orlando Norie but only rarely reached his quality. R. Wymer, by comparison, may have had a higher technical standard but was erratic in his production and never challenged Simkin. Of course R. Caton Woodville was famous, but as an oil-painter (and not always accurate in his details), but that was not a field for Simkin, and neither was military portraiture. But Simkin's output and results were much above others like Stansell and Brennan, two artists who made a living in the military field. It is important to appreciate that Simkin made a vast amount of information available with a higher than average standard of quality and detail.

It is interesting to look into the sources which Simkin may have used. Although some of his work is obviously based on personal observation, in many cases the information was given to him by specialists in the field. Even in this book some pictures are

Gentleman-at-Arms
1911.

Plate 1a

Royal Company of Archers
Archer 1911.

Plate 1b

1ST REGIMENT OF FOOT GUARDS,
PIKEMAN – 1660.

a

1ST REGIMENT OF FOOT GUARDS.
SERGEANT – 1742.

b

Plate 2

acknowledged to be after Harry Payne, no doubt because Simkin was commissioned to do so. The many pictures of the Royal Artillery are from the illustrations in the *History of the Dress of . . . the Artillery* by R. J. Macdonald and the uniforms of the Artificers and the Sappers and Miners are from the plates in the books by T. W. J. Connolly. The Highland regiments no doubt would have supplied him with the intricate details of the uniforms that they commissioned.

When Simkin had to find uniforms of certain periods he often took a well-known print and changed the facings or lace. He would have found the task of researching time-consuming and a financial drain; therefore he chose the simplest and easiest methods for a quick result. Today military research has grown into almost a science and whereas in the past a passable depiction might do, in modern days a minor error could call for general condemnation from certain 'experts'. However, Simkin's vast output remains an invaluable resource.

Preceding pages:
1*a*
Gentleman-at-Arms, 1911
1*b*
Royal Company of Archers, 1911

2.
1st Foot Guards
a   1660, pikeman
b   1742, sergeant

Gentlemen-at-Arms

It was Henry VII who in 1485 created a special bodyguard which still exists today as the Yeomen of the Guard. When Henry VIII succeeded to the throne in 1509 he created a new Royal Body Guard which was mounted and drawn from the gentry. Originally they were known as the 'King's Speres' but by 1540 the corps was named the 'Band of Gentlemen Pensioners' in imitation of those serving the French king and known as the *Gentilhommes de l'Hotel du Royou Pensionnaires*'. In William IV's reign the name was changed to the 'Gentlemen-at-Arms' and it has also been known by every sovereign since as 'Our Nearest Guard and Principal Military Corps of Our Household'. Although it was in the Army Lists up to the First World War it is not today, despite the fact that all the Gentlemen-at-Arms hold a military commission and have honourable service (or a title).

At first, armour was worn and the men carried spears or lances but later when the numbers performing dismounted duties increased from forty to a hundred, they wore livery gowns of silk and carried 'poll-axes' when they went before the King. Their dress was the height of fashion, sometimes in white and sometimes in black but by 1551 they were wearing red damask. Later the green and white, the colour of the Tudor house, was worn. The French king Charles V said that his Honourable Band of fifty Gentlemen Pensioners were not obliged to wear any habit or livery other than such as they themselves considered fit. At the Coronation of Queen Anne in 1702, the Band of Pensioners were 'clad in scarlet cloth with gold lace, holding halberds with gold tops like pickaxes'. When in mourning or at funerals, black trimmings and under-garments were worn. Scarlet stockings were ordered for birthdays but in 1736 the stockings were to be of light grey or white, an order repeated in 1745. Obviously the main dress changed with the fashions, but little detail has come to light.

In 1805 new clothing was ordered for the Installation of the Garter: '[the] Pattern of the Epaulette, Lapelles, etc., to be seen at ——. The Hats to have the same Lace as the Coat, and a white feather in lieu of a Red one.' Thus a military type of dress was being worn. A shako seems to have been approved by George IV, and this type of head-dress appears in the Dubois Drahonet oil-painting of 1833 where the red coat is double-breasted and the cuff has a three-buttoned cuff flap. At the funeral of George IV in 1830 the Band of Pensioners are said to have worn 'Guards uniform' with black breeches and buckles as a sign of mourning but a woodcut in the periodical the *Mirror* gives them fore-and-aft cocked hats with large plumes. By 1834 they were being ordered to wear dark blue trousers with gold lace stripes from October to May and white trousers from May to October, the latter to be of the same material and pattern as the officers of the Guards.

But in 1838 Her Majesty Queen Victoria commanded an alteration in the uniform of the corps; the coat was now to be single-breasted with skirts the same as those worn by heavy dragoons, cocked hat with Star loop, Cavalry bullion, tassels and plume. The coat had gold lace but the badge of the Portcullis on each side of the collar was silver. The change to a cavalry helmet was approved in August 1848 when it was noted in the *Illustrated London News* of 8 March: 'a new helmet of classical design; it is of burnished gold, highly-embossed, and ornamented with the Royal Arms and a star of burnished silver in front; the whole surmounted by a white plume' (this was made of the famous swan-feathers). Another change was made in 1850 when a cavalry sash was introduced instead of the girdle and in 1867 the height of the stem of the plume was to be nine inches with the feather seventeen inches long.

The painting by Richard Simkin dated 1911 depicts the uniform (1a) as it had evolved and the *Dress Worn at His Majesty's Court* issued with the authority of the Lord Chamberlain, describes it as follows: 'coatee, scarlet cloth, single-breasted. Blue velvet collar, cuffs and turnbacks on the skirts. Gold embroidery on collar and cuffs. Gold embroidered Wreath and Crown and Portcullis in silver on back skirts. Nine buttons down front and two at waist behind. Skirts lined blue silk.' The epaulettes are of gold bullion with the Tudor portcullis embroidered in silver; gold aiguillettes for officers only; the helmet is as described above with an eighteen-inch-long plume; and there are many other minute details.

The King's Body Guard for Scotland (Royal Company of Archers)

The origin of this body, according to its own history, 'if not quite lost in the mists of antiquity' is involved in considerable obscurity. However the Army Lists before the First World War say that it 'originated in the year 1676, re-constituted in 1703'. It was at that first date that Edinburgh's citizens formed themselves into 'a particular society and company for Archery and Shutting with Bowes and Arrowes, to be called His Majesty's Company of Archers in time comeing'. A letter to Queen Anne in October 1703 requested Her Majesty to grant a new establishment of the Royal Company of Archers, which was granted the next year.

The practice of archery and the shooting for prizes continued, but it was not until 1822 when King George IV visited Edinburgh that the Royal Company of Archers acted as his Body Guard. In 1825 a court dress was proposed for the Company and the King presented the Captain-General with a gold stick, which gave him permission to appear at His Majesty's courts. There were further gifts of two silver sticks and seven ebony sticks for other officers, granted by King William IV and Queen Victoria. Practically every notable Scottish family was represented in the Royal Company of Archers and it was considered most exclusive – each archer had to dwell in Scotland and be of noble birth. There was also a minimum height requirement of 5 feet 8 inches, but despite these limitations there were up to 400 bowmen who could be mustered, a much greater number than the Gentlemen-at-Arms.

In the beginning no special uniform was worn, 'the Company's Seal and Arms on their Hatts or Bonnetts' being sufficient. In Queen Anne's reign tartan lined with white shalloon was approved for the 'habit' and the blue bonnet had a cockade of white and green ribbons. The tartan was red or 'dress' but later in the century it became the same as that of the '42nd' Regiment, which was a hunting tartan both darker and greener.

In 1789 a new uniform with a short green frock with yellow-gilt buttons was worn with white waistcoat, breeches and stockings. The shooting uniform was the short tartan jacket ornamented with blue, green and white silk. The blue bonnet had green and white ribbons with a painted badge which included St Andrew. The metal button carried the design of a Royal Crown, a pair of crossed arrows with a thistle below. The waistcoat and breeches were white cloth with small metal buttons. There were also white silk stockings and small black cloth half-gaiters, the latter for the shooting dress. The distinctions for officers were the different coloured feathers in the bonnet.

When George IV made his famous visit to Scotland in 1822 and brought the great upsurge in fashion of Scottish dress, the Company of Archers did duty in green tartan for both jackets and trousers. Their dark green bonnets carried single long dark feathers. All wore a broad white sash over the right shoulder and held the long yew bow in the left hand. Just above the low shoes could be seen the red and white hose.

In 1825 a Court dress was proposed and the Captain-General of the Company was given a Gold Stick so that he might appear at His Majesty's Court in London. The new Court dress had a single-breasted scarlet coat with green velvet collar and cuffs while the gold embroidery was of thistles and arrows, these devices appearing on the collar, cuffs, skirt ornaments and wings. A cocked hat with gold ornaments had a large green feather.

In 1831 the scarlet coat was discontinued for a double-breasted green garment and about the same time the tartan shooting dress was changed to one of 'Border-green' cloth, somewhat similar to the present garment. The dark green coat or coatee had gold epaulettes and a gold and crimson waist sash tied on the left hip, and was worn with dark green trousers.

Simkin's water-colour of 1911 (1b) shows the items, described in the *Dress Worn at Court*, in great detail. The field-dress bonnet for Gentlemen of the Body Guard was green trimmed with black braid and had a crimson tuft or toorie, the white and green silk cockade continued in wear and there were ribbons at the back. A single eagle's feather indicated a Gentleman, two feathers marked the officers, while three were worn by the Captain-General. Officers also had two rows of gold braid on the band and a gold button instead of the crimson tuft. The particular ranks of the officers was denoted by the special gold-embroidered badges on the collar.

The Foot Guards

1st Foot Guards or the Grenadier Guards

When Charles II was in exile on the Continent he had many officers in his court and in 1656 raised his Royal Regiment of Guards who returned to England with him in 1660. In 1685 it had become known as the 1st Regiment of Foot Guards, which title it retained until 1815 when it was re-named the Grenadier Guards, having defeated Napoleon's Imperial Guards at Waterloo.

The early dress of the Foot Guards is not well recorded and reconstructions have had to be made. An early illustration had appeared in the well-documented *History of the Grenadier Guards* by Sir F. W. Hamilton, based on the B. Clayton prints of 1854. An officer, pikeman and musketeer of 1660 are shown in elaborate detail and these Simkin has copied most carefully, like that of the pikeman (2a). The picture of the officer and musketeer he used to illustrate the Coldstream Guards (7a,c). The appearance of these soldiers is quite theatrical and although based on contemporary information is only a compilation. The famous painting by William Hogarth of 'the March of the Guards to Finchley' (1745) is a good source for uniform and the soldiers in that were used by B. Clayton for the prints of the Grenadier Guards. Simkin carefully copies Clayton for the sergeant, 1742 (2b) and the drummer (3a). There are of course other contemporary sources like the grenadiers of Bernard Lens c. 1740 and the 1742 *Representation of Cloathing* book.

The men's red coats had blue lapels, cuffs and turn-backs to the skirts. The breeches were blue as was the case in Royal Regiments and the waistcoats were red. The men's lace on buttonholes and elsewhere was plain white and that of the sergeants was gold (2b). This n.c.o. carried a halberd as a sign of rank but the uprising hook at the back does not seem right. Grenadiers had cloth caps with a small red flap carrying the White Horse of Hanover. The tall blue front had an embroidered crown over the Star of the Garter with the red cross of St George in the middle.

The drummer (3a) is based on the Hogarth picture but also agrees with the 1751 oil-painting by David Morier. The slightly shortened mitre cap does not have the tassel at the top (as in the case of grenadiers) of the blue front, because the red bag which was loose falls to the right. The embroidered front has a crown over a trophy of colours and drums. Whereas the drummers of line regiments are said to have had coats of 'reversed facings' to show the livery of the commanding officer, in the case of Royal Regiments the red coat with blue facings was the livery of the sovereign as was the coat of the men. So the main distinction of royal drummers was the heavy lace, blue with yellow edges, which was laid down the seams, round the edges and wherever possible. 'Wings' on the shoulders marked the place where the hanging sleeves of the old doublet once fell behind.

Although the basic distinctions of the 1st Foot Guards did not change, in the last half of the eighteenth century the style and fit did alter. The garments became closer-fitting and civilian fashions had their influence. The paucity of 1st Foot Guards paintings of other ranks restricts descriptions but the story of uniform given for other Foot Guards may cover the gaps. An innovation for the Foot Guards was the introduction of light infantry companies (4a) raised to fight in Flanders 1793. A striking feature of this dress was the top hat, the brim held up with stays, a fur crest over the top and a large dark green plume at the side to indicate a light infantry man. Small wings on the shoulders were blue, also indicating a flank company. Although Simkin indicates high white gaiters with black garters, the latter are not shown in contemporary prints and it is reasonable to suppose that one-piece gaiter-overalls were worn.

Battalion company men wore the black hat with three sides turned up, developing various cockings. Towards the end of the century it had really become a 'bicorn' and had lost the white lace on the brim (3b). This portrait of an officer is copied carefully from the October 1798 coloured print in the *British Military Library*. The large feather was white with a red base and there was a gold loop on the black rosette and one gold tassel in each corner. The scarlet coat was no longer worn open to show the white waistcoat but buttoned over, with the crimson silk sash around the waist offering better protection in cold weather. The blue collar and cuffs had gold lace on the edges but the loops were now discontinued for the service garment. The skirts were also reduced to small white turn-backs. Black gaiters to below the knee were worn by officers (except for full dress when white was still the rule) but mounted field officers had high boots.

The conversion of the 1st Foot Guards to Grenadier Guards in 1815 gave all ranks the fur cap or bearskin. As grenadier companies of line battalions had white plumes on the left of their fur caps, these were also worn by all men of the Grenadier Guards (6). The officer of 1912 wears the full dress with the State sash of crimson and gold introduced in Edward VII's reign. The buttons are set 'regular' or at equal intervals to indicate the '1st'. The officer in the blue undress frock coat has black braid ornamentation and his rank is indicated on the shoulder-straps. He wears a plain crimson waist sash. The blue forage cap had been introduced early in the reign of Edward VII, replacing the stiff 'cheese-cutter' type. The guardsman wears the garments as seen today (subject to minor alterations) and the heavy white leather equipment, now reduced as much as possible for ceremonial occasions.

Musicians of the Foot Guards had their own special dress, quite different from that of the line, usually with much gold lace. The musician of the 1st Foot Guards (4b) was a fairly recent addition, for coloured musicians were employed at the end of the eighteenth century. The illustration is based on the original water-colour by N. Finart in the Royal Collection at Windsor Castle. One may wonder how Richard Simkin was able to make so careful a copy. The original is named 'musicien nègre du grenadiers de la Garde Royale Anglaise 1816'. Simkin has added cymbals whereas the original gives no indication of what this 'time-beater' may have carried. The oriental head-dress with the voluminous turban may be exaggerated but the gold lace on the back of the jacket and the blue band on the sleeve show careful observation of distinctions carried on until modern times in the Grenadier Guards.

The bass-drummer (5) depicts another exotic dress which presents another problem. Such a dress is known to have been worn in the Scots Fusilier Guards but on the shell of this drum Simkin clearly writes '1st Battn. Grenadier Guards'. Contemporary evidence for this has not been found. The loose upper sleeves in the oriental Turkish style are known in the Scots Fusilier Guards, where such articles cost £6 14s 5d in 1864. There were three of these specially dressed time-beaters wearing the shako, but only in the Scots Fusilier Guards; this information appeared as late as 1866 when the dress was simplified.

Overleaf:
3.
1st Foot Guards
a 1742, drummer
b 1798, officer

2nd Foot Guards or the Coldstream Guards

In 1650 George Monk was given men from two regiments of the New Model Army who became Monk's Regiment of Foot. He concentrated his forces at Coldstream and then marched to London, where he waited for Charles II to return to England as King. His regiment theoretically laid down its arms as a Parliamentary unit and then took them up again as a regiment known as the Lord General's Regiment of Foot Guards. On his death in 1670 it was known as the Coldstream Regiment of Foot Guards, changing in 1817 to the Coldstream Guards. Although sometimes officially referred to as the 2nd

1ST REGIMENT OF FOOT GUARDS.
1742.

a

1ST FOOT GUARDS.
1798.

b

Plate 3

1ST FOOT GUARDS
(LIGHT COMPANY 1798)

a

1ST FOOT GUARDS
1813

b

Plate 4

Foot Guards, the Coldstream Guards resisted taking second place, their motto being 'Nulli Secundus'. When in 1831 they were offered the title of Coldstream Fusilier Guards, it was not accepted although they did take the proffered fur caps.

The three figures of 1660 (7a,b,c) were taken from the Clayton prints of 1848 and used by Richard Simkin for both English Foot Guards. The basic items are possible but the details and dating are not precise. The elaborate armour of the pikeman is much earlier and the cut of the officer's coat may be styled as 'theatrical' rather than contemporary. It is also said that Monk's regiment had green facings until 1670 when he died and the blue facings were taken after that date. However, the details of the private of 1742 (7d) are much more reliable as they are taken from the hand-coloured guardsman in the 1742 Cloathing book. At this time there were only subtle differences between the uniforms of the two Foot Guards, one being the shape of the buttonhole loops.

The man of the grenadier company 1751 (7e) is also taken from a good source, the series of oil-paintings by David Morier in the Royal Collection. The cloth grenadier cap had reached its most developed form at this time; from a low cap with embroidered devices, it had grown in height, and only in 1749 had the colour of the small flap in front been changed from blue to red. Pictures of a slightly earlier date show the full skirts of the coat hanging freely. Although they were warm in cold weather, the clinging bulk of cloth, especially in wet weather, made marching difficult and so the front corners were fastened back. The long white gaiters reached the knees but in fine weather they could be left off to show the white stockings reaching to just below the knees. By the outbreak of the American revolution the grenadier cloth caps had been replaced by ones of black fur with a metal plate in front carrying the Royal Arms. By this time the Coldstream Guards had their buttonholes in pairs (while those of the 1st Foot Guards were set 'regular').

There are many portraits extant which show what the officers wore. The scarlet coat had dark blue lapels which could be worn turned back on each side, thus showing the white waistcoat, or they could be fastened across negligently on two or three buttons. The gold laced buttonholes were so wide that often only a small segment of blue showed on the lapels. But eventually the loops were arranged in pairs to make a regimental distinction. On the less expensive 'lace-less' frock, only the buttons remained in pairs to show their distinction.

The officer (7f) of 1792 is taken from the beautiful hand-coloured print by E. Dayes, each detail and pose being carefully repeated. The old three-cornered hat had given place to the 'bicorn' without lace on the brim. The coat has the single epaulette on the right shoulder which replaced the earlier shoulder-knot. The neat white waistcoat has lost its long flaps and the crimson sash rests on the waist. The tight-fitting white breeches have small gilt buttons at the knee and just below the sword may be seen an indication of the front flap. Simkin indicates buttons down the outside of the legs as though gaiters were worn but these are not shown on the original print, but rather high boots instead.

The guardsman of 1792 (7h) is from the same group of prints. The hat has white tape or stays to keep the front flap in position and above the black cockade rises a white tuft with a black top. At this time various colours and patterns of plumes were put on the hat but there were no overall rulings. As

Preceding page:
4.
1st Foot Guards
a   1798, private, light company
b   1813, cymbal-player

there were so many variations in a few years, regulations were made giving battalion companies white over red (the colour of St George) tufts or feathers, white for grenadiers and green for light infantry. The belt-plates on the bayonet- or sword-belt had proliferated at the time of the American war and practically every unit had its own plate, brass for the men but gilt and enamel for the officers of the Coldstream Guards. Within a few years the open coat had been ordered to be closed and fastened over so that the waistcoat could not be seen. Also in the Dayes prints were examples of the grenadier company dress, of drummers and of sergeants. The battalion sergeant had the old axe-headed halberd (soon to be replaced by the simple spontoon) but both he and the grenadier sergeant had a long and heavy cane hanging from a button on the left side.

When the shako was introduced into the British Army the Foot Guards also wore it, although the officers clung to their hats as long as possible. Light company officers found the 'stove-pipe' shako much better for actual combat. Trousers or overalls now went over the breeches and gaiters and the Napoleonic wars brought reforms and simplification of uniform. Among the changes of 1812 a new 'false-fronted' shako came in use and remained until the end of these conflicts. Charles Hamilton Smith in his prints showed the dress of the period with a certain amount of authority, as he was then in the Quartermaster's Department. The officer (7i) depicts the service dress. The shako has a gilt regimental plate in front and gold and crimson cords but in bad weather a black oilskin cover would be worn. The double-breasted jacket could be worn with the lapels showing or turned back. The men of the period (7m) had brass plates on their shakos and white cords. Their equipment was that carried into action and their light blue water-bottles usually had white painted letters indicating the unit and other details.

At the end of hostilities a new pattern broad-topped shako was introduced and the coatee, a coat with cutaway skirts, was worn. The State dress of the officer (7j) is taken from an original water-colour by Denis Dighton in the Royal Library at Windsor. The pose has been slightly altered, as the officer originally had a sword in his right hand. This officer with epaulettes belongs to a battalion company; the officers of the flank companies wore wings, and the officers of the grenadier companies had imposing bearskin caps with white plumes.

In 1831 the Coldstream Guards were given grenadier caps for all ranks and as they no longer had a separate grenadier company the regimental plume became red, and as a difference was worn on the right side of the fur cap. For a time officers wore a crowned rose badge in front but even this was discontinued before the Crimean War.

Overleaf:
5.
Grenadier Guards, 1855, bass-drummer

When the Foot Guards went to the Crimea to fight the Russians, they wore their tight coatees, awkward epaulettes and top-heavy fur caps. The officer (7l) wore the same dress as for some duties at home and although he preferred to wear undress cap and coat, during the actions at Inkerman and elsewhere he had to wear the complete uniform to be recognized when he led his men. The corporal (7k) is shown ready to march into action with his knapsack looking regimental, though in later months the fur cap gave place to the forage cap and the overcoat was the popular garment.

Before the war finished, a new double-breasted tunic had been approved which gave protection to the stomach and had no tiresome epaulettes. This was soon followed by a single-breasted tunic on which the cuff flaps were

GRENADIER GUARDS.
1855.

Plate 5

GRENADIER GUARDS.
1912

Plate 6

retained and in fact is similar to that worn today, slightly varied by contemporary cutting.

The lieutenant (8b) of 1913 has a scarlet cut feather six inches long in his bearskin. His scarlet tunic has ten buttons down the front and four bars of embroidery, two and two, on each skirt and coat flap. Underneath the white piping on the cuff is a row of gold embroidery. The embroidered badge on each side of his collar is the Cross of St George within the Garter on a silver star, the elongated Garter Star.

The mounted officer (7g) is a lieutenant-colonel and although dressed like the lieutenant would have extra embroidery, including a second row on each cuff. He, of course, wears pantaloons (better known as breeches) and high boots. Although Simkin shows the spurs as white metal, the Dress Regulations of 1911 state 'brass', the normal metal for field officers. His saddle-cloth is dark blue edged with two laces of gold for field officers with the embroidered Crown and Star in silver wire. The horse's brow-band and rosette are in blue silk for review order.

The drum-major wears 'State Dress' which in fact is not regimental dress but that worn by State musicians of the Sovereign going back to the seventeenth century. The materials and the complicated design of the gold lace date back to that time and this type of coat is worn by bandsmen of the Household Cavalry, drum-majors of the Foot Guards and trumpeters. The velvet skull-cap is said to have been inspired by the caps of racing men so encouraged by Charles II. But the crimson silk sash and the drum-major's staff or mace are 'regimental'. Although all drum-majors of the Foot Guards have the scarf or sash with a six-inch gold fringe, each regiment has its own brooch, in this case with the enamelled badge of the Garter Star. The belt, as is the case for all drum-majors, has a pair of small drum-sticks. The ground is dark blue edged with gold lace which has a central crimson stripe. The embroidered devices are regimental, the Crown above the Garter Star, the silver Sphinx for the Egyptian Campaign of 1811 and many scrolls bearing battle honours.

3rd Foot Guards, Scots Fusilier Guards or Scots Guards

The 'Lyffe Guarde' of Charles II raised in 1650 from the Argyll Regiment of 1642 fought against the Parliamentary troops but were in Scotland when reformed in 1661. They became the new regiment of Foot Guards in Scotland 'to His Majesty' in 1662 and remained in that country. In February 1712 the 'Scotch Regiment of Foot Guard' became the 3rd Regiment of Foot Guards and in 1713 both its battalions moved to London. In 1831 the two junior regiments of Foot Guards were granted special change of title and the 3rd became the Scots Fusilier Guards, thus acquiring the right for all to wear the fusilier (or grenadier) cap. In 1877 the title was simplified to the Scots Guards.

Unfortunately, there are not many Simkin water-colours of the Scots Guards available and so the early uniforms may be described but not illustrated. The Scots Guards originally had white facings to their red coats. In 1686 their breeches and stockings were also noted as white. When blue facings were taken into wear is not known but it was possibly in 1707 when

Preceding page:
6.
Grenadier Guards 1912, officer in undress, officer in State dress, private in full dress

the Scots Guards could be considered to be on the 'English' establishment. At one period the grenadiers of the regiment appear to have had the Crown and Star of St Andrew embroidered on the cloth cap but the Morier painting does not show this. The plate on the fur cap, when introduced, had the Royal Arms device like the other two regiments. By 1774 at least the loops on the lapels were three and three. The broad gold-lace loops of the officers also took this regimental spacing.

In 1790 the King approved that in future the men's hats 'should be without lace round the edge and a feather being worn in them'. The beautifully coloured prints by E. Dayes show the grenadier's plume as white, the battalion men as white with a black top and the drummers with a dark red feather, but by the end of the century the various companies were indicated by white, white over red, and green. The changes of uniform followed the normal patterns — closing of the coats, introduction of the jacket, the shako replacing the hat for the men and the new pattern shako of 1812.

The uniforms after Waterloo were most grandiose and the officer of 1827 (9a) is based on a print by W. Heath which shows three officers, one in full dress, the second in undress and the third in back view. The broad-topped shako not only had gold lace and gilt-scaled chin-strap but gold cords and 'festoon'; no doubt the top-heavy item was expected to fall off at some time. The full-dress coat was scarlet with blue cuffs and lapels (the collar was red) and the heavy gold-lace loops were named 'bastion-shaped' by tailors and placed in threes. The undress coat had a blue collar and although the double-breasted plastron front was edged with gold lace, buttonhole loops were omitted and only one strip of lace went around the top of the collar. The single epaulette indicates a subaltern officer and his sword and scabbard hung from the white leather shoulder-belt. Trousers were white for summer and grey for other times.

By 1829 a new pattern coat had been designed. This was double-breasted with the two rows of buttons placed close together, a Prussian collar and the round cuffs ornamented with a patch or flap bearing three buttons. The officer (9b) wears this new coat but little else is changed in his dress. For some time the Grenadier Guards had been allowed to wear a grenade on each side of the collar, but the other Guards regiments had not been allowed any special badge. Simkin, however, shows the 'Scotch Star' in this water-colour.

In 1831 the 3rd Foot Guards were renamed the Scots Fusilier Guards, thus acquiring the right for all men to wear the bearskin cap and for a time the new fusilier caps had a white plume on the left side, and in fact this is quoted in the 1831 Dress Regulations. Officers had a gilt crown and thistle on the front and two gold tassels on the right. The water-colour by Simkin (12) is based on the Dubois Drahonet oil-painting of Lord Rokeby 1832 in the Royal Collection at Windsor which clearly shows the white plume, not only on the officer but also on the painting of the drummer by the same artist. The white feather was not discontinued until 1838. The plain red coatee has a pair of gold epaulettes as befits a field officer and the cuff slashes or flaps have three gold-buttoned rectangles. The trousers are dark blue with gold side-stripes for winter wear.

The uniforms shown in the group (11) are practically the same as those worn today. In the centre is an officer in full dress, his bearskin without ornaments or plume, his scarlet tunic with buttons in threes (nine down the

Overleaf:
7.
Coldstream Guards
a 1660, musketeer
b 1660, pikeman
c 1660, officer
d 1742, private
e 1751, grenadier
f 1792, officer
g 1912, officer in undress frock, officer mounted full dress
h 1792, private
i 1815, officer
j 1821, officer
k 1854, corporal
l 1854, officer
m 1815, private

a 1660

b 1660

c 1660

d 1742

e 1751

f 1792

g 1912

COLDSTREAM GUARDS

h 1792

i 1815

j 1821

k 1854

l 1854

m 1815

R. Simkin.

Plate 7

COLDSTREAM GUARDS.
1912.

a

COLDSTREAM GUARDS.
1913.

b

Plate 8

front) and three bars of embroidery with buttons on the skirts and cuff flaps. His blue collar, besides gold embroidery on each side, has the thistle in silver on a gold lace ground. The blue cloth trousers have scarlet side-stripes two inches wide. The web sword-belt is under the crimson waist-sash and the gold lace sword-slings hang from the left to support the steel scabbard.

The mounted officer differs only in wearing blue pantaloons (breeches) and high boots with brass spurs (steel spurs were worn with service dress). The gold stripes in the sash denote the 'State occasion' sash. The blue saddle-cloth has the special devices for the Scots Guards, is three feet long, two feet two inches at the top and one foot two inches deep. The field officer had two stripes of gold lace and the silver-embroidered badges denote the rank.

The officer in undress has a blue cloth forage cap of universal pattern with gold cord around the crown and the regimental badge in front. The diced band denoted the Scottish origin and no chin-strap or buttons were worn by officers of this regiment. The blue cloth frock coat was of regimental pattern with black mohair trimmings. In the lower right-hand corner the senior n.c.o. wears a uniform of almost officer's quality but has shoulder-straps of blue edged with gold. His sash is over the left shoulder and his sword is from a white leather waist-belt. On his right upper arm he carries the elaborately embroidered badge of the Royal Arms. Beside him stands a colour-sergeant wearing the other ranks' tunic but with gold patches on the cuff flaps and the crowned Regimental Colour badge on three gold chevrons.

In the lower left-hand corner is a guardsman, his tunic having white piping and braid as well as an embroidered thistle on each side of the collar. The guardsman standing beside him has the white fatigue jacket which now was only worn by the Foot Guards and Highland regiments. His forage cap has the diced band with a red piping around the crown. The regimental badge is worn in front and the single row of brass on the peak marks him as a guardsman or private.

In the upper right-hand corner is a musician or bandsman, his scarlet tunic having band wings (gold on blue) and elaborate gold lace loops in threes down the chest. With him is a drummer boy, his scarlet tunic being elaborately laced with white and blue braid, the blue devices being the fleur-de-lys, a vestige recalling Britain's ancient claim to France.

In the upper left-hand corner is a drum-major of the Scots Guards, dressed in his State clothing, already described. There is little difference from the earlier picture, apart from the enamelled regimental badge on the crimson sash and the devices on the shoulder-belt which include the Sphinx for Egypt. The pipe-major is somewhat reduced in size with details being lost – those in the larger picture (10) giving a much better idea.

In 1856 a pipe-major and five pipers were officially added to each battalion of the Scots Fusilier Guards and at last Highland dress appeared in the regiment. The pipe-major painted by Simkin was Pipe-Major Fraser, 1st Battalion, originally the piper to Lord Lovat, chief of the Fraser clan. The water-colour is closely based on a photograph by Gregory and Co. The glengarry is dark blue with a silver badge and black-cock's feathers. The blue doublet has the buttons grouped in threes and the silver lace around the collar and down the front is broad for pipe-majors but thin for other pipers. A pipe-major should have a silver crown over four silver chevrons

Preceding page:
8.
Coldstream Guards
a   1912, drum-major
b   1913, officer, State dress

on the right forearm but as this was hidden in the original photograph, Simkin failed to include these distinctions in his picture.

Pipe-majors of the Scots Guards had crimson banners (not blue as for other pipers) and the Scottish devices for the 1st Battalion include a crown over the Scottish coat-of-arms and the motto 'En Feris Hostis' over the 'Egypt and the Sphinx', but Simkin portrays the Victorian type of crown as shown in the c. 1897 photograph although he dates his photograph '1912', when the crown should have been the Tudor or Imperial design. The Highland dress of the pipers is much the same today but in 1938 the Scots Guards pipers were given black feather bonnets with a cut-feather plume on the left in red and blue being King George's own colours.

Irish Guards

It was not until 1900 that the Irish Guards were formed, after the Queen had expressed a desire to commemorate the bravery of the Irish regiments during the operations in South Africa in the years 1899–1900, and by 1901 the first men were in the Irish Guards Mounted Infantry section on duty in South Africa.

The dress of the Irish Guards officers (13) followed that of the other three Foot Guards by being scarlet for the tunic, dark blue for the facings with gold lace and buttons. To mark the fourth in rank, the buttons were in fours down the front, on the cuffs and the flaps on the back of the skirts. The regimental device was the Star of the Order of St Patrick with the motto 'Quis Separabit' (which dates from 1783), to be seen on the cap badges and coloured belt-plate. The bright blue feather plume was on the right side, so that when the four regiments lined up – the Grenadier Guards on the right, the Scots Guards in the middle, the Irish Guards next to the Coldstream Guards on the left – all plumes would be visible to an inspecting officer in front.

The officer wears a state sash, crimson with gold vertical stripes and his sword is hooked up to leave both hands free to handle the regimental colour. What colour Simkin intends to display is not clear. All regimental badges are carried on the Union which acts as the regimental colour. But the badge he displays is the Star of the Order of St Patrick ensigned with the Crown, which should be displayed on the all 'gules' (crimson) colour of the 2nd Battalion. It is not a 'regimental' badge.

The dress of the men of course followed the pattern set by the other Foot Guards but was distinguished by the buttons in fours, the blue hackle on the right and the shamrock collar-badges. For undress they wore the short white fatigue jacket and the new cap – which is sometimes quoted as a 'brodrick' but is actually a broad-topped forage cap without a peak and with a dark green band around it. No badge is shown in early photographs.

Overleaf:
9.
3rd or Scots Guards
a 1827, officer
b 1830, officer

Infantry of the Line

Apart from the personal Foot Guards of the Sovereign there were the troops needed for national defence, the main part of which was infantry. The return of Charles II to England saw the disbandment of the old Parliamentary or Roundhead troops of the Revolution. Although extremely limited in number, the infantry battalions were then gradually reformed and were

3RD FOOT GUARDS - 1827.
(NOW SCOTS GUARDS)

a

3RD FOOT GUARDS - 1830.
(NOW SCOTS GUARDS)

b

Plate 9

SCOTS GUARDS
1912.

Plate 10

usually named after the colonel who raised them. There were also other names such as the Royal Scots, or the Tangier Regiment which was specially created to defend an overseas possession brought as part of the dowry of Catherine of Braganza when she married Charles in 1662. Many regiments were recruited for a short time only, perhaps a year, and then further re-employment had to be permitted by Parliament. Many regiments of this period had a brief life and were not heard of again but others continued often with a new colonel. Regiments followed a precedence among themselves; this was sometimes determined by the oldest colonel and later by seniority, according to which was raised earliest in England.

Scotland as an ancient kingdom had its own army on a separate establishment but in 1707, when England and Scotland were united, the Scottish troops were placed on the combined establishment, which unfortunately did not always give the desired seniority in precedence or rank. New regiments were constantly being formed for fighting, at home or on the Continent, normally to be disbanded in time of peace, but the total always increased. Problems sometimes occurred when a regiment which had been disbanded after peace was achieved was reraised when war broke out again with the same officers, but with the regiment taking a lower precedence. However, by the time of the 1742 *Cloathing* book the precedence was well established and after the ten marine regiments transferred from the Army to the Navy in 1748 a fixed precedence was published in 1751, which numbered the regiments from 1 to 49 with other honorific titles added. There were some 'Royal' and 'Ancient' regiments which had specially permitted titles such as the 1st or Royal, the 2nd or Queen's, the 3rd or Buffs, and so on. The advent of the Highland Regiment brought that title into use.

In 1780 the House of Commons suggested that existing regiments might be given county titles to help in recruiting but that did not come about until August 1782 when the permanent regiments of infantry acquired these distinctions (see the Brief Outlines, pp. 36–108). The wording quoted in these titles is taken from contemporary Army Lists but the use of 'or' and 'The' varied over the years, even in official publications. Some regiments are particular regarding the capital 'T', although this is by no means a universal custom. In times of warfare many new regiments were needed and these took the higher numbers. But many hundreds disappeared and are not mentioned because they had no connection with the regiments of Simkin's day.

Improvements were being made continually to the organization of infantry regiments and battalions. The number of regiments increased to 109. Even in times of peace the continuing expansion of the British Empire meant that regiments were needed for stations abroad and that the replacement of men, not only from conflict, but also from bad health and age, brought problems. The system of a regiment having men serving abroad and a depot at home to build up reserves was one answer. After various trials a new system introduced in 1881 linked together two battalions (taken from existing regiments) with a new 'territorial' connection. Thus the two battalions could be numbered 1st and 2nd and linked with the local Militia regiments, also numbered as battalions, while the local volunteer rifle corps were part of the scheme, although not permanently until 1908.

The two World Wars brought many new battalions to each regiment, to

Preceding page:
10.
Scots Guards, 1912, pipe-major

be followed by drastic disbandments of some in the succeeding peace. But it was the 'financial' reductions of the 1950s and 1960s that brought about the disappearance of the names of famous regiments. However, 'precedence' had to be maintained and the modern Army Lists give the complicated reduction of units with the old pre-1881 regimental numbers in brackets after the title, although only a few regiments have reintroduced the numerals into their titles or distinctions. In the Brief Outlines below, the original regiment with the lowest (oldest) number continues the tradition and descent while the higher (and younger) number on amalgamation is absorbed into the senior battalion.

The following Brief Outline of each infantry regiment from the 1st Royal Scots to the 109th Bombay Infantry and the Rifle Brigade gives the dates of the founding of each regiment, of the official changes of name and the linkage with other regiments or battalions, not only up to the time of Richard Simkin's water-colours but later through the tortuous and complicated amalgamations and reductions up to the present day, thus permitting a serving soldier to trace his unit through the intertwined branches of the family tree.

This is not the place to record the activities and histories of the regiments (which may be found in the several hundred regimental records and histories); even to list all the granted battle honours (reaching several thousands) would be overwhelming here, and they are easily available in past and current Army Lists. But there are certain ancient awards which must not be overlooked – the Castle, Key and motto for service in Gibraltar during the Great Siege, the Sphinx for service in Egypt, the Dragon for China, the Elephant for India and so on. These are cited here because they have a distinctive influence and are or were perpetuated on the uniform or appointments. So of course are royal awards, such as the Royal Crest, the Prince of Wales's Coronet and Feathers and motto, the Dragon for Queen Elizabeth I and so on. But the plethora of variations in regimental badges – especially the designs of the swiftly changing units of modern days – has been omitted.

As Richard Simkin's work in this book is mainly concerned in depicting the changing uniforms of regiments, so the text of this book must concentrate on that aspect. But the subject is so vast, that it must be broken down into 'digestible' sections. Originally the dress of the soldier was based on that worn by civilians and also adopted the quirks of passing fashions as they appeared. But apart from the normal evolution of fashion and cutting over the centuries there were, even in the infantry, separate fields of development, such as for Highlanders, riflemen, grenadiers and light troops, besides the need of specialist soldiers.

The Brief Outlines cover the basic elements of the common soldier and where the complete uniform varies from the basic, later sections deal with these. These can be found by referring to the index. The uniform information in these outlines is kept simple, giving the colour of the dress garment (coat, coatee, tunic or jacket) with distinguishing facings which needed 'regularizing' at intervals, leading up to the drastic reductions in 1881, when four colours only were thought necessary (no doubt to reduce costs): blue for royal regiments, white for all English and Welsh regiments, yellow for Scottish and green for Irish. Even this simplistic plan had its pitfalls. Many English and Scottish regiments were extremely discontented with the changes and plagued the authorities for a return to their original

Overleaf:
11.
Scots Guards, 1912
a drum-major and pipe-major
b musician and drummer
c officer in frock coat, officer (dismounted) and officer mounted, full dress
d privates, full and undress
e colour-sergeant and senior n.c.o. full dress

a   b

c

Scots Guards - 1912

R. Simkin

d   e

Plate 11

Scots Fusilier Guards
1832.

Plate 12

IRISH GUARDS.
1913.

2ND QUEEN'S ROYAL REGIMENT.
1828.

Plate 13   **Plate 14**

facings. As to the Irish regiments, several were royal (with blue), one was rifles, and that left only the Connaught Rangers with the Irish green.

One of the first regiments to break the colour rulings was the Buffs, who tinted their white facings at their own expense. Some Scottish regiments then requested a return to their buff facings, thus reducing the number with the Scottish yellow. Despite this apparent disarray, permission to return to the original facings was difficult to obtain, but before the First World War many had achieved victory.

Brief Outlines of the Regiments of Foot 1–109 and the Rifle Brigade

These brief outlines are arranged under the regimental title used by Simkin, but they go back to the raising of the regiment and cover the main changes of name and amalgamations up to the modern successor. Where no references to illustrations are given, no Simkin water-colours are available. Names of the regiments in Simkin's time are indicated in italic.

1st Foot
1633   Raised as Sir John Hepburn's Regiment, then known by succeeding colonels' names.
1684   Also known as the Royal Regiment of Foot.
1751   1st or Royal Regiment of Foot.
1812   1st Regiment of Foot or Royal Scots.
1821   1st or Royal Regiment of Foot.
1871   1st or Royal Scots Regiment.
1881   *The Lothian Regiment (The Royal Scots).*
1920   The Royal Scots (The Royal Regiment).
1968   In the Scottish Division.

Scottish infantry served in France in 1590 and later in 1613 in the service of Gustavus Adolphus of Sweden but it was not until 1633 that Hepburn's regiment was formed and served in Europe, returning to England in 1661 for a brief time and finally returning to England in 1678 to take a full place in the new army of Charles II and his successors.

The first uniform was red with white facings and although made royal in about 1684 continued to have white facings up to the last years of the seventeenth century, perhaps not taking the royal blue until the time of Queen Anne or even George I. The earliest information on officers' lace and buttons indicates gold. Special distinctions include the Royal Cypher and the Order of St Andrew (the Star of the Order of the Thistle). The uniform was that of the basic infantryman until 1880 when a diced border was introduced for undress caps and the next year a 'Lowland' dress was adopted (see the Lowland section on uniform).

See also the officer, full dress, 1913 (*96*)

2nd Foot
1661   Raised as the Tangier Regiment by the Earl of Peterborough, then known by succeeding colonels' names.
1685   The Queen Dowager's Regiment.
1703   The Queen's Royal Regiment.

Preceding page:
12.
Scots Fusilier Guards, 1832, colonel in State dress

13.
Irish Guards, 1913, officer with colour

14.
2nd Queen's Royal Regiment, 1826, officer

1715   The Princess of Wales's Own Regiment.
1727   The Queen's Regiment of Foot.
1751   The 2nd (Queen's Royal) Regiment of Foot.
1881   *The Queen's (Royal West Surrey Regiment).*
1900   The Queen's Royal Regiment (West Surrey).
1959   Linked with the East Surrey Regiment, as the Queen's Royal Surrey
        Regiment.
1966   Linked with three other regiments (Queen's Own Buffs, Royal
        Sussex and the Middlesex) as the Queen's Regiment.
1968   Part of the Queen's Division.

Catherine of Braganza brought as her wedding dowry to Charles II the
possessions of Tangier and Bombay. On his death she became the Queen
Dowager.

The red coat was traditionally given facings of sea green and was green
for many years although by 1768 it was blue (a grenadier cap *c.* 1766 had
light blue velvet). Officers' lace and buttons were silver until 1830 when all
regular officers had gold. Special distinctions include the Paschal Lamb
associated with Catherine of Braganza, the Sphinx for Egypt, 1801, the
'Naval Crown' for sea-service under Lord Howe, 1794, as well as the
Queen's Cipher in early days. The uniform always followed the traditional
dress of line infantry.
See also officer, 1826 (*14*)

3rd Foot

1665   The Holland Regiment under Richard Sidney.
1680   Prince George of Denmark's Regiment under Colonel Charles
        Churchill.
1708   Known by name of colonel, also (by 1743) as the Buffs.
1751   The 3rd (or the Buffs).
1782   3rd (East Kent) Regiment of Foot (The Buffs).
1881   *The Buffs (East Kent Regiment).*
1935   The Buffs (Royal East Kent Regiment).
1961   Amalgamated with the Queen's Own Royal West Kent to form the
        Queen's Own Buffs (The Royal Kent Regiment).
1966   Amalgamated with the Queen's Royal Surrey Regiment, the Royal
        Sussex, and Middlesex Regiment to form the Queen's Regiment.
1968   In the Queen's Division.

In May 1572 Queen Elizabeth inspected the London Trained Bands in
Greenwich Park from which a company was raised to fight for the Flemish
cause. This Holland regiment continued in being until recalled to England
in May 1655, thus coming on the English establishment. From its ancient
origins the Buffs were permitted to parade and recruit in the City of
London. As the regiment in 1665 was intended for sea-service, it would not
have had any pikemen. In 1667 it became a land regiment again and was
noted as having red coats with yellow linings. Later the facings were
described as 'flesh' colour and then as buff or ash. When the nickname of
'Buffs' was introduced is not known but it was many years before the
official use was made (1747).

The Green Dragon was officially recognized as an ancient badge of the
regiment, although its origins are not known for certain. The first Queen
Elizabeth had a dragon supporter to her coat-of-arms. The historian Cannon
suggests that when the Buffs were in Bruges *c.* 1707 they adopted the

dragon which that city had captured in the Crusades; I suggest that the Griffin from the arms of General Wills, once their colonel, might also be a source. The Rose and Crown was also a badge used in the eighteenth century. The uniform followed that of infantry but with the distinctive buff facings until 1881 when white the colour for English regiments was imposed. But in 1890, after the white facings had been unofficially coloured buff, the ancient facings were again permitted. The officers' metal was silver but soon after Waterloo was changed to gold.
See also the group (*15*)

4th Foot

1680   The 2nd Tangier Regiment raised by Charles Earl of Plymouth.
1684   The Duchess of York and Albany's Regiment of Foot.
1685   The Queen's Own Regiment.
1702   The Queen's Own Regiment of Marines.
1710   The Queen's Own Regiment of Foot.
1715   The King's Own Regiment of Foot.
1751   4th or the King's Own Regiment of Foot.
1815   The 4th (The King's Own) Regiment of Foot.
1865   The 4th (The King's Own Royal) Regiment of Foot.
1881   *The King's Own (Royal Lancaster Regiment).*
1920   The King's Own Royal Regiment (Lancaster).
1959   Amalgamated with the Border Regiment to form the 1st Battalion the King's Own Royal Border Regiment.
1968   Part of the King's Division.

Although specially raised for Tangier service, the regiment returned home when the colony was abandoned. When in Africa all-red coats may have been worn but back in England the red coats were given yellow facings, a colour which James II frequently chose, in this case for his wife. When the change to royal blue facings took place is not known but it must have been early in the eighteenth century. Silver lace was worn by officers at Culloden and continued until 1807 when gold was taken into wear. For a time officers had blue velvet facings. The Lion of England was their ancient badge with the later addition of the Red Rose of Lancashire. The uniform followed the normal changes as may be expected in a royal regiment.
See also the officer, 1852 (*16*)

5th Foot

1685   Colonel T. Monk's Regiment of Foot, and then known by succeeding colonels' names.
1751   The 5th Regiment of Foot.
1782   The 5th (Northumberland) Regiment of Foot.
1836   The 5th (Northumberland) (Fusiliers) Regiment of Foot.
1881   *The Northumberland Fusiliers.*
1935   The Royal Northumberland Fusiliers.
1968   Amalgamated with the Royal Warwickshire Fusiliers, the Royal Fusiliers and the Lancashire Fusiliers as the Royal Regiment of Fusiliers.
1968   In the Queen's Division.

The English Brigade formed in Holland in 1674 had four regiments two English, one Scottish and one Irish. In 1685 at the time of the Monmouth Rebellion, James II recalled the men in this brigade and the regiment of

Colonel T. Monk became eventually the 5th Foot and that of Sir Henry Bellasis became the 6th Foot, taking seniority from the date of their first employment in England.

Traditionally the first dress was a red coat with yellow facings with green breeches and linings. By 1742 the facings are shown as yellow-green but officially in 1751 they were known as 'gosling-green', and this distinction has been kept to the present day. But in 1881 the 'English' white facings were worn, although in 1899 the traditional facings were restored. The officers' lace was silver until 1830, when gold was worn.

St George and the Dragon was an early device of the regiment. Later they used the King's Crest and the Red and White Rose as well as the Rose and Crown. In 1778 at St Lucia the men are said to have taken white plumes from the defeated French troops, enough to equip the regiment, and they kept this distinction for many years, receiving official approval in 1826. In 1836 the regiment was named fusiliers, and as all other fusiliers were permitted white feathers, they were given an extra distinction in having the upper half of the feather coloured red. When the ball-tuft was introduced, this had the upper half red and the lower half white, a special colour distinction, which is continued in modern times on the beret. The dress was the basic uniform up to 1836 when they were made fusiliers. For that development see the section on fusiliers' uniform (p. 125).

See also the group (59), the group, 1910 (60), and the drummer, 1751 (61a)

6th Foot

1685 Raised by Colonel Sir Henry Bellasis, and known by succeeding colonels' names.
1751 The 6th Regiment of Foot.
1782 The 6th (1st Warwickshire) Regiment of Foot.
1832 The 6th (Royal 1st Warwickshire) Regiment of Foot.
1881 *The Royal Warwickshire Regiment.*
1968 Amalgamated with the Royal Northumberland Fusiliers, Royal Fusiliers and Lancashire Fusiliers to form the 2nd Battalion the Royal Regiment of Fusiliers.

Some of the regiments formed in the English Brigade 1674 were then in the service of Holland. They were called back by James II at the time of the Monmouth Rebellion but soon had to return to the Netherlands. Bellasis's regiment with Monk's regiment (later to be the 5th Foot) returned to England with William, Prince of Orange in 1688 to fight against James II. They entered the English Army taking precedence from their visit in 1685.

The coat was red with facings of deep yellow, which might have been inspired either by the house of Orange or by James II. When the regiment was made royal in 1832 the facings became blue. The officers' buttons and lace were silver until 1830 when all regular infantry had gold. The dress followed the basic infantry patterns until 1832, when the royal aspects were added. The Antelope was the 'Ancient' badge of the regiment and like the George and Dragon of the sister regiment, its original sources are not known, but as they are royal devices they were allowed to continue as such in regulations.

See also the group (18) and the bandsman, 1852 (17)

7th Foot

1685 Royal Regiment of Fusiliers (or Fuzileers).

1751   The 7th or Royal Fusiliers.
1881   *The Royal Fusiliers (City of London Regiment)*.
1968   Amalgamated with the Royal Northumberland Fusiliers, the Royal Warwickshire Fusiliers and the Lancashire Fusiliers to form the Royal Regiment of Fusiliers in the Queen's Division.

Originally raised to guard the Artillery, they were armed with fusils (flint-locks) instead of match-locks (burning matches) as a safeguard for use near gunpowder. The men wore caps instead of hats so that their firearms could be slung on their backs. There were no pikemen in the regiment but there was a company of miners.

The ancient badge of the Royal Fusiliers was the Rose with the Garter Crowned, a device which also appeared on the barrels of the cannon that they guarded. The bursting grenade is the badge for all fusilier regiments in the British Army and it is interesting to note that the original companies of the Royal Fusiliers did not have grenadiers – no doubt they were too dangerous among barrels of gunpowder. From 1688 they were considered as normal infantry and fought as such. The miner company was detached and lived a separate life.

The original dress was red with yellow lining and grey breeches and stockings. The yellow facings seem to indicate a preference by James II. Lord Dartmouth, who was the colonel, had interesting regimental colours: some had the red cross of St George and all had golden suns or trophies painted on the white field. Heraldically gold on silver (white) was not proper; only the Pope could adopt such rules, which may be an indication of James's religious preferences. When the facings changed to blue is not clear, but by 1702 blue linings were known. The officers' lace and buttons were golden. The dress, although following the normal development, had special fusilier extras (see the fusilier section, p. 125).
See also the drummer, 1852 *(61b)* and the group *(62)*

8th Foot

1685   Princess Anne of Denmark's Regiment of Foot, under Robert, Lord Ferrers.
1702   The Queen's Regiment of Foot.
1716   The King's Regiment of Foot.
1751   8th (The King's) Regiment of Foot.
1881   *The King's (Liverpool Regiment)*.
1920   The King's Regiment (Liverpool).
1958   Amalgamated with the Manchester Regiment to be the King's Regiment (Manchester and Liverpool).
1968   In the King's Division.

The badge of the White Horse, with the Garter and the Crown above, was authorized as the regimental device possibly when the regiment became the King's in 1716. The Sphinx for Egypt was granted in 1802. The regimental history quotes the first uniform as being with yellow distinctions which may have been a dark hue. The officers' lace was gold. The uniform was that of infantry of the line (see p. 29) with royal distinctions (blue facings from 1716).
See also the private, 1742 *(19)*

9th Foot

1685   Henry Cornwall's Regiment of Foot, then known by succeeding colonels' names.

1751 The 9th Regiment of Foot.

1782 9th (The East Norfolk) Regiment of Foot.

1881 *The Norfolk Regiment*.

1935 The Royal Norfolk Regiment.

1959 Amalgamated with the Suffolk Regiment to form the 1st East Anglian Regiment (Royal Norfolk and Suffolk).

1964 Amalgamated with the 2nd and 3rd East Anglian and Royal Leicestershire as part of the Royal Anglian Regiment.

1968 In the Queen's Division.

Although not one of the early regiments to be permitted to have a badge, that of Britannia was claimed as an early distinction. The first official recognition came in a letter from the Horse Guards in 1799. The first dress of the regiment had orange distinctions but at an unknown date it changed to green. However, in 1733 official permission was given to change from bright green back to light orange. By 1747 this was called yellow which remained until 1881 when the 'English' white facings were ordered. In 1925 the yellow facings were restored. The officers' lace and buttons were silver until the general adoption of gold for the regular army in 1830. After 1881 officers adopted a black line in their lace. The men's dress followed the accepted infantry patterns.

See also the grenadier, 1768 (*20*)

10th Foot

1685 John, Earl of Bath's Regiment of Foot, then known by succeeding colonels' names.

1751 The 10th Regiment of Foot.

1782 The 10th (North Lincoln) Regiment of Foot.

1881 *The Lincolnshire Regiment*.

1946 The Royal Lincolnshire Regiment.

1960 Amalgamated with the Northamptonshire Regiment to form the 2nd East Anglian (Duchess of Gloucester's Own Royal Lincolnshire and Northamptonshire).

1964 Amalgamated with the 1st and 3rd East Anglian and Royal Leicestershire to form the 2nd Battalion the Royal Anglian Regiment.

1968 In the Queen's Division.

This regiment was unusual in having blue coats when it was raised in 1685. These were faced with red, and waistcoats and stockings were also red. The reason for blue is not known but the livery for the Earl of Bath at this time was blue with red cuffs and linings, so he may have had some garments available. The regimental history states that the blue coats were changed to red with red facings in 1691. It must be mentioned that blue-coated infantry did appear in England as a compliment to the Prince of Orange when he arrived in 1688 as his troops wore this colour, but the 'Bath' uniform cannot be attributed to so early a date. The blue coat became discontinued in England and this may have brought back the red coat of the Stuarts. The linings may have been changed to yellow in William's reign; and yellow facings continued until the change to white in 1881. The Sphinx for service in Egypt was granted in 1802. The men's dress followed the normal changes.

See also the officer, Earl of Bath's Regiment (*21*)

Overleaf:

15.

The Buffs (East Kent Regiment)

a 1768, grenadier
b 1751, grenadier
c 1742, battalion private
d 1792, officer
e 1792, private
f 1814, officer
g 1905, private, officer and drummer, all in full dress
h 1814, private
i 1826, officer
j 1852, officer
k 1864, bandsman
l 1861, officer
m 1832, private

a 1768

b 1751

c 1742

d 1792

e 1792

f 1814

g
1905
The Buffs (East Kent Regt.)

R.Simkin.

h 1814

i 1826

j 1852

k 1864

l 1861

m 1832

Plate 15

4TH KING'S OWN ROYAL REGIMENT
1852.

Plate 16

6TH ROYAL FIRST WARWICKSHIRE REGIMENT,
1852.

Plate 17

11th Foot

1685   Raised by Henry, Duke of Beaufort, and then known by succeeding colonels' names.

1751   The 11th Regiment of Foot.

1782   The 11th (North Devonshire) Regiment of Foot.

1881   *The Devonshire Regiment.*

1958   Amalgamated with the Dorset Regiment as the 1st Battalion Devonshire and Dorset Regiment.

1968   In the Prince of Wales's Division.

When raised, the regiment's red coats were faced with 'tawny' with the same colour for the breeches and stockings. Early in the next century yellow was the distinguishing colour, but this was changed to dark green. This was the colour shown in the 1742 *Cloathing* book, with red waistcoat and breeches. The shade of green may have varied but this colour remained until 1881 when white became the official colour for all English regiments. By determined efforts Lincoln green was restored in 1905. There were no special distinctions in uniforms but the Castle of Exeter was chosen in 1883 as a distinctive badge.

See also the group, 1686 to 1914 (*22*) and the private, 1792 (*23*)

12th Foot

1685   Henry, Duke of Norfolk incorporated his company this year into the regiment later to be known as the Suffolk; then known by succeeding colonels' names.

1751   The 12th Regiment of Foot.

1782   12th (or the East Suffolk) Regiment of Foot.

1881   *The Suffolk Regiment.*

1959   Amalgamated with the Royal Norfolk to form the 1st East Anglian Regiment (Royal Norfolk and Suffolk).

1964   Amalgamated with the 2nd and 3rd East Anglian and the Leicestershire Regiments to form the Royal Anglian Regiment.

1968   In the Queen's Division.

In 1686 the regimental coat was lined with white and the breeches and stockings were blue. When the change to yellow facings was made is not known, but it was so in 1742 when the waistcoat and breeches were red. Yellow remained the facing colour until 1881 when white was ordered, but the yellow was restored in 1899. The officers' lace had been gold since the eighteenth century. The uniforms followed the basic infantry development and having served in Gibraltar 1778–83 the regiment was granted later the distinction of the Castle and Key with the motto '*Montis Insignia Calpe*'. The regiment also wore roses in its head-dress in honour of Minden Day (1 August).

See also the grenadier, 1751 (*24*)

Preceding page:
16.
4th King's Own Royal Regiment, 1852, officer

17.
6th Royal 1st Warwickshire Regiment, 1852, bandsman

13th Foot

1685   Raised by Theophilis, Earl of Huntingdon, and then known by succeeding colonels' names.

1751   The 13th Regiment of Foot.

1782   13th (or the 1st Somersetshire) Regiment of Foot.

1822   13th (1st Somersetshire Light Infantry) Regiment.

1842   13th (1st Somersetshire) (Prince Albert's Regiment of Light
        Infantry).
1881   *Prince Albert's (Somersetshire Light Infantry).*
1912   Prince Albert's (Somerset Light Infantry).
1920   The Somerset Light Infantry (Prince Albert's).
1953   Amalgamated with the Duke of Cornwall's Light Infantry to form
        the Somerset and Cornwall Light Infantry.
1968   Amalgamated with the King's Own Yorkshire Light Infantry, the
        King's Shropshire Light Infantry and the Durham Light Infantry to
        form the Light Infantry in the Light Division.

The regiment began with yellow facings and breeches with grey hose. Yellow facings continued although the colour was sometimes called light yellow or philemot. On being named 'Prince Albert's' the regiment was given blue facings. The officers' lace had been silver but changed to gold in 1830 and had a black line. The dress followed normal infantry practice, taking on light infantry distinctions in 1822. Badges for this regiment included the Sphinx for Egypt, the bugle-horn for light infantry and the special Mural Crown for Jellahabad.

See also the group, 1742–c. 1914 (*68*), the picket, 1777 (*69a*), and the pioneer, 1812 (*69b*)

14th Foot

1685   Sir Edward Hales raised this regiment at the time of the Monmouth
        Rebellion; it was then known by succeeding colonels' names.
1751   The 14th Regiment of Foot.
1782   The 14th (Bedfordshire) Regiment of Foot.
1809   The 14th (Buckinghamshire) Regiment of Foot (title exchanged with
        16th Foot).
1876   The 14th (Buckinghamshire or the Prince of Wales's Own) Regiment
        of Foot.
1881   *The Prince of Wales's Own (West Yorkshire Regiment).*
1920   The West Yorkshire Regiment (The Prince of Wales's Own).
1958   Amalgamated with the East Yorkshire Regiment to form the Prince
        of Wales's Own Regiment of Yorkshire.
1968   In the King's Division.

Apart from the fact that the regiment wore red coats and grey stockings little more is known until 1742 when buff facings were worn, and these continued until 1881. The obligatory white facings were then worn until they were replaced in 1900 by buff. The officers' lace, which had been silver, changed to gold in 1830. The basic infantry dress was worn. Distinctions in the way of badges included the White Horse and '*Nec Aspera Terrent*', the 'Royal Tiger superscribed India' and, of course, the Prince of Wales's Feathers and '*Ich Dien*' from 1876.

See also the grenadier, 1685 (*25*)

15th Foot

1685   Sir William Clifton raised this regiment in Nottingham; it was then
        known by succeeding colonels' names.
1751   The 15th Regiment of Foot.
1782   The 15th (Yorkshire, East Riding) Regiment of Foot.

Overleaf:
18.
Royal Warwickshire Regiment
a 1768, grenadier
b 1742, private
c 1688, officer
d 1751, grenadier
e 1792, officer
f 1808, private
g 1905, officer, frock coat, officer
     and private full dress
h 1813, officer
i 1826, officer levée dress
j 1852, officer
k 1875, private marching order
l 1860, officer
m 1832, private

a *1768*

b *1742*

c *1688*

d *1751*

e *1792*

f *1868*

g *1905*

ROYAL WARWICKSHIRE REGT.

h *1813*

i *1826*

j *1852*

k *1875*

l *1860*

m *1832*

R. SIMKIN.

10.

Plate 18

THE KING'S REGIMENT- 1742.
(now the 8TH King's Liverpool Regt.)

Plate 19

1881 *The East Yorkshire Regiment.*
1935 The East Yorkshire Regiment (the Duke of York's Own).
1958 Amalgamated with the West Yorkshire Regiment (the Prince of Wales's) as the Prince of Wales's Own Regiment of Yorkshire.
1968 In the King's Division.

In the reign of James II the uniform was red lined red with white stockings. When the yellow facings (first shown *c.* 1742) were first worn is not known, but they were retained until 1881, when white became regulation. In the seventeenth century the officers' lace was silver but changed to gold in 1830, taking on a black line after 1881. The regimental uniform followed the normal practices.
See also the private, 1792 (*26*)

16th Foot

1688 Raised by Colonel Archibald Douglas, and then known by succeeding colonels' names.
1751 The 16th Regiment of Foot.
1782 The 16th (Buckinghamshire) Regiment of Foot.
1809 The 16th (Bedfordshire) Regiment of Foot (exchanged titles with the 14th Foot).
1881 *The Bedfordshire Regiment.*
1919 The Bedfordshire and Hertfordshire Regiment.
1958 Amalgamated with the Essex Regiment to form the 3rd East Anglian Regiment (16/44th).
1964 Amalgamated with the 1st and 2nd East Anglian Regiment to form the Royal Anglian Regiment.
1968 In the Queen's Division.

In 1689 the red coat of the regiment was lined red but the lining changed in 1691 to white. Some time before 1742 the facing colour changed to yellow, but in 1881 it went back again to white. Officers' lace had been silver and changed in 1830 to gold. The uniform followed normal infantry fashions and the distinctive badge of the Hart came after 1881.
See also the private, 1822 (*27*)

17th Foot

1688 Raised by Colonel Solomon Richards, and then known by succeeding colonels' names.
1751 17th Regiment of Foot.
1782 17th (or the Leicestershire) Regiment of Foot.
1881 *The Leicestershire Regiment.*
1946 The Royal Leicestershire Regiment.
1964 Became the Tiger Company of the 4th Battalion Royal Anglian Regiment.
1968 In the Queen's Division.

It is said that the regiment had grey coats in the early days, but the 1742 *Cloathing* book is the best information for the pearl-grey facings quoted in regulations up to 1768. However, the inspection reports of 1769 speak of white facings, so the tint may have been very subtle. The ruling of white for English regiments in 1881 made a firm decision, but the pearl-grey facings were not forgotten and in 1931 they were restored. The officers' lace was silver and early in the nineteenth century was noted as having a black line in the centre. Gold lace and buttons came in 1830 but the black line was

Preceding page:
19.
The King's Regiment (later 8th;
The King's Liverpool Regiment),
1742, private

eventually placed on each side of the new 'rose' pattern lace. The dress followed normal developments and the badge of the Royal Tiger was granted in 1825.

See also the private, 1798 (*28a*) and the bandsman, 1828 (*28b*)

18th Foot

1684   The independent company raised by the Earl of Granard was the nucleus of a regiment which eventually came on the English establishment; it was known at first by the succeeding colonels' names.

1695   The Royal Regiment of Ireland.

1751   The 18th (The Royal Irish) Regiment of Foot.

1881   *The Royal Irish Regiment.*

1922   Disbanded.

Even before being named royal, this Irish regiment had red coats lined blue and they wore white stocks. The royal blue facings continued throughout the life of the regiment, as did the gold lace and buttons for the officers. It was the assault on the Fortress of Namur in 1695 that brought them not only the royal title from William III but also the right to have the Harp of Ireland with the Crown and the Lion arms of Nassau. Later the Sphinx was gained for Egypt (1802) as well as the Dragon for China (1843).

See also the officer, 1913 (*29*)

19th Foot

1688   Raised by Francis Lutterell, and then known by succeeding colonels' names.

1751   19th Regiment of Foot.

1782   19th (or the 1st Yorkshire North Riding) Regiment of Foot.

1875   19th (1st Yorkshire North Riding) (Princess of Wales's Own) Regiment of Foot.

1881   *The Princess of Wales's Own (Yorkshire Regiment).*

1902   Alexandra, Princess of Wales's Own Yorkshire Regiment.

1920   The Green Howards (Alexandra, Princess of Wales's Own Yorkshire Regiment).

1968   In the King's Division.

As officers' coats in the seventeenth century were blue, it may be that the men also were clothed in blue, possibly with yellow facings, for yellow was the colour of the facings in 1709. When the facings changed to green is not known, but it may have been *c.* 1738 when Sir Charles Howard became their colonel, for the 1742 *Cloathing* book shows full green facings. The shade varied later from yellow-green to dull green. In 1881 white facings for English regiments were the rule but in 1899 grass green was restored. The officers' lace was gold from the earliest days. The White Rose of York was a distinction but later the Cipher of Princess Alexandra and the Coronet on the Danneborg Cross became the distinctive badge.

See also the officer, 1792 (*30a*), and the colour-sergeant (*30b*)

Overleaf:
20.
9th Foot, 1768, grenadier

20th Foot

1688   Sir Richard Peyton raised the regiment in Devon; it was then known by succeeding colonels' names.

1751   20th Regiment of Foot.

1782   20th (or East Devonshire) Regiment of Foot.

9TH FOOT.
(Grenadier)-1768.

Plate 20

a

b

c

d

e

f

g

DEVONSHIRE REGT
(11th Foot)

h

i

j

k

l

m

Plate 22

1881   *The Lancashire Fusiliers.*

1968   Amalgamated with the Royal Northumberland Fusiliers, the Royal Warwickshire Fusiliers and the Royal Fusiliers to form the 4th Battalion Royal Regiment of Fusiliers in the Queen's Division.

The early uniform is not known. At the beginning of the eighteenth century it was said to be red, lined and faced with white, but by 1740 the facings were yellow and remained so until 1881 when they became white. The officers' lace began as silver but changed to gold in 1830. The uniforms followed that of infantry of the line until 1881 when the fusilier distinctions were adopted. The Sphinx for Egypt and the Laurel Wreath were badges of the old 20th Foot but after 1881 the Red Rose of Lancaster was added to the grenade. Roses were worn on the head-dress on Minden Day.

See also the officer with King's Colour, 1913 (*63*)

21st Foot

1678   Raised by the Earl of Mar, and then known by succeeding colonels' names.

1691   O'Farrell's Fusiliers and then known by succeeding colonels' names.

1707   Regiment of Scots Fuzileers.

1712   Royal North British Fusiliers.

1715   Lord Orrery's Regiment of Scotch Fusiliers.

1751   21st Regiment of Foot (or Royal North British Fusiliers).

1877   The 21st Royal Scots Fusiliers.

1881   *The Royal Scots Fusiliers.*

1959   Amalgamated with the Highland Light Infantry and became the Royal Highland Fusiliers (Princess Margaret's Own Glasgow and Ayrshire Regiment).

1968   In the Scottish Division.

Towards the end of the seventeenth century the red coats were lined and faced red but on being made royal the facings changed to blue and remained so. The officers' lace was gold at least from 1739 and the uniforms developed like those of other fusiliers. The Scottish Thistle with the Circle of St Andrew was worn on the cloth caps as was the Scottish motto '*Nemo me impune lacessit*'. When formed, they were nicknamed 'greybreeks'.

See also the group, 1742–1905 (*64*)

22nd Foot

1689   Henry, Duke of Norfolk raised this regiment in the vicinity of Chester; it was then known by succeeding colonels' names.

1751   22nd Regiment of Foot.

1782   22nd (or the Cheshire) Regiment of Foot.

1881   *The Cheshire Regiment.*

1968   Part of the Prince of Wales's Division.

Buff facings may have been worn from earliest days, although the exact shade varied. White facings were worn in 1881 as an English regimental distinction, but in 1904 the buff facings were restored. Officers' lace and buttons were gold and the dress followed normal infantry practice. The Prince of Wales's Feathers were adopted in 1881 coming from the now-associated Cheshire Militia. The badge of the Acorn was taken into wear from 1881 and was said to be a reminder of an incident at Dettingen. However, the oak sprig with an acorn can be traced back to 1689 when the

Preceding page.
22.
Devonshire (11th Foot) Regiment
a   1686, officer, grenadier co.
b   1742, private
c   1751, grenadier
d   1768, grenadier
e   1792, officer
f   1814, officer
g   1914, other rank dress, man and officer service dress, mounted officer full dress
h   1826, officer
i   1832, private
j   1852, officer
k   1860, officer
l   1864, bandsman
m 1864, private

two original colonels of the regiment, the Duke of Norfolk and Henry Bellasis, both had this device in their coat-of-arms.
See also the officer, 1806 (*31a*) and the private, 1812 (*31b*)

23rd Foot

1688   Raised by Henry, Lord Herbert in the Welsh Marches, and then known by succeeding colonels' names.
1714   The Prince of Wales's Own Royal Regiment of Welsh Fusiliers.
1727   The Royal Welsh Fusileers.
1751   23rd (Royal Welsh Fusileers) Regiment of Foot.
1881   *The Royal Welsh Fusiliers.*
1920   The Royal Welch Fusiliers.
1968   In the Prince of Wales's Division.

As the regiment was raised to support the cause of King William III, it was dressed in blue coats (thus imitating the Dutch troops) with white facings and linings. When it changed to red coats is not known, nor even when the facings were changed, but it could possibly be in 1714 that the blue facings were taken into wear, and they have remained to the present day. Officers would have gold embroidery, lace and buttons that went with the royal livery. The dress followed that of fusiliers. On the cloth 'grenadier' caps were embroidered the three feathers of the Prince of Wales issuing from a coronet, with the motto '*Ich Dien*'. Later the Sphinx for Egypt was granted, and when pigtails were cut off about 1808 these fusiliers retained the black ribbon or 'flash' which held the hair in place, as a neck ornament. (The development of dress is also noted in the uniform section on the uniform of fusiliers and grenadiers, pp. 125 and 117).
See also the group, 1742 to *c.* 1914 (*65*)

24th Foot

1689   Raised by Sir Edward Dering, and then known by succeeding colonels' names.
1751   The 24th Regiment of Foot.
1782   24th (or the 2nd Warwickshire) Regiment of Foot.
1881   *The South Wales Borderers.*
1969   Joined with the Welch Regiment to form the Royal Regiment of Wales (24/41) in the Prince of Wales's Division.

No information is available for the first uniform but by 1742 the facings were green with skirt linings of white. 'Willow green' was an early description of the facings but later 'grass green' was quoted, and it was this colour which was restored in 1905 after the facings had been changed temporarily to white in 1881. Officers' distinctions were silver until the ruling for gold was made in 1830. The uniforms followed the general rules and fashions. The Sphinx for Egypt was granted in 1802 and in 1880 Queen Victoria authorized a 'Wreath of Immortelle' but a laurel wreath had been worn on appointments many years before.
See also the group, 1742 to *c.* 1914 (*32*)

25th Foot

1689   David, Earl of Leven raised this Edinburgh regiment for William III in a matter of hours; it was then known by succeeding colonels' names.
1751   25th Regiment of Foot.

Overleaf:
23.
11th North Devonshire Regiment, 1792, private
24.
12th East Suffolk Regiment, 1751, grenadier
25.
Hales's Regiment of Foot (later 14th; the Prince of Wales's Own West Yorkshire Regiment), 1685, grenadier

11ᵀᴴ NORTH DEVONSHIRE REGIMENT, 1792.

Plate 23

12ᵀᴴ EAST SUFFOLK REGIMENT, 1751.

COLONEL SIR EDWARD HALES REGIMENT OF FOOT,
(NOW THE PRINCE OF WALES'S OWN WEST YORKSHIRE REGT)
GRENADIER-1685.

Plate 24   **Plate 25**

15TH YORKSHIRE EAST RIDING REGIMENT
1792

Plate 26

16TH BEDFORDSHIRE REGIMENT
1828

Plate 27

1782   25th (or the Sussex) Regiment of Foot.
1805   25th (or the King's Own Borderers) Regiment of Foot.
1881   *The King's Own Borderers.*
1887   The King's Own Scottish Borderers.
1968   In the Scottish Division.

The earliest-known facings are deep yellow, which in the third quarter of the eighteenth century were almost orange. When it was made the King's Own Borderers in 1805 blue facings were given to the red coat. The officers' distinctions were gold. The dress was that of line regiments but occasionally Scottish distinctions were to be seen, such as the 'Scottish company' *c.* 1776 and the pipers who are said to have worn the Royal Stuart tartan after 1805. In 1882 it became a Lowland regiment wearing doublets and trews. The uniform had been basic infantry up to that date and its developments followed the Lowland. In 1802 the Sphinx for Egypt was granted, in 1805 the Royal Crest and in 1832 the Castle of Edinburgh was allowed on the appointments.
See also the group, 1742–1914 (*97*)

26th Foot

1689   James, Earl of Angus raised the Cameronian Regiment of Foot; it was then known by succeeding colonels' names.
1751   26th Regiment of Foot.
1782   26th (or Cameronian) Regiment of Foot.
1881   *The Cameronians (Scottish Rifles).*
1968   Disbanded.

It is possible that the early red coats were faced with white but evidence is lacking on this point. In 1742 pale yellow facings were known. These continued until 1881 when the regiment became rifles, wearing green doublets with dark green facings. The officers' distinctions had been silver up to 1830 and then gold, but in 1881 they took black buttons and braid. The uniform at the beginning had been mainly that of Infantry of the Line but occasionally Scottish items were worn (see the Lowland section, pp. 156–165), but after 1881 it is the Rifle section which should be consulted. Among the badges are the Sphinx for Egypt in 1802, the Dragon for China, and the Mullet or spur rowel adopted in the late nineteenth century which had its origins from the crest of the Graham of the 90th Foot.
See also the group, 1688–1914 (*98*)

27th Foot

1689   Zachariah Tiffin's commission for raising the regiment is dated 1689, but it was formed from independent companies that had been raised earlier in Enniskillin. It was then known by succeeding colonels' names.
1751   27th (or Inniskilling) Regiment of Foot.
1881   Linked with the 108th Regiment to form the 1st Battalion of the *Royal Inniskilling Fusiliers.*
1968   Amalgamated with the Royal Ulster Rifles and the Royal Irish Fusiliers to form the Royal Irish Rangers in the King's Division.

It was once thought that the Inniskilling Regiment had grey uniforms at its creation but evidence now exists for red coats and blue breeches being brought from London in 1689, and as a quantity of red shalloon was sent in a list of 1690 it may have been used as lining to the scarlet cloth sent at the

Preceding page:
26.
15th Yorkshire East Riding Regiment, 1792, private

27.
16th Bedfordshire Regiment,
1822, private

same time for officers. What the first facings were is not known but by 1742 they were buff and continued so until 1881 when they were changed to blue. The officers' lace and buttons had been silver but in 1768 gold was quoted. The special ancient badge was the Castle with three turrets, St George's colours flying, with the name 'Inniskilling'. The Sphinx for Egypt was granted in 1802, and when the regiment became fusiliers in 1881 they took the grenade badge. The uniforms up to this date had been the normal infantry patterns but thereafter they had the fusilier distinctions.

See also the piper, 1900 (*66b*) and the musketeer, 1680 (*66a*).

28th Foot

1694   Sir John Gibson first raised this regiment in Portsmouth where it was disbanded in 1698 but it was reraised in 1702, having maintained its ancestors from a detachment of sixty men remaining in Newfoundland. It was then known by succeeding colonels' names.

1751   28th Regiment of Foot.

1782   28th (or the North Gloucestershire) Regiment of Foot.

1881   Linked with the 61st Foot and became the 1st Battalion *The Gloucestershire Regiment*.

1968   In the Prince of Wales's Division.

The first uniform had a red coat faced with bright yellow. The facings were changed to white in 1881 but in 1929 they were permitted to be primrose yellow (a compromise between the yellow of the 28th and the buff of the 61st). Officers' lace had been silver in 1768 but changed to gold in 1830. The uniforms were those of Infantry of the Line. The Sphinx for Egypt was granted in 1802 and at the same time achieved a unique honour when they fought an enemy attacking both the front and rear, thus gaining the special honour of the 'Back Badge', the sphinx within a laurel wreath. This badge continued to be worn on the back of the head-dress to modern times.

See also the private, 1913 (*33*).

29th Foot

1694   This regiment was raised by Thomas Farrington in 1694 but was broken in 1698. It was reraised in 1702 and was known by succeeding colonels' names.

1751   29th Regiment of Foot.

1782   29th (or the Worcestershire) Regiment of Foot.

1881   Amalgamated with the 36th Foot and became the 1st Battalion *Worcestershire Regiment*.

1970   Amalgamated with the Sherwood Foresters to form the Worcestershire and Sherwood Foresters Regiment in the Prince of Wales's Division.

In 1694 the regiment was supplied with coats of white kersey faced with yellow and blue breeches, but two years later red coats with yellow facings were being worn. Yellow facings were worn until 1881 when the obligatory white was worn. But in 1920 the facings became grass green (from those of the old 36th or 2nd Battalion). The officers' lace had been silver but in 1830 became gold. The uniforms followed the normal practices.

See also the officer, 1842 (*34*).

Overleaf:
28.
17th Leicestershire Regiment
a   1798, private
b   1828, bandsman

29.
Royal Irish Regiment (late 18th), 1913, officer

17ᵀᴴ LEICESTERSHIRE REGIMENT.
1798.

17ᵀᴴ LEICESTERSHIRE REGIMENT.
1828.

Plate 28 a

Plate 28 b

THE ROYAL IRISH REGIMENT
(18ᵀᴴ FOOT) 1913.

Plate 29

19ᵀᴴ FIRST YORKSHIRE NORTH RIDING REGIMENT.
1792

a

19ᵀᴴ FIRST YORKSHIRE, NORTH RIDING REGIMENT.
1860.

b

Plate 30

30th Foot

1694   Colonel Thomas Saunderson raised the regiment but it was disbanded in 1698.

1702   Colonel Saunderson and his half-pay officers re-raised the regiment which at first acted as marines; it was then known by succeeding colonels' names.

1751   30th Regiment of Foot.

1782   30th (or the Cambridgeshire) Regiment of Foot.

1881   Joined the 59th Foot and became the 1st Battalion *East Lancashire Regiment*.

1958   Amalgamated with the South Lancashire Regiment to form the Lancashire Regiment (Prince of Wales's Volunteers).

The facings of the 30th Foot were yellow and became white in 1881. The officers' lace and buttons were silver until 1830 and then became gold. The uniforms followed the normal developments and the regiment gained the Sphinx for Egypt in 1802.

See also the officer, light infantry company, 1852 (*35*)

31st Foot

1702   The regiment raised by George Villiers was another of the six regiments destined for sea-service and although disbanded in 1715 was restored and placed on the establishment. It was then known by succeeding colonels' names.

1751   The 31st Foot.

1782   31st (or the Huntingdonshire) Regiment of Foot.

1881   Joined the 70th Foot to become the 1st Battalion *East Surrey Regiment*.

1959   Amalgamated with the Queen's Royal Regiment (West Surrey) to form the Queen's Royal Surrey Regiment.

1968   In the Queen's Division.

When enlisted for sea-service as marines they are said to have worn 'high crowned leather caps' and the red coats were lined with yellow. On re-raising, the red coats had buff facings but these became white in 1881. The officers' lace and buttons were silver until 1830 when they became gold. The uniforms developed no special features but in 1881 the Arms of Guildford became their special badge.

See also the grenadier, 1751 (*36*)

Preceding page:
30.
19th 1st Yorkshire North Riding Regiment
a   1792, officer
b   1860, colour-sergeant

32nd Foot

1702   This third marine regiment was raised by Edward Cox and was also broken at the peace of 1715. It was re-formed at once and was then known by succeeding colonels' names.

1751   32nd Regiment of Foot.

1782   32nd (or the Cornwall) Regiment of Foot.

1858   32nd (Cornwall) Light Infantry.

1881   Joined the 46th Foot to become the 1st Battalion *The Duke of Cornwall's Light Infantry*.

1959   Amalgamated with the Somerset Light Infantry to become the Somerset and Cornwall Light Infantry.

1968   In the Light Division.

The uniform of Fox's marines was red faced and lined green but the later uniform was slightly different. There was a green lining to the coat but there were no lapels and the cuffs were white. In 1751 white facings were regulation and remained so until the end of full dress. Officers' lace was gold in regulations from 1768 onwards. The uniforms followed basic infantry patterns until 1858 when light infantry distinctions were added, although this brought little change apart from the green horse-hair plume, the whistle and chain for the sergeant, and buglers instead of drummers. The bugle badge was now worn.

See also the private, 1864 (*70a*) and the officer, 1870 (*70b*)

33rd Foot

1702   Regimental histories quote the Earl of Huntingdon as having raised the regiment but old Army Lists give James Stanhope as the colonel in February 1702 and the Earl in 1703. The regiment was then known by succeeding colonels' names.

1751   33rd Regiment of Foot.

1782   33rd (or the 1st Yorkshire West Riding) Regiment of Foot.

1853   33rd (or the Duke of Wellington's) Regiment of Foot.

1881   Joined with the 76th and became the 1st Battalion *The Duke of Wellington's (West Riding Regiment)*.

1920   The Duke of Wellington's Regiment (West Riding).

1968   In the King's Division.

The dress of the Earl of Huntingdon's regiment in 1702 had a red coat lined with yellow and yellow breeches, that being 'the regiment's livery'. Later the same century the coats had red facings but white linings (showing in the turn-backed skirts), and the 1742 print has red cuffs, waistcoat and breeches. Red or scarlet facings were retained until 1881 when the 'English' white had to be assumed. But in 1905 the scarlet facings were restored. Officers' lace and buttons had been silver but took the regulation gold in 1830. The uniforms followed the normal development and after 1893 the badge of the Duke of Wellington was worn.

See also the officer, 1872 (*37*)

34th Foot

1702   The Lieutenant of the Tower of London, Robert Lord Lucas, raised in the Southern counties a regiment which among other duties guarded the Tower of London. It was known by succeeding colonels' names.

1751   The 34th Regiment of Foot.

1782   34th (or the Cumberland) Regiment of Foot.

1881   Joined the 55th Foot to become the 1st Battalion the *Border Regiment*.

1959   Amalgamated with the King's Own Royal Regiment (Lancaster) to form the King's Own Royal Border Regiment.

1968   In the King's Division.

Lord Lucas's regiment had red coats lined with grey though later the lining was changed to white; the grey of the facings also applied to the waistcoats and breeches. Later the facings were made light yellow and the waistcoat and breeches red. As in the case of other regiments, the facings were the regulation white in 1881 but in 1913 yellow came back again. The officers' lace and buttons which had been silver changed to gold in 1830. The dress followed the infantry development. When the white ball-tuft was introduced for shakos in 1835 for battalion companies, the 34th were

Overleaf:
31.
22nd Cheshire Regiment
a   1806, officer
b   1812, private

22ⁿᵈ CHESHIRE REGIMENT.
1808.

a

22ⁿᵈ CHESHIRE REGIMENT.
1812.

b

Plate 31

a 1742

b 1751

c 1768

d 1792

e 1792

f 1814

g

SOUTH WALES BORDERERS

R. SIMKIN

h 1826

i 1840

j 1852

k

l

m 1879

13

Plate 32

permitted to have one which was half-red and half-white. This distinction was due to the capture of the 34th French infantry in a Peninsular War battle. When about 1846 all battalion companies were permitted a tuft two-thirds white and one-third red, the 34th continued their half-and-half distinction; one continued even as a backing to their modern metal badges. Officers' lace and buttons were silver up to 1830, then gold.

See also the officer, 1814 (*38*)

35th Foot

1701   This regiment was raised in Belfast by Arthur, Earl of Donegal who had commanded a regiment in the reign of William III. In 1702 it came on the British establishment and was known by succeeding colonels' names.

1751   35th Regiment of Foot.

1782   35th (or the Dorsetshire) Regiment of Foot.

1804   35th (or the Royal Sussex) Regiment of Foot.

1881   Joined the 107th Regiment to become the 1st Battalion the *Royal Sussex Regiment*.

1966   Amalgamated with the Queen's Royal Surrey Regiment, the Queen's Own Buffs and the Middlesex Regiment as a battalion of the Queen's Regiment.

1968   In the Queen's Division.

When formed in Ireland the red coats had orange facings in honour of King William's House of Orange. The orange facings continued until 1832 when the royal blue was permitted. The officers had silver distinctions until 1830 when gold was regulation. The Roussillon plume said to have been taken from that French regiment was allowed as a regimental badge in 1880. The uniform changes followed those of the infantry of the line and of royal regiments.

See also the officer, 1825 (*39*)

36th Foot

1701   This regiment was also raised in Ireland, the colonel being William, Viscount Charlemont. It came on the British establishment the following year and was then known by succeeding colonels' names.

1751   36th Regiment of Foot.

1782   36th (or the Herefordshire) Regiment of Foot.

1881   Joined the 29th Regiment and became the 2nd Battalion the *Worcestershire Regiment*.

This regiment had sea-service for many years and there is no evidence of the green facings until 1742. Later the shade was gosling green, grass green or other shades, until 1881 when white was authorized. A regimental motto 'Firm' is known to have been worn from 1773 at least, and it appeared on regimental devices. The uniform had no unusual developments.

See also the grenadier, 1768 (*40*)

37th Foot

1702   Thomas Meredith raised this regiment in Ireland and it was known by succeeding colonels' names until 1751.

1751   37th Regiment of Foot.

1782   37th (or North Hampshire) Regiment of Foot.

1881   Joined the 67th Regiment and became the 1st Battalion *The*

Preceding page:
32.
South Wales Borderers (late 24th)
a   1742, private
b   1751, grenadier
c   1768, grenadier
d   1792, officer
e   1792, private
f   1814, officer
g   1905, officer service dress, officer full dress mounted
h   1826, officer levée dress
i   1840, officer
j   1852, private
k   1856, private
l   1875, officer
m   1879, private, Zululand dress

Hampshire Regiment.

1946   The Royal Hampshire Regiment.

1968   In the Prince of Wales's Division.

The early uniform is not recorded but by 1742 the facings were yellow. When they changed to white in 1881 efforts were made to restore the yellow and this was achieved in 1903. The officers appear to have had gold appointments in the early seventeenth century but in 1768 they had silver, and this was retained until 1830 when the regulation gold was worn. The uniforms were according to regulation and the Hampshire Rose as a badge was not adopted until 1881. The winning of the battle honour for Minden allowed the wearing of roses on Minden Day.

See also the group, 1742–c. 1914 (*41*)

38th Foot

1702   13 February is the date given in early Army Lists for the commission of Luke Lillingston, who raised the regiment, but in another source April 1705 is given as the official date of raising the regiment.

1751   38th Regiment of Foot.

1782   38th (or 1st Staffordshire) Regiment of Foot.

1881   Joined with the 80th to become the 1st Battalion *The South Staffordshire Regiment.*

1959   Amalgamated with the North Staffordshire Regiment to form the Staffordshire Regiment (The Prince of Wales's).

1968   In the Prince of Wales's Division.

Grey undress garments seem to have been worn in the early days but by 1742 bright yellow facings were established in the regiment for the red coats. In 1881 white facings were authorized but in 1936 the yellow facings were restored. Because of the fifty-seven years spent in the West Indies when they had to wear ticking under-garments and linings to the coats, brown linen has been worn traditionally on mess dress and service dress. Officers' lace and buttons were silver up to 1830, then gold. The 'Sphinx for Egypt' was granted in 1802 and the Stafford Knot frequently appeared on appointments.

See also the group, 1742–c. 1914 (*42*)

39th Foot

1702   Colonel Richard Coote raised the regiment in Ireland and it was named after several colonels before it was numbered.

1751   39th Regiment of Foot.

1782   39th (or East Middlesex) Regiment of Foot.

1809   39th (Dorsetshire) Regiment of Foot.

1881   Joined the 54th Foot and became the 1st Battalion *The Dorsetshire Regiment.*

1951   The Dorset Regiment.

1958   Amalgamated with the Devonshire Regiment to form the Devonshire and Dorset Regiment.

1968   In the Prince of Wales's Division.

In 1707 the men mounted mules to be at the battle of Almanza and gained the nickname 'Sankey's Horse'. A few years later they acted as marines. No distinctive facings may be quoted before 1742, when pale green was used for the facings and the waistcoat. The green was later named as 'willow green', 'popinjay', 'light green' and other variations, no doubt because a

Overleaf:
33.
The Gloucestershire Regiment (late 28th), 1913, private

34.
29th Worcestershire Regiment, 1842, officer

THE GLOUCESTERSHIRE REGIMENT (28TH)
1913.

Plate 33

29TH WORCESTERSHIRE REGIMENT.
1842.

Plate 34

30TH CAMBRIDGESHIRE REGIMENT.
LIGHT COMPANY - 1852.

Plate 35

31ST FOOT.
1751.

Plate 36

fixed shade of green was hard to find in those days when dyes changed under battle conditions. White facings were ordered in 1881, but in 1904 gave place to grass green. Officers' lace and buttons, which had been silver, changed to gold in 1830. The regiment received distinctions for being at Gibraltar, 1777–83, and for being the first regular regiment seen in India. The uniforms followed the normal developments.

See also the drummer, 1875 (*43*)

40th Foot

1717   Colonel Richard Philipps (his spelling) formed this regiment from four independent companies in Nova Scotia and four in Newfoundland; it was then known by succeeding colonels' names.

1751   40th Regiment of Foot.

1782   40th (or 2nd Somersetshire) Regiment of Foot.

1881   Joined the 82nd Regiment and became 1st Battalion *The Prince of Wales's Volunteers (South Lancashire Regiment)*.

1920   The Prince of Wales's Volunteers (South Lancashire).

1938   The South Lancashire Regiment (The Prince of Wales's Volunteers).

1958   Amalgamated with the East Lancashire Regiment to form the Lancashire Regiment (Prince of Wales's Volunteers).

1970   Amalgamated with the Loyal Regiment (North Lancashire) to form the Queen's Lancashire Regiment in the King's Division.

The red coat may have had buff facings from the beginning but confirmation only comes in 1742. White facings were obligatory in 1881 but buff was restored in 1928. As the regiment served in America, permission was sought to discontinue the coloured braid on the buttonholes of the men, but this was refused as this privilege was only granted to the 60th Royal Americans. Officers' lace and buttons were known to have been gold from 1768 onwards. Dress would have followed the normal developments, but local variations were expected in North America. The flank companies earned the Sphinx for Egypt, 1801.

See also the officer, grenadier company, 1832 (*44*)

41st Foot

1719   It was decided to form a regiment of invalid soldiers who were not too disabled or too old, and Colonel Edmund Fielding raised ten companies capable of performing garrison duties.

1751   41st Regiment of Invalids.

1787   41st Regiment of Foot.

1831   41st (Welsh) Regiment of Foot (1852–62 spelt 'Welch').

1862   The 41st the Welsh Regiment of Foot.

1881   *The Welsh Regiment*, on linking with the 69th Foot.

1920   The Welch Regiment.

1969   Amalgamated with the South Wales Borderers as the Royal Regiment of Wales (24/41 Foot) in the Prince of Wales's Division.

The uniform of the invalids was loose-fitting as may be expected for handicapped soldiers and was much like that worn today in the Royal Hospital, Chelsea. The voluminous red coat had blue cuffs and blue baize lining to the skirts which were not fastened back. The waistcoat and breeches were blue and no lace was worn. The men's buttons were brass. Officers had a similar uniform without lace but later gold epaulettes were worn. After 1769 silver was to be the metal for epaulettes and hat. In 1787 the 41st became a 'duty' regiment and the invalids were removed. The facings were now red and regimental lace was worn by the men. The officers' lace and buttons were silver but before Waterloo changed to gold. The white facings were adopted in 1822, and they remained in use until the end of full dress.

See also the private, 1751 (*45*)

42nd Foot

1739   Independent companies of Highlanders were regimented in this year by John, Earl of Crawford and were then known as the Highland Regiment.
1751   42nd Highland Regiment.
1758   42nd Royal Highland Regiment.
1861   42nd Royal Highland Regiment (the Black Watch) Regiment of Foot.
1881   Joined with the 73rd Foot and became the 1st Battalion *The Black Watch (Royal Highlanders)*.
1934   The Black Watch (Royal Highland Regiment).
1968   In the Scottish Division.

This was the first Highland regiment to be put on the British establishment and it wore the regimental or government tartan. The red short-coat had buff facings until 1758 and then had the royal blue. Officers' lace was gold; the uniform is described fully in the Highland section (pp. 137–156). The badge and motto of St Andrew as well as the Egyptian Sphinx were worn on appointments.

See also the group, 1742–1906 (*75*), and the pipers, 1814 (*76a*), 1852 (*76b*)

43rd Foot

1741   Thomas Fowke raised this regiment which bore his name and those of two others until 1751.
1751   43rd Regiment of Foot.
1782   43rd (or Monmouthshire) Regiment of Foot.
1803   43rd (Monmouthshire Light Infantry) Regiment.
1881   Linked with the 52nd and became the 1st Battalion *Oxfordshire Light Infantry*.
1908   The Oxfordshire and Buckinghamshire Light Infantry.
1958   1st Green Jackets (43 and 52).
1966   Amalgamated with the 2nd and 3rd Green Jackets to form the Royal Green Jackets.
1968   In the Light Division.

The facings of the regiment were white, said to have been chosen by their colonel because he wore the same when in the 7th Dragoons. The officers had silver lace and buttons until 1830, then gold. The men's uniform was the normal infantry type until 1803 when light infantry distinctions were worn (see also the uniform sections on light infantry companies and regiments).

See also the group, 1741–c. 1914 (*71*)

44th Foot

1741   Raised by Colonel James Long and then known by succeeding colonels' names until 1751.

Overleaf:
37.
33rd Duke of Wellington's Regiment, 1872, officer

38.
34th Cumberland Regiment, 1814, officer

33ᴿᴰ DUKE OF WELLINGTON'S REGᵗ.
1872.

Plate 37

34ᵀᴴ CUMBERLAND REGIMENT.
1814.

Plate 38

36TH SUSSEX REGIMENT.
1828.

Plate 39

36TH HEREFORDSHIRE REGIMENT
1768.

Plate 40

1751 44th Regiment of Foot.

1782 44th (or East Essex) Regiment of Foot.

1881 Linked with 56th Foot and became the 1st Battalion *The Essex Regiment*

1958 Amalgamated with the Bedfordshire and Hertfordshire Regiment to become the 3rd East Anglian Regiment (16/44).

1964 Amalgamated with 1st and 2nd East Anglian Regiments and the Royal Leicestershire to form the Royal Anglian Regiment.

1968 In the Queen's Division.

The red coat had yellow facings which lasted until the white, as ordered in 1881. In 1936 the facings were changed to purple, a distinction of the 2nd battalion. The officers' lace and buttons were silver until 1830, then gold. The uniforms followed the normal changes of infantry. The 'Sphinx for Egypt' was granted in 1802 but the Eagle for the capture of an eagle or French colour at Salamanca was not granted until 1902.

See also the private, 1832 *(46)*

45th Foot

1741 Colonel Daniel Houghton formed this regiment in England which was known by his name and one other until 1751.

1751 45th Regiment of Foot.

1782 45th (or Nottinghamshire) Regiment of Foot.

1866 45th (the Nottinghamshire Sherwood Foresters) Regiment.

1881 Linked with the 95th Regiment and became the 1st Battalion the *Sherwood Foresters (Derbyshire) Regiment*.

1902 The Sherwood Foresters (Nottinghamshire and Derbyshire) Regiment.

1970 Amalgamated with the Worcestershire Regiment as the Worcestershire and Sherwood Foresters Regiment in the Prince of Wales's Division.

The original facings were deep green, later Lincoln green and then white in 1881, but Lincoln green was again restored in 1913. The officers' lace was silver until 1830, when regulation gold was worn. There were no important distinctions in the uniforms.

See also the colour-sergeant, 1913 *(47)*

46th Foot

1741 Colonel James Price of the 1st Foot Guards raised this regiment which was known by his name and that of the succeeding colonel until 1751.

1751 46th Regiment of Foot.

1782 46th (or South Devonshire) Regiment of Foot.

1881 Linked with the 32nd Regiment and became the 2nd Battalion *Duke of Cornwall's Light Infantry*.

The first uniform shown in 1742 had no lapels on the red coat but the cuffs and linings were yellow. Yellow became the established facing colour and continued until 1881 when the new regiment took white. The officers' lace and buttons had been silver but became gold in 1830. When fighting in America *c.* 1777 the light company wore red feathers, a distinction continued on the ball-tufts of shakos until the flank companies were discontinued, when it was granted to the whole regiment. Otherwise the uniform of the regiment followed normal practices.

See also the sergeant, light company, 1854 *(48)*

Preceding page:
39.
35th Sussex Regiment, 1828, officer

40.
36th Herefordshire Regiment, 1768, grenadier

47th Foot

1741 Colonel John Mordaunt raised this regiment but Peregrine Lascelles took command two years later and the regiment was known by these men's names.

1751 47th Regiment of Foot.

1782 47th (or Lancashire) Regiment of Foot.

1881 Linked with the 81st Regiment to become the 1st Battalion of the *Loyal North Lancashire Regiment.*

1920 The Loyal Regiment (North Lancashire).

1970 Amalgamated with the Lancashire Regiment (Prince of Wales's Volunteers) to form the Queen's Lancashire Regiment in the King's Division.

The first uniform had white facings on the red coat and these facings continued unchanged. The officers' lace was silver with black stripes before 1830, when it became gold. The men's uniform followed normal changes.

See also the private, 1832 (*49*)

48th Foot

1741 The regiment was raised by the Honourable James Cholmondeley, and known by his name and those of five other colonels before 1751.

1751 48th Regiment of Foot.

1782 48th (or Northamptonshire) Regiment of Foot.

1881 Linked with the 58th Regiment and became the 1st Battalion the *Northamptonshire Regiment.*

1960 Amalgamated with the Royal Lincolnshire Regiment to form the 2nd East Anglian Regiment (Duchess of Gloucester's Own Royal Lincolnshire and Northamptonshire).

1964 Amalgamated with 1st and 3rd East Anglian Regiments to form the Royal Anglian Regiment.

1968 In the Queen's Division.

The facings and linings of the red coat were buff, which changed in 1881 to white but in 1926 the buff facings were restored. The officers' lace and buttons were gold. There were no special changes in the men's uniforms.

See also the officer, 1913 (*50*)

49th Foot

1743 This regiment was raised and named after Colonel Edward Trelawny.

1751 49th Regiment of Foot.

1782 49th (or the Hertfordshire) Regiment of Foot.

1816 49th (or the Princess Charlotte of Wales's or the Hertfordshire) Regiment.

1881 Linked with the 66th Regiment and became the 1st Battalion *Princess Charlotte of Wales's (Berkshire Regiment).*

1885 Princess Charlotte of Wales's (Royal Berkshire Regiment).

1920 The Royal Berkshire Regiment (Princess Charlotte of Wales's).

1959 Amalgamated with the Wiltshire Regiment (Duke of Edinburgh's) as the Duke of Edinburgh's Royal Regiment (Berkshire and Wiltshire).

1968 In the Prince of Wales's Division.

The early facings of the regiment were named as 'full green', later called

Overleaf:
41.
The Hampshire Regiment (late 37th and 67th)
a 1742, private 37th
b 1751, grenadier 37th
c 1792, officer 37th
d 1814, sergeant 37th
e 1826, officer 37th
f 1832, private 37th
g 1905, drummer, private and officer, all full dress
h 1758, private 67th
i 1852, officer 67th
j 1862, private 67th
k 1864, bandsman 67th
l 1875, officer undress 67th
m 1875, officer full dress 67th

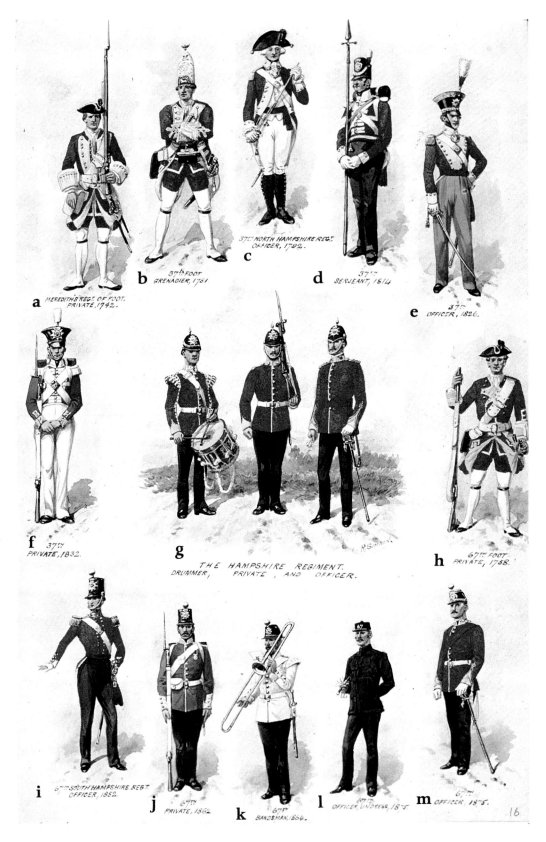

a MEREDITH'S REGT. OF FOOT.
PRIVATE, 1742.

b 37TH FOOT
GRENADIER, 1751

c 37TH NORTH HAMPSHIRE REGT.
OFFICER, 1792.

d 37TH
SERJEANT, 1814

e 37TH
OFFICER, 1826.

f 37TH
PRIVATE, 1832.

g THE HAMPSHIRE REGIMENT.
DRUMMER, PRIVATE, AND OFFICER.

h 67TH FOOT
PRIVATE, 1758.

i 67TH SOUTH HAMPSHIRE REGT.
OFFICER, 1852.

j 67TH
PRIVATE, 1862.

k 67TH
BANDSMAN, 1864.

l 67TH
OFFICER, UNDRESS, 1875.

m 67TH
OFFICER, 1875.

16

Plate 41

39TH DORSETSHIRE REGIMENT
1875.

Plate 43

40TH SECOND SOMERSETSHIRE REGIMENT
GRENADIER COMPANY 1832.

Plate 44

Lincoln green. In 1881 the facings were made white but on becoming royal, blue facings were awarded. Officers' lace and buttons were gold from the earliest days. The 'Dragon for China' was awarded in 1843.

See also the officer, 1793 (*51*)

50th Foot

1755   When raised by James Abercromby this regiment was numbered 52.
1757   Renumbered 50th Regiment of Foot.
1782   50th (or the West Kent) Regiment of Foot.
1827   50th (The Duke of Clarence's) Regiment of Foot.
1831   50th (or the Queen's Own) Regiment of Foot.
1881   Linked with the 97th Foot and became the 1st Battalion *The Queen's Own Royal West Kent Regiment*.
1920   The Royal West Kent Regiment (Queen's Own).
1921   The Queen's Own Royal West Kent Regiment.
1961   Amalgamated with the Buffs (Royal East Kent Regiment) to form the Queen's Own Buffs, The Royal Kent Regiment.
1966   Amalgamated with the Queen's Royal Surrey Regiment, the Royal Sussex Regiment and the Middlesex Regiment to form the Queen's Regiment.
1968   In the Queen's Division.

The black facings of the 52nd were continued in the 50th Foot and remained until 1831 when blue facings were authorized. The officers' lace and buttons had been silver but changed to gold 1830–31. The 'Sphinx for Egypt' was granted in 1802 and the Duke of Clarence's Cypher and Coronet was authorized in 1828. The uniforms followed the normal infantry developments.

See also the officer, levée dress (*52*)

51st Foot

1755   Raised by Lieutenant-General Robert Napier as the 53rd Regiment of Foot.
1757   Became the 51st Regiment of Foot.
1782   51st (or 2nd Yorkshire West Riding) Regiment of Foot.
1809   51st (or 2nd Yorkshire West Riding) Light Infantry Regiment.
1821   51st (2nd Yorkshire West Riding) or 'The King's Own' Light Infantry Regiment.
1881   Linked with the 105th Regiment and became the 1st Battalion *The King's Own Light Infantry*.
1887   The King's Own (Yorkshire Light Infantry).
1920   The King's Own Yorkshire Light Infantry.
1968   Amalgamated with the Somerset and Cornwall Light Infantry, the King's Shropshire Light Infantry and the Durham Light Infantry to form the Light Infantry in the Light Division.

The sea-green facings of the 53rd were carried into the 51st, although they were later called 'dull green'. In 1821 the facings were changed to the royal blue. The officers' buttons and lace were gold. The 51st regiment could wear the roses for Minden and later the French bugle-horn as its light infantry badge. The uniforms followed the basic infantry changes up to 1809 when the regiment became light infantry.

See also the bandsman, 1830 (*72a*) and the officer, 1832 (*72b*)

Preceding page:
43.
39th Dorsetshire Regiment, 1875, drummer

44.
40th 2nd Somersetshire Regiment, 1832, officer, grenadier company

52nd Foot

1755 When Hedworth Lambton raised the regiment it was numbered 54th.
1757 52nd Regiment of Foot.
1782 52nd (or Oxfordshire) Regiment of Foot.
1803 52nd (Oxfordshire Light Infantry) Regiment.
1881 Linked with the 43rd Foot and became the 2nd Battalion *Oxfordshire Light Infantry*.

The facings of the regiment were buff until 1881 and then white. The officers' buttons and lace were silver until 1830 when gold was the rule for regular regiments. The dress was normal infantry until 1803 when it took light infantry attributes such as wings and the bugle-horn.
See also the officer, 1812 (*73*) and the group, 1755–1875 (*71*)

53rd Foot

1755 The regiment that William Whitmore raised was first numbered 55th.
1757 The 53rd Regiment of Foot.
1782 53rd (or Shropshire) Regiment of Foot.
1881 Linked with the 85th and became the 1st Battalion *The King's Light Infantry (Shropshire) Regiment*.
1882 The King's (Shropshire Light Infantry).
1920 The King's Shropshire Light Infantry.
1968 Amalgamated with the Somerset and Cornwall Light Infantry, the King's Own Yorkshire Light Infantry and the Durham Light Infantry as the Light Infantry in the Light Division.

The red coat originally had red facings and yellow linings but in 1768 the regiment was ordered white linings. In 1881 the facings were made blue. The officers' buttons and lace had always been gold. The uniform followed normal infantry changes until it was made light infantry.
See also the officer, 1857 (*53*)

54th Foot

1755 Raised by John Campbell as the 56th Regiment.
1757 The 54th Regiment of Foot.
1782 54th (or the West Norfolk) Regiment of Foot.
1881 When linked with the 39th Regiment became the 2nd Battalion the *Dorsetshire Regiment*.

The original popinjay green facings continued in the 54th Regiment although they later became known as 'grass green'. In 1881 the facings in the new Dorsetshire Regiment became white. Officers' lace and buttons had been gold. The regiment gained the Egyptian Sphinx in 1802. The dress followed normal infantry developments.

55th Foot

1755 Raised by George Perry as the 57th Regiment of Foot.
1757 The 55th Regiment of Foot.
1782 55th (or Westmoreland) Regiment of Foot.
1881 Linked with the 34th Regiment to become the 2nd Battalion the *Border Regiment*.

The dark green facings of the 57th continued into the 55th Regiment but became Lincoln green before submitting to the white of England in 1881.

41ST ROYAL INVALIDS.
1751.

Plate 45

44TH EAST ESSEX REGIMENT
1832.

THE SHERWOOD FORESTERS (NOTTINGHAMSHIRE & DERBYSHIRE REGT)
1913.

Plate 46

Plate 47

46TH SOUTH DEVONSHIRE REGIMENT
LIGHT COMPANY 1854

Plate 48

The officers' lace and buttons were gold. The uniforms followed the normal developments. The Imperial Dragon of China was granted as a badge in 1843.

56th Foot

1755   Raised by Lord Charles Manners as the 58th Regiment.
1757   The 56th Regiment of Foot.
1782   The 56th (or the West Essex) Regiment of Foot.
1881   On linking with the 44th Regiment became the 2nd Battalion the *Essex Regiment*.

The facings were originally called 'deep crimson' but about 1764 changed to purple, which because of the 'fugitive' nature of the dye varied considerably. Despite this problem the colour, derived from the Madame de Pompadour, continued in use up to 1881 when it was lost to the English white. However, vestiges of this unusual colour continued on modern uniforms. The uniform followed the normal developments. The officers' lace and buttons were silver until 1830, then gold.

57th Foot

1755   Raised by John Arabin as the 59th Regiment.
1757   The 57th Regiment of Foot.
1782   57th (or the West Middlesex) Regiment of Foot.
1881   Linked with the 77th Regiment and became the 1st Battalion *the Duke of Cambridge's Own (Middlesex Regiment)*.
1920   The Middlesex Regiment (Duke of Cambridge's Own).
1966   Amalgamated with the Queen's Royal Surrey Regiment, the Queen's Own Buffs and the Royal Sussex Regiment to form The Queen's Regiment.
1968   In the Queen's Division.

From the beginning the facings were yellow but for a short time, 1881–1902, they were white, and the lemon-yellow facings were then restored. The officers' buttons and lace were gold. The uniforms followed the normal changes. The regiment was granted the device of a laurel wreath and the honour 'Albuhera' for action in that battle.

58th Foot

1755   Raised by Robert Anstruther as the 60th Regiment.

Preceding page:
48.
46th South Devonshire Regiment,
1854, sergeant, light company

1757   The 58th Regiment of Foot.
1782   58th (or the Rutlandshire) Regiment of Foot.
1881   Linked with the 48th Foot to become the 2nd Battalion *the Northamptonshire Regiment*.

The facings of both the early 60th and the 58th were black; these were kept in wear up to 1881 when the 'English' white facings were introduced. The officers' lace and buttons were gold from the beginning and for a time the officers had black velvet facings. The regiment gained the Castle and Key for Gibraltar and later the Egyptian Sphinx. The uniforms followed those laid down for infantry.

59th Foot

1755   Raised by Charles Montague as the 61st Regiment of Foot.
1757   The 59th Regiment of Foot.
1782   59th (or the 2nd Nottinghamshire) Regiment of Foot.

1881   Linked with the 30th Regiment to become the 2nd Battalion the *East Lancashire Regiment*.

The original facings were light crimson and later called purple. This colour continued to be quoted in Army Lists long after although officially it had changed to white in 1776, which continued after 1881. The officers' lace and buttons had been silver but in 1798 were permitted to be changed to gold. The uniforms followed the normal developments.

60th Foot

1755   John, Earl of Loudoun raised the Royal American Regiment on that continent and it was at first numbered 62nd.

1757   The 60th (Royal American) Regiment of Foot.

1815   60th (Royal American) (Light Infantry) Regiment.

1819   60th (Royal American), 1st Battalion Rifle Corps, 2nd Battalion Light Infantry.

1824   60th Duke of York's Own Rifle Corps (light infantry became Rifle Battalion).

1830   60th or the King's Royal Rifle Corps.

1881   *The King's Royal Rifle Corps.*

1920   The King's Royal Rifles.

1921   The King's Royal Rifle Corps.

1958   Redesignated the 2nd Green Jackets (the King's Royal Rifle Corps).

1968   Amalgamated with the 1st and 3rd Green Jackets to form the Royal Green Jackets in the Light Division.

When first raised the four battalions all had red coats with blue facings and had special permission to be without lace or braid. The officers had silver lace and buttons. The uniforms followed the normal infantry practices with allowances for rough service in North America. At the end of the eighteenth century the addition of a fifth battalion consisting of foreigners in green coats or jackets introduced a new element into the British Army which was so successful that the red coats of the 60th were obsolete by 1815. The 'red coat' followed infantry practice; for the rifle battalions and corps see also the uniform section of rifles.

See also group, 1759–1914 (*91*), the sergeant-major, 1854 (*92a*) and the bandsman, 1854 (*92b*)

61st Foot

1756   The 3rd Foot (the Buffs) raised a second battalion at Chatham which, after overseas service, became

1758   61st Regiment of Foot.

1782   61st (or South Gloucestershire) Regiment of Foot.

1881   Linked with the 28th Foot and became the 2nd Battalion the *Gloucestershire Regiment*.

When formed from the 2nd battalion of the Buffs the regiment continued to wear the buff facings until 1881, when the white of English infantry was worn. Silver lace and buttons were worn by officers up to 1830, when gold was adopted. The 61st gained the Sphinx for services when fighting in Egypt in 1801 and this honour appeared on appointments as from 1802.

62nd Foot

1756   The 4th King's Own Regiment raised in this year a second battalion.

1758   The 62nd Regiment of Foot.

Overleaf:
49.
47th Lancashire Regiment, 1832, private

50.
The Northamptonshire Regiment (late 48th), 1913, officer

51.
49th Hertfordshire Regiment, 1793, officer

47TH LANCASHIRE REGIMENT
1832.

Plate 49

THE NORTHAMPTONSHIRE REGIMENT
(48TH) 1913.

49TH HERTFORDSHIRE REGIMENT
1793

Plate 50

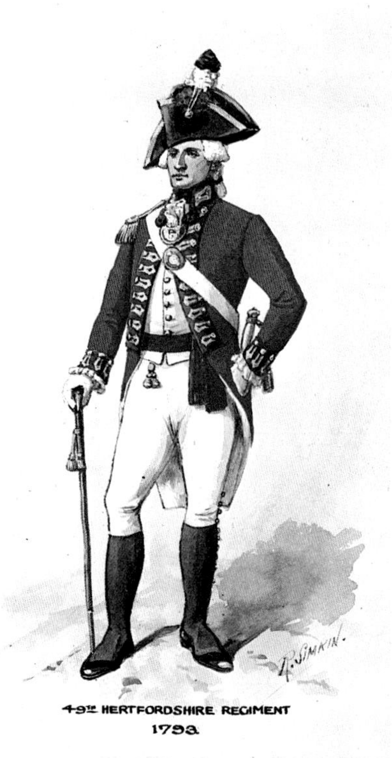

Plate 51

50^D THE QUEEN'S OWN REGIMENT.
(LEVÉE DRESS) 1874.

Plate 52

53^D SHROPSHIRE REGIMENT.
1857.

Plate 53

The Manchester Regiment
1900.

Plate 54

1782　62nd (or the Wiltshire) Regiment of Foot.

1881　Linked with the 99th Foot and became the 1st Battalion *The Duke of Edinburgh's (Wiltshire Regiment)*.

1920　The Wiltshire Regiment (Duke of Edinburgh's).

1959　Amalgamated with the Royal Berkshire Regiment to form the Duke of Edinburgh's Royal Regiment (Berkshire and Wiltshire).

1968　In the Prince of Wales's Division.

This newly formed regiment did not take the blue facings of its parent regiment but had yellow-buff facings and linings. Buff was worn up to 1881 when the white facings became regulation. In 1905 the desired buff facings were restored. Silver lace and buttons were the officers' distinctions up to 1830, then gold. For a time the officers' lace had blue mixed with it. The uniforms followed the normal developments.

63rd Foot

1756　A second battalion of the 8th King's Regiment was raised in the West of England.

1758　The 63rd Regiment of Foot, under David Watson.

1782　63rd (or the West Suffolk) Regiment of Foot.

1881　Linked with the 96th Foot to become the 1st Battalion the *Manchester Regiment*.

1958　Amalgamated with the King's Regiment (Liverpool) to form the King's Regiment (Manchester and Liverpool).

1968　The King's Regiment in the King's Division.

The new regiment had very dark green facings and buff linings to the red coats. The buff lining would have been ruled out by 1767 when white became regulation. The green was later called 'Lincoln green' and was worn until 1881. White was then worn until 1937 when the dark green facings were restored. Officers' lace and buttons were silver until 1830, then gold. Black stripes had been worn in the silver lace and for a time in the gold but this distinction ceased in 1832. The uniform of the men followed the normal developments.

See also the officer, 1900 (54)

64th Foot

1756　A second battalion of the 11th Foot was raised.

1758　The 64th Regiment of Foot.

1782　64th (or the 2nd Staffordshire) Regiment of Foot.

1881　Linked with the 98th Regiment to become the 1st Battalion the *Prince of Wales's (North Staffordshire Regiment)*.

1920　The North Staffordshire Regiment (the Prince of Wales's).

1959　Amalgamated with the South Staffordshire Regiment to form the Staffordshire Regiment (Prince of Wales's).

1968　In the Prince of Wales's Division.

The new 64th Regiment did not take the green facings of its parent but chose black with white linings. These facings became white in 1881 until in 1937 the black was restored. For a period in the nineteenth century officers had black velvet facings which went well with their gold lace and buttons. Needless to say, the Stafford Knot appeared as a regimental badge. The uniforms followed the normal developments.

65th Foot

1756　A second battalion of the 12th Foot was formed.

Preceding page:

52.
50th The Queen's Own Regiment, 1874, officer levée dress

53.
53rd Shropshire Regiment, 1857, officer

54.
The Manchester Regiment (late 63rd), 1900, officer

1758   The 65th Regiment of Foot.

1782   65th (or the 2nd Yorkshire North Riding) Regiment of Foot.

1881   Linked with the 84th Foot to become the 1st Battalion of the *York and Lancashire Regiment*.

1968   The York and Lancashire Regiment in the King's Division (disbanded).

The new 65th took white facings and linings, not the yellow of the parent regiment, and these remained throughout the regiment's life. The officers had silver buttons and lace but by the end of the eighteenth century had changed to gold. In later times the gold rose lace had black stripes on both sides. The badge of the Royal Tiger signified the regiment's service in India from 1796 to 1819. There were no unusual features in the men's dress except that required for service in India.

66th Foot

1756   A second battalion of the 19th Foot was formed.

1758   The 66th Regiment of Foot.

1782   66th (or the Berkshire) Regiment of Foot.

1881   Linked with the 49th Regiment and became the 2nd Battalion *Princess Charlotte of Wales's (Berkshire Regiment)*.

The new 66th Regiment had coats with yellow-green facings and linings, the same facings of the parent regiment. Later the facings were described as 'gosling green' and also 'emerald', all variations giving place to the white of 1881. The officers' lace and buttons had been gold but in 1778 changed to silver, only to revert to the original metal in 1824 by a special order. The men's uniforms followed the normal developments.

67th Foot

1756   A second battalion of the 20th Foot was formed.

1758   67th Regiment of Foot.

1782   67th (or the South Hampshire) Regiment of Foot.

1881   Linked with the 37th Foot and became the 2nd Battalion of the *Hampshire Regiment*.

The facings of the 20th Foot were yellow at this time and so the new 67th took the same yellow facings and linings. The linings would have changed to white by 1767 but the yellow facings continued until the white of 1881. The officers' buttons and lace were silver until 1830, then gold. The distinction of the Royal Tiger and 'India' was granted for the regiment's service on that sub-continent from 1805 to 1826. Normal dress was worn except for warm climates.

See also the group, 1750–1876 (*41*)

Overleaf:
55.
Infantry of the Line, 1815, drum-major

68th Foot

1756   A second battalion of the 23rd Fusiliers was formed.

1758   68th Regiment of Foot.

1782   68th (or the Durham) Regiment of Foot.

1808   68th (Durham Light Infantry) Regiment.

1881   Linked with the 106th Regiment to become the 1st Battalion the *Durham Light Infantry*.

1968   Amalgamated with the Somerset and Cornwall Light Infantry, the King's Own Yorkshire Light Infantry and the King's Shropshire Light Infantry to form the Light Infantry in the Light Division.

INFANTRY OF THE LINE.
1815.

Plate 55

INFANTRY OF THE LINE.
1815.

INFANTRY OF THE LINE.
1815.

Plate 56

Plate 57

INFANTRY OF THE LINE.
1815.

Plate 58

As the parent regiment was 'royal' and a fusilier one as well, the new 68th could not expect to follow such a parent and so chose dark green facings and linings for the infantry coats. The green lining would have disappeared in the general order of 1767 which ordered white waistcoats and breeches for all regiments of infantry. The green facings were later known as 'bottle green' and gave way in 1881 to the regulation white. However, the dark green facings were restored in 1932. The officers' buttons and lace had been silver, but gold after 1830. The normal infantry uniforms were worn up to 1808 after which the light infantry differences were taken into wear.

69th Foot

1756   The 2nd Battalion of the 24th Regiment of Foot was formed.
1758   69th Regiment of Foot.
1782   69th (or the South Lincolnshire) Regiment of Foot.
1881   Linked with the 41st Regiment and became the 2nd Battalion the *Welsh Regiment*.

The 24th Regiment of Foot had willow-green facings in 1756 and no doubt it was thought economical to continue the old coats with the same facings, because this shade of green remained in use. However, green was often a fugitive colour and the exact shade varied in the years, including grass green until the white of 1881. Officers' buttons and lace were gold. Men's uniforms had no special variations.

70th Foot

1756   A second battalion of the 31st Foot was raised.
1758   70th Regiment of Foot.
1782   70th (or the Surry) Regiment of Foot (the 'e' in Surrey was omitted in early lists and was still spelt so in 1812).
1812   70th (Glasgow Lowland) Regiment of Foot.
1825   70th (or Surrey) Regiment of Foot (later the 'or' was omitted).
1881   Linked with the 31st Foot to become the 2nd Battalion of the *East Surrey Regiment*.

The grey facings chosen by the new 70th Regiment of Foot had no connection with its progenitor and the linings of the coat were white. By 1763 the facings were black and continued as such until the white of 1881. The officers' lace was gold and included a black stripe to match the facing colour. The officers had black velvet facings and their buttons were gilt. Although the regiment was quartered in Glasgow in 1813 there seems to have been no change in the uniform towards a Scottish tendency. Instead the uniforms followed the normal infantry of the line development.

71st Foot

1777   There had been other regiments numbered '71' and disbanded before the one that became the Highland Light Infantry. It had begun life as the 73rd, a Highland regiment raised by John, Lord Macleod.
1786   71st (Highland) Regiment of Foot.
1808   71st (Glasgow Highland) Regiment of Foot.
1810   71st (Highland) (Light Infantry).
1881   Linked with the 74th Regiment and became the 1st Battalion the *Highland Light Infantry*.
1923   The Highland Light Infantry (City of Glasgow Regiment).

Preceding page:
56.
Infantry of the Line, 1815, bandsman

57.
Infantry of the Line, 1815, bass-drummer

58.
Infantry of the Line, 1815, cymbalist

1958 Amalgamated with the Royal Scots Fusiliers to become the Royal Highland Fusiliers (Princess Margaret's Own Glasgow and Ayrshire Regiment).

1968 In the Scottish Division.

The regimental facings were buff and continued so until 1881 when the Scottish yellow were ordered, but in 1899 the buff facings were restored. The officers' lace and buttons were silver until 1830, then gold. Highland dress was worn until 1809, then normal infantry dress was worn. See also the Highland and Lowland uniform sections.

See also the group, 1815–c. 1914 (*99*)

72nd Foot

1778 There were other regiments numbered '72' before Kenneth, Earl of Seaforth raised this regiment. It was then numbered '78' but after other regiments were disbanded, it became

1786 72nd (Highland) Regiment of Foot.

1809 72nd Regiment of Foot.

1823 72nd (Duke of Albany's Own Highlanders).

1881 Linked with the 78th Highlanders and became the 1st Battalion *Seaforth Highlanders (Ross-shire Buffs)*.

1881 Seaforth Highlanders (Ross-shire Buffs, The Duke of Albany's).

1961 Amalgamated with the Queen's Own Cameron Highlanders to form the Queen's Own Highlanders (Seaforth and Camerons).

1968 In the Scottish Division.

The facings were yellow from the beginning until 1881 when the yellow for Scottish regiments was the rule (despite the fact that the new title included the word 'Buffs'). However, the claims of the 2nd battalion were such that in 1899 their buff facings were restored to the whole regiment. Officers' buttons and lace were silver until 1830, then gold. Highland dress was worn from 1778 to 1809 when the Highland dress was discontinued. In 1823 a modified form of Highland dress was adopted. See also the Highland and Lowland uniform sections.

See also the group, 1809–c. 1914 (*77*)

73rd Foot

1780 Earlier '73rd' regiments had been formed and disbanded, but the 2nd Battalion of the 42nd Royal Highlanders became

1786 the 73rd Highland Regiment of Foot.

1809 73rd Regiment of Foot.

1862 73rd (Perthshire) Regiment.

1881 Linked with the 42nd Royal Highlanders (Black Watch) to become the 2nd Battalion the *Black Watch (Royal Highlanders)*.

The new 73rd did not carry on the royal blue as worn in the 2nd battalion of the Royal Highlanders but took dark green, which continued until the linkage of 1881 when the royal blue returned. The gold lace and buttons of the officers were worn all the time. The Highland dress was worn until 1809 when so many Highland regiments lost the kilt in the economic changes. But the restoration of a Scottish title in 1862 brought back some Highland distinctions, though not the kilt. See also the Highland and Lowland uniform sections. The Arms of Perth were permitted on officers' appointments after 1862.

Overleaf:
59.
Northumberland Fusiliers (late 5th)
a 1688, officer
b 1742, private
c 1751, grenadier
d 1768, grenadier
e 1792, officer
f 1814, private
g (c.1912) colour-sergeant full dress, officer service dress, officer full dress
h 1814, officer
i 1838, officer
j 1852, private
k 1858, bass-drummer
l 1858, private
m 1878, sergeant

a 1686.

b 1742.

c 1751.

d 1768.

e 1792.

f 1814.

g 1902.

1901.

1910.

h 1814.

NORTHUMBERLAND FUSILIERS

i 1838.

j 1852.

k 1855.

l 1858.

m 1878.

Plate 59

Plate 60

74th Foot

1787   Sir Archibald Campbell raised the 74th Highland Regiment as one of four for East India service.

1816   74th Regiment of Foot.

1845   74th (Highlanders).

1881   Linked with the 71st Highland Light Infantry to become the 2nd Battalion of the *Highland Light Infantry*.

The facings were white from the beginning until 1881 when the yellow for Scotland was ordered. Officers' lace and buttons were gold, with black edges on the lace up to 1840. At the start, full Highland dress was expected to be worn, but no doubt the eighteen years in India brought modifications. Full Highland dress was ordered when the regiment returned to Scotland but in the reductions of 1809 normal infantry of the line dress was ordered. In 1845 some elements of the Highland dress were restored but not the kilt. See also the Highland and Infantry uniform sections. In 1817 the Elephant for India was granted for certain distinctions.
See also the group, 1808–c. 1914 (*100*)

75th Foot

1787   There were three previous regiments which were numbered '75' and disbanded before Colonel Robert Abercrombie raised this second regiment for East India service, then known as the 75th (Highland) Regiment of Foot.

1809   75th Regiment of Foot.

1862   75th (Stirlingshire) Regiment of Foot.

1881   Linked with the 92nd Gordon Highlanders and became the 1st Battalion the *Gordon Highlanders*.

1968   In the Scottish Division.

This regiment began with full Highland dress with yellow facings to the red coat (which continued after joining the Gordon Highlanders). The officers had silver buttons and lace up to 1830 when gold took over. Unfortunately the Highland dress was lost from 1809 to 1862. Even then the restoration was not complete and the kilt did not return. Traces of the Highland origins were to be seen in badges and some head-dress. The rank and file as well as officers wore standard infantry dress up to 1881.
See also the officer, 1809 (*78a*), the officer, 1913 (*78b*) and the group, 1809–1914 (*79*)

Preceding page:
60.
Northumberland Fusiliers (late 5th), 1910, drummer and private in full dress, officer service dress, officer full dress, officer mounted and officer undress

76th Foot

1787   Previous regiments numbered '76' had been disbanded and the third regiment to be raised for East India service was an English one, the 76th Regiment of Foot under Thomas Musgrave.

1807   76th (Hindostan) Regiment of Foot.

1812   76th Regiment of Foot.

1881   Linked with the 33rd Foot to become the 2nd Battalion of the *Duke of Wellington's (West Riding Regiment)*.

The facings were red and stayed so until 1881 when the English white took over, but the combined battalions received scarlet facings in 1905. Silver was the distinctive metal for officers' buttons and lace up to 1830, when gold became the rule. The service in India brought the badge of the Elephant with Howdah plus 'Hindostan'.

77th Foot

1787 The last of the four regiments raised for East India service was an English one, the 77th Regiment of Foot.

1807 77th (East Middlesex) Regiment of Foot.

1876 77th (East Middlesex) (or Duke of Cambridge's Own) Regiment of Foot.

1881 Linked with the 57th Regiment and became the 2nd Battalion the *Duke of Cambridge's Own (Middlesex Regiment)*.

Yellow facings were worn from the beginning until the linkage with the 57th in 1881 when white was regulation. By 1820 the special lemon-yellow shade of the facings was changed to the darker shade of yellow ordered for all regiments. Officers' buttons and lace were silver until 1830, then gold. The Prince of Wales's Plumes, Coronet and motto were granted in 1810 but this almost royal honour did not bring the royal facings. The Duke of Cambridge's Cypher and Coronet were granted in 1876. The basic infantry dress was worn with the usual exceptions brought about by service abroad.

78th Foot

1793 There had been other regiments numbered '78', one of 1778–86 which had been the Seaforth Highlanders and was renumbered 72nd, but this one was raised as the 78th Highlanders by F. H. Mackenzie (later the Earl of Seaforth) and was commonly known as the Ross-shire Buffs.

1881 Linked with the 72nd Highlanders and became the 2nd Battalion *Seaforth Highlanders (Ross-shire Buffs, The Duke of Albany's)*.

The facings of the regiment were buff until 1881 when the yellow for Scotland prevailed, but in 1899 the buff was restored. Officers' buttons and lace were gold. The Highland dress was worn from the beginning; see also the section on Highland uniform. The badge of the Elephant and the honour 'Assaye' were granted in 1807.

See also the group, 1793–1915 *(80)*, the piper, 1799 *(81a)* and the pipe-major, 1869 *(81b)*

79th Foot

1793 There had been two other '79th' Regiments of Foot before the 79th (Cameronian Volunteers) Regiment of Foot was raised.

1804 79th (Cameron Highlanders) Regiment of Foot.

1873 79th (Queen's Own Cameron Highlanders) Regiment of Foot.

1881 Did not link with any other regiment and was known as *The Queen's Own Cameron Highlanders*.

1961 Amalgamated with the Seaforth Highlanders to become the Queen's Own Highlanders (Seaforth and Cameron).

1968 In the Scottish Division.

The facings were dark green from the beginning until 1873 when, on becoming the Queen's, the regiment acquired blue facings. The officers had gold lace and buttons. The kilt was worn continuously; see also the section on Highland uniform. The Sphinx superscribed 'Egypt' was granted in 1802 and the Scottish Thistle ensigned with the Imperial Crown came in 1873.

See also the group, 1815–c. 1914 *(82)*, the officer, 1854 *(83a)* and the drum-major, 1854 *(83b)*

Overleaf:
61a
5th Foot, 1751, drummer

61b
7th Royal Fusiliers, 1852, drummer

5TH FOOT.
1781.

a

7TH ROYAL FUSILIERS.
1852.

b

Plate 61

a 1742
b 1742
c 1792
d 1792
e 1792
f 1812
g 1914
ROYAL FUSILIERS
h 1826
i 1832
j 1852
k 1860
l 1860
m 1916

Plate 62

80th Foot

1793   Two previous regiments were numbered '80' before the one that was formed at Chatham by Henry, Lord Paget, later to be the Marquess of Anglesey, who then as an officer in the Staffordshire Militia brought that county's name into the 80th (Staffordshire Volunteers) Regiment of Foot.

1881   Linked with the 38th Regiment to become the 2nd Battalion *South Staffordshire Regiment*.

The facings were yellow until the white of the amalgamation. The officers' distinctions were gold. The Stafford Knot was an early badge of this regiment, which followed the usual infantry fashions and changes.
See also the group, 1793–1875 (*42*)

81st Foot

1794   The third regiment to be numbered '81' was raised in Lincoln by Major-General Albemarle Bertie and was known also as the 'Loyal Lincoln Volunteers'.

1881   Linked with the 47th Regiment and became the 2nd Battalion of the *Loyal North Lancashire Volunteers*.

The regimental facings were buff until the amalgamation, when the English white took over. The officers had silver buttons and lace until 1830 when gold was worn. The fact that many of the original men came from the Lincoln Militia was the reason why the Arms of the City of Lincoln later appeared on their buttons. The dress followed the normal infantry changes.

82nd Foot

1793   The third regiment to be numbered '82' was raised by Major-General Leigh who had been in the staff of the Prince of Wales (later King George IV) and thus took the supplementary title of the 'Prince of Wales's Volunteers'.

1881   Linked with the 40th Regiment to become the 2nd Battalion of the *Prince of Wales's Volunteers (South Lancashire Regiment)*.

The facings were buff while the officers' lace and buttons were silver up to 1830 and then gold. The Prince of Wales's Feathers, Coronet and motto appeared on appointments. The uniform followed the normal developments.

83rd Foot

1793   There were two previous regiments numbered '83'; this 83rd Regiment of Foot was raised by Colonel William Fitch in Dublin.

1859   83rd (County of Dublin) Regiment of Foot.

1881   Linked with the 88th Regiment to become the 1st Battalion the *Royal Irish Rifles*.

1922   The Royal Ulster Rifles.

1968   Amalgamated with the Royal Inniskilling Fusiliers and the Royal Irish Fusiliers (Princess Victoria's) to form the Royal Irish Rangers (27th [Inniskilling] 83rd and 87th) in the King's Division.

The regimental facings were yellow until the amalgamation of 1881 when the regiment was converted to rifles. At first the facings were light green but in 1882 they became rifle green. The lace and buttons of officers were originally gold but on becoming rifles they took black distinctions. Thus the story of their uniforms is to be found firstly under the section on the infantry of the line and then in the rifle uniform section.

See also the group, 1793–c. 1914 (*94*) and the officer, 1913 (*95*)

84th Foot

1793 The third regiment to be numbered '84' was raised in Yorkshire by General George Bernard as the 84th Regiment of Foot.

1809 84th York and Lancaster Regiment of Foot.

1881 Linked with the 65th Regiment and became the 2nd Battalion *York and Lancaster Regiment*.

The facings were pale yellow until 1820 when the various shades of yellow facings were to be simplified to plain yellow. In 1881 the 'English' white was taken into wear. The buttons of officers were silver and their lace was silver with black edges until 1830, when they became gold. For badges the coronet of the Duke of Lancaster was worn c. 1811 and the Union Rose in 1820, a late recognition of the White Rose of Yorkshire and the Red Rose of Lancashire, as the union had taken place in 1809. The uniforms followed the normal developments.

85th Foot

1793 Other regiments were numbered '85' and disbanded; this one was raised by Sir George Nugent on the Marquess of Buckingham's estates and thus had the name of the 85th (Bucks Volunteers) Regiment of Foot.

1808 85th (Bucks Volunteers) (Light Infantry) Regiment.

1815 85th (Bucks Volunteers, Duke of York's Own Light Infantry) Regiment.

1821 85th (Bucks Volunteers) (The King's Light Infantry) Regiment.

1827 85th (The King's Light Infantry) Regiment.

1881 Linked with the 53rd Regiment to become the 2nd Battalion *The King's Light Infantry (Shropshire Regiment)*.

The original facings were yellow but in 1821 became blue and remained so. The officers' buttons had been silver until 1830 and then gold, the lace following the same change. The regiment wore normal infantry garments until 1808 and then had the light infantry dress with the stringed bugle-horn.

86th Foot

1793 The third regiment to be numbered '86' was raised by Cornelius Cuyler. It was originally known as the 'Shropshire Volunteers' as it was raised in that shire and nearby and had much overseas service before it returned home.

1806 86th (Leinster) Regiment of Foot (renamed while in India).

1812 86th (Royal County Down) Regiment.

1881 Linked with the 83rd Regiment as the 2nd Battalion the *Royal Irish Rifles*.

When formed, the 86th had yellow facings but in 1812 took blue upon becoming a royal regiment. On being converted to rifles, the facings became green, which was the then chosen colour for Ireland. Officers had silver buttons and lace until 1812 and then gold until the regiment was made rifles. The 86th acquired the 'Sphinx for Egypt' in 1802 and the Crowned

Harp and motto in 1832. See also the infantry of the line and rifles uniform sections.

See also the group, 1793 1879 *(94)*

87th Foot

1793   The third regiment to be numbered '87' was raised in Ireland by Sir John Doyle as the 87th (Prince of Wales's Irish) Regiment.

1811   87th (The Prince of Wales's Own Irish) Regiment of Foot.

1827   87th Prince of Wales's Own Irish Fusiliers.

1881   87th (or Royal Irish Fusiliers) Regiment of Foot.

1881   Linked with the 89th Regiment and became the 1st Battalion *Princess Victoria's (Royal Irish Fusiliers).*

1920   The Royal Irish Fusiliers (Princess Victoria's).

1968   Amalgamated with the Royal Inniskilling Fusiliers and the Royal Ulster Rifles to become the Royal Irish Rangers (27th [Inniskilling] 83rd and 87th) in the King's Division.

Green facings were originally worn, no doubt to indicate Ireland, but in 1827 the facings became blue. The lace and buttons of officers were gold. The Harp and Crown was an old badge and in 1811 'the Eagle with a Wreath of Laurel' was granted to mark the capture of a French eagle. The dress was that of infantry up to 1827 when the dress of fusiliers was worn (see also the infantry of the line and fusilier sections).

See also the group, 1793–c. 1914 *(67).*

88th Foot

1793   Two regiments numbered '88' had been disbanded before the 88th (or Connaught Rangers) was raised in Connaught.

1881   Linked with the 94th Regiment and became the 1st Battalion the *Connaught Rangers.*

1922   Disbanded.

The facings of the regiment were yellow until 1881 when green facings for Ireland were adopted (the Irish green was scarce, as many other Irish regiments were royal and had blue, and another was a rifle regiment). The buttons and lace of officers were silver until 1830, then gold. Black stripes were added to the gold lace of officers. As a badge the Sphinx for Egypt was granted in 1802. The Harp and Crown with '*Quis Separabit*' had been worn for some time but authority to retain and to confirm the use was granted in 1830. The uniforms followed the normal developments.

89th Foot

1793   This 89th Regiment of Foot was the third to be numbered '89'. It was raised in Ireland.

1866   89th (Princess Victoria's) Regiment of Foot.

1881   Linked with the 87th Regiment to become the 2nd Battalion *Royal Irish Fusiliers (Princess Victoria's).*

When the regiment was raised it had black facings which were changed to blue in 1881. The facings for the officers were black velvet and their lace and buttons gold. The regiment saw much overseas service, gaining the Sphinx for Egypt, the honour of 'Niagara' for serving in America, 'Java' in 1818 and 'Sevastopol' in 1855. In 1866 the distinction of the Cypher and Coronet of Princess Victoria was granted in memory of the presentation of the regimental colours by Queen Victoria when a girl. The usual infantry uniforms were worn with the expected differences for serving abroad in all weathers.

90th Foot

1794   Two regiments were numbered '90' before the 90th (Perthshire Volunteers) Regiment was raised in that Scottish county.

1815   90th (Perthshire Volunteers) (Light Infantry).

1881   Linked with the 26th Regiment and became the 2nd Battalion *The Cameronian Regiment (Scottish Rifles)*.

The scarlet coats of the 90th had buff facings until 1881 when the regiment became rifles. The officers had gold buttons and lace until 1881. The nickname of the regiment when raised was the 'Perthshire Greybreeks', indicating the colour of their nether-wear at that time. From the beginning there may have been a preference for light infantry which was confirmed in 1815. The regiment gained the Sphinx for Egypt when fighting in 1801, the distinction being granted the next year. See also the light infantry and Lowland uniform sections.

See also the private, 1832 (*74*)

91st Foot

1794   There had been three regiments numbered '91' and disbanded. This regiment began life as the 98th Argyllshire Highlanders Regiment.

1798   The 91st Argyllshire Highlanders Regiment of Foot.

1809   91st Regiment of Foot.

1820   91st (or Argyllshire) Regiment of Foot.

1863   91st (Argyllshire) Highlanders.

1872   91st (Princess Louise's Argyllshire) Highlanders.

1881   Linked with the 93rd Highlanders and became the 1st Battalion *Princess Louise's (Sutherland and Argyll Highlanders)*.

1882   Princess Louise's (Argyll and Sutherland Highlanders).

1920   The Argyll and Sutherland Highlanders (Princess Louise's).

1968   In the Scottish Division.

The facings of these Highlanders were yellow and the officers had gold lace. Although they began wearing the kilt, the change in 1809 meant that Highland distinctions were lost and the regiment was clothed as ordinary infantry of the line. However, in 1863 they again became Highlanders. The badge of the Boar's Head of the Argyll family was authorized in 1872, and the silver Label of Three Points to indicate the cadency of Princess Louise also came in 1872. The development of the Highland dress is traced in the section on Highland dress but the full Highland dress with the kilt was not restored until 1881.

See also the group, 1809–c. 1914 (*84*)

92nd Foot

1794   There were three regiments numbered '92' which were disbanded before the 100th Regiment was raised by the Marquess of Huntley, the last Duke of Gordon, as the 100th (Gordon Highland) Regiment of Foot, but after reductions in the Army it became the 92nd.

1798   The 92nd (Highland) Regiment of Foot.

1861   The 92nd (Gordon Highlanders) Regiment of Foot.

1881   Linked with the 75th Regiment it became the 2nd Battalion the *Gordon Highlanders*.

From the beginning the facings had been yellow and the officers' lace was silver and black, the black being continued in the gold lace of 1830 but discontinued about 1861. The 92nd did not suffer the indignity of losing the kilt and wore it continuously from the beginning. Unusually, in the 1881 linkings the 2nd Battalion brought its dress to the regiment with the Gordon tartan sett. Among the badges for the regiment was the Sphinx for Egypt (granted 1802), the 'Head of the Stag, being the crest of the Marquess of Huntley', and the 'Ivy of the Gordons'. See also the Highland uniform section.

See also the drummer, 1813 (*85a*), the officer, 1828 (plate *85b*), the colour-sergeant, 1838 (*86a*), the bandsman, 1838 (*86b*) and the group, 1794–1915 (*87*)

93rd Foot

1800   Major-General Wemyss raised the 93rd Highlanders mainly from the 3rd Sutherland Fencibles. It was sometimes known as the '93rd' or 'Sutherland Regiment of Highlanders' but usually as the 93rd Highlanders.

1861   The 93rd (Sutherland Highlanders) Regiment of Foot.

1881   Linked with the 91st Highlanders and became the 2nd Battalion *Princess Louise's (Sutherland and Argyll Highlanders)*.

The facings were always yellow. The buttons and lace of the officers were silver up to 1830, then gold. Theoretically, the 93rd wore the kilt from earliest times, but in America, 1814–15, they wore trews of tartan as foreign service had made demands on their clothing. A distinctive feature of the regimental dicing was the omission of a central green square and the distinctive red and white dicing was worn even after amalgamation. Among special badges was the Wild Cat indicating the Sutherland clan. The main story of their dress is to be found in the Highland uniform section.

See also the group, 1814–1914 (*88*), the corporal at Lucknow, 1957 (*89*), the lance-corporal, 1862 (*90a*) and the pipe-major, 1889 (*90b*)

94th Foot

1823   There had been three previous regiments numbered '94', including the famous Scots/Scotch Brigade which had been in the Netherlands since 1685, but when it returned to British service in 1793 it was numbered '94th', but it disbanded in 1818. The present 94th was revived in Glasgow with many officers from the Scotch Brigade and the men from the Veteran Battalions merely as a regiment of foot.

1881   On linking with the 88th Regiment it lost any Scottish distinction and became the 2nd Battalion the *Connaught Rangers*.

The facings were bluish-green and the officers' lace was gold. In general, the infantry uniform was worn. But suggestions may be made for a Scottish connection, for when the distinctions of the old Scottish Brigade were restored in 1875 – the Caparisoned Elephant as well as the honours for Peninsula and India – an application asked that a diced band be added to the shako but the copious Regimental Records tell that it was not adopted.

95th Foot

1823   There had been several other regiments numbered '95'; this 95th Regiment of Foot was the second of six regiments raised over the 1823–4 period.

1825   95th (the Derbyshire) Regiment of Foot.

1881   Linked with the 45th Regiment and became the 2nd Battalion the *Sherwood Foresters (Derbyshire) Regiment*.

The regimental facings were yellow until 1881, when white was to be worn. The buttons and lace of officers were silver until 1830, then gold. The uniforms followed the normal infantry developments.

96th Foot

1824   There were several previous regiments of foot numbered '96' before this third of six raised for general service, the 96th Regiment of Foot.

1881   Linked with the 63rd Regiment to become the 2nd Battalion of the *Manchester Regiment*.

The regimental facings were yellow until 1881, when white was worn. Lace and buttons for officers were silver until 1830, then gold. In 1874 the Sphinx worn by a previous 96th Foot was permitted to be worn as a badge. Otherwise the uniforms followed the normal developments.

97th Foot

1824   There were five previous regiments numbered '97' before this fourth of the six regiments was raised as an Irish corps.

1826   97th (Earl of Ulster's) Regiment of Foot. The title being one of those borne by the Duke of Cambridge.

1881   Linked with the 50th Regiment and became the 2nd Battalion of the *Queen's Own (Royal West Kent Regiment)*.

The sky-blue facings of the regiment were based on the Ribbon of the Order of St Patrick, which brought the nickname of the 'Celestials'. The buttons and lace of the officers were silver until 1830, then gold. The dress followed the normal infantry practice with local variations when serving abroad.

98th Foot

1824   The sixth regiment to bear the number '98' was the fifth of the six new regiments raised at this time and was known simply as the 98th Regiment of Foot.

1876   98th (The Prince of Wales's) Regiment of Foot (after the 98th of 1815–18).

1881   Linked with the 64th Regiment and became the 2nd Battalion of the *Prince of Wales's (North Staffordshire Regiment)*.

The facings were white, and the officers' buttons and lace silver until 1830, then gold. In 1876 the Prince of Wales's Feathers, Coronet and motto were authorized, and the Dragon of China was authorized in 1843 for their services in the Far East.

Overleaf:
63.
The Lancashire Fusiliers (late 20th), 1913, officer

99th Foot

1824   The last of the six regiments raised at this time was the 99th Regiment of Foot, the sixth and last to carry this number.

1832   99th (Lanarkshire) Regiment of Foot.

1874   99th (The Duke of Edinburgh's) Regiment of Foot.

1881   Linked with the 62nd Regiment to become the 2nd Battalion of the *Duke of Edinburgh's (Wiltshire Regiment)*.

The regimental facings were yellow and would have continued in 1881 if the regiment had remained in Scotland, but since they were Wiltshire the

THE LANCASHIRE FUSILIERS.
1913.

Plate 63

a 1792

b 1751

c 1742

d 1768

e 1792

f 1814

g 1905

ROYAL SCOTS FUSILIERS

h 1826

i 1852

j 1859

k 1868

l 1859

m 1852

R. Simkin.

Plate 64

'English' white facings were regulation. The officers' buttons and lace were silver until 1830, then gold. In 1874 the Duke of Edinburgh's Coronet and Cypher were permitted as badges. When serving as a Lowland regiment, a diced border (with a yellow central square) was worn on the head-dresses and there were pipers in full Highland dress; this disappeared after 1881.

100th Foot

1855   Even such a high number as '100' had been given to five regiments raised and disbanded before the 100th (Prince of Wales's Royal Canadian) Regiment of Foot was raised.

1881   Linked with the 109th Regiment and became the 1st Battalion *The Prince of Wales's Leinster Regiment (Royal Canadians)*.

1922   Disbanded.

The regiment had royal blue facings from the beginning and gold lace and buttons for the officers. Being raised in Canada, old uniforms of the Canadian Militia were issued and worn until arrival in England. In 1860 the badge of the Prince of Wales's Feathers was part of the appointments. The uniform followed the normal infantry changes but after 1881 the Irish connection was noted with the appointment of pipers in Irish dress wearing saffron kilts.

101st Foot

1861   There had been several regiments numbered '101' before this one, but the regiment due to take this number had an ancient lineage, as it had been an East India Company regiment raised in Bengal in 1756. After the Indian Mutiny, the European regiments were brought home. Thus the 1st Bengal Fusiliers of 1858–61 became the 101st (Royal Bengal Fusiliers) Regiment on the British establishment.

1881   Linked with the 104th Regiment and became the 1st Battalion *Royal Munster Fusiliers*.

1922   Disbanded.

Being a royal regiment, the facings were blue and the officers' lace gold. The uniform in the British service was that of fusiliers and after 1881 the regiment had the Arms of Munster as well as the Royal Tiger as badges.

102nd Foot

1861   Another of the European regiments from India taken on the British establishment, the 1st Madras Fusiliers of 1858–61 became the 102nd (Royal Madras Fusiliers) Regiment.

1881   Linked with the 103rd Regiment to become the 1st Battalion *Royal Dublin Fusiliers*.

1922   Disbanded.

As a royal regiment the facings were blue and the officers' distinctions were gold. On the new badges of 1881 were the Arms of the City of Dublin and the Royal Tiger for earlier battles in India. The dress was fusiliers.

103rd Foot

1861   The third in rank of the regiments from India was the 1st Bombay Fusiliers of 1858–61 who became the 103rd (Royal Bombay Fusiliers).

1881   Linked with the 102nd Foot and became the 2nd Battalion the *Royal Dublin Fusiliers*.

Following the precedence of the first two European regiments, the uniform was that of fusiliers with royal blue facings, but with the badge of the Royal Tiger and later the Arms of Dublin.

104th Foot

1861   The 2nd Bengal Fusiliers, a European regiment of 1858–61, became the 104th (Bengal Fusiliers).

1881   Linked with the 101st Regiment and became the 2nd Battalion the *Royal Munster Fusiliers*.

1922   Disbanded.

The facings had been blue when the regiment was Bengal Fusiliers so the uniforms were similar to those of the previous three regiments, specially the 1st Battalion Royal Munster Fusiliers.

105th Foot

1861   Another of the nine European regiments from India, the 2nd Madras European Regiment of 1858–61 became the 105th (Madras Light Infantry) Regiment.

1881   Linked with the 51st Regiment and became the 2nd Battalion the *King's Own Light Infantry (South Yorkshire Regiment)*.

The facings were pale buff and as it had been a light infantry regiment it was linked with an existing light infantry regiment, when the facings were changed to white. Before amalgamation the badge had been a curled bugle-horn with the motto '*Cede nullis*'.

106th Foot

1861   The sixth regiment to return from India was the 2nd Bombay Light Infantry Regiment of 1858–61 which became the 106th Bombay Light Infantry Regiment.

1881   Linked with the 68th Light Infantry and became the 2nd Battalion of the *Durham Light Infantry*.

The facings had been white and so as a former light infantry regiment, linking did not change the uniform very much. Until amalgamation the regimental badge had been the French bugle-horn with '106' within the curl.

107th Foot

1862   The seventh regiment from India was the 3rd (Bengal European Light Infantry) Regiment of 1858–61. All Indian Presidencies had three regiments of white European troops who returned to Great Britain and this one was named the 107th (Bengal Infantry Regiment).

1881   When linked with the 35th Regiment it became the 2nd Battalion of the *Royal Sussex Regiment*.

The facings were white until linking and the number '107' was worn within a Garter on the buttons. Uniforms followed the normal developments.

108th Foot

1862   The eighth regiment from India was the 3rd (Madras) European

Overleaf:
65.
Royal Welch Fusiliers (late 23rd)
a   1715, private
b   1742, private
c   1751, private
d   1768, private
e   1792, officer
f   1822, officer
g   (c.1914) goat and goat-major, officer back view, officer mounted all full dress
h   1832, sergeant
i   1852, officer
j   1852, private
k   1856, officer
l   1862, officer
m   1868, corporal

a *1715*

b *1742*

c *1751*

d *1768*

e *1792*

f *1822*

g Royal Welch Fusiliers

h *1832*

i *1852*

j *1852*

k *1856*

l *1862*

m *1868*

Plate 65

COLONEL ZACHARIAH TIFFIN'S REGIMENT OF FOOT.
(NOW 1ST BATTALION ROYAL INNISKILLING FUSILIERS.
MUSKETEER - 1689.

a

PIPER, 3RD INNISKILLING FUSILIERS, 1900.

b

Plate 66

Infantry Regiment of 1858–61 which became the 108th (Madras Infantry) Regiment.

1881   Linked with the 27th Regiment and became the 2nd Battalion of the *Royal Inniskilling Fusiliers.*

Facings had been deep yellow and the uniforms followed those of the line. When other Irish regiments were disbanded in 1922, the 2nd Battalion was also re-formed in 1924 in the Royal Irish Fusiliers and in 1938 again became the 2nd Battalion of the Royal Inniskilling Fusiliers.

109th Foot

1861   The ninth and last regiment to come from India was the 3rd (Bombay) Regiment of 1858–61 which was taken on the British establishment as the 109th (Bombay Infantry) Regiment.

1881   Linked with the 100th Regiment and became the 2nd Battalion of the *Prince of Wales's Leinster Regiment (Royal Canadians).*

The regimental facings were white and the normal infantry of the line uniforms were worn.

The Rifle Brigade

1800   The Rifle Corps.
1803   The 95th or Rifle Regiment.
1816   The Rifle Brigade.
1862   The Prince Consort's Own (Rifle Brigade).
1881   *Rifle Brigade (Prince Consort's Own).*
1920   The Rifle Brigade (Prince Consort's Own).
1958   The 3rd Green Jackets (the Rifle Brigade).
1966   Amalgamated with the 1st Green Jackets (43 and 52) and the 2nd Green Jackets (The King's Royal Rifle Corps) to form the Royal Green Jackets.
1968   In the Light Division.

The distinctive rifle green jackets were worn from the beginning and the developments of the Rifle Brigade uniforms are given in the rifle section of uniforms. The stringed bugle-horn was an original badge in the regiment and the Maltese Cross became a belt-plate for the officers.

See also the group, 1806–1914 *(93)*

The Development of Infantry Uniform

Infantry uniform followed a developing pattern over the years and the separate articles of uniform are described below. The variations needed to cover grenadiers, light infantry, riflemen, and so on are covered later in appropriate sections.

Head-dress

In the beginning the normal head-dress was the civilian hat with a wide brim. Rain made the brim weak and floppy so that later it was bound on the edge with tape. The fashion of turning the brim up on one side also gave strength. When the other side was turned up and finally the back it became a 'tricorn'. This development had various fashions of cocking and towards

Preceding page:
66a
Tiffin's Regiment (later 1st Battalion Royal Inniskilling Fusiliers [late 27th]), 1689, musketeer

66b
Royal Inniskilling Fusiliers (late 27th and 108th), 1900, piper

the end of the eighteenth century the hat evolved into the 'bicorn', the flap being being very large and the front fastened up with a loop, rosette and finally a plume. Eventually this plume became white and red for the battalion companies, white for the grenadier companies and green for the light infantry.

By 1800 the shako (already accepted in Europe) was being introduced as the basic cap for infantry. The word was spelt in many ways. Later in the nineteenth century the spelling was 'chaco' or 'chakot' but to avoid confusion, the word shako is used here to cover all periods. The 'stove-pipe' pattern changed in 1812 to the false-fronted cap, later called the 'Belgic' or 'Waterloo' pattern. In 1816 a broad-topped version was introduced, based on the French or Prussian style, and was worn with variations until 1844 when the 'Albert' pattern (tubular with back and front peaks) was being worn. In 1855 a tapering version, after the French fashion, was worn and this changed in 1861 to a lower type. Another low pattern in 1869 saw the last of the basic shakos in wear because in 1878 a more militant form of head-dress, a Prussian version of helmet, became the last full-dress infantry head-dress.

Body Garments (coats and jackets)

The distinguishing red coats of the English troops had been well established even in the days of Elizabeth I, the red hue having a national connection with the red cross of St George, which was the English flag at that time. When Charles II returned to England the Parliamentary army had to be disbanded and a new force created. The earliest Royalist troops of the Restoration were to be found among those who had accompanied the King in exile. Thus red coats with blue facings were worn by the Royal troops – infantry, cavalry and even the artillery.

The jacket was at first short but officers were quick to adopt the long cassock or surtout worn on the Continent, and the men soon followed. Although the coats were ample, the cloth for the common soldier was not suitable in cold weather and needed a warmer lining or facing, sometimes red but often another colour. The long sleeves reached to the knuckles of the hand and in warm weather were turned back to make cuffs of the facing colour, blue for royal regiments and yellow, white or other colours for non-royal regiments. Buttons and buttonholes with braid were needed to keep the cuff in place. Then a slit in the sleeve and further buttoning made a closer fit and produced a new style. This eventually developed into the buttoned flap which is still seen today on the Foot Guards' tunics. As the material on the early coats was of poor material, the buttonholes soon became enlarged and had to be strengthened. Stitching was insufficient and so lace or braid was sewn all around the holes and eventually on other parts of the coats.

When James II came to the throne he brought a preference for yellow facings (perhaps connected with his support for the Catholic religion) but a radical change came when blue coats were worn by some regiments in William III's time. The Dutch Foot Guards wore dark blue coats with orange-yellow facings and for a time it was a fashion to clothe newly raised English troops in blue, like Lord Lisburne's and Lord Herbert's Welshmen (later the 23rd). For a period in Ireland, grey coats were being worn but by the end of the century red again became the distinctive English colour.

Being a single-breasted garment the lower parts of the skirts often parted

Overleaf:
67.
Princess Victoria's Royal Irish Fusiliers (late 87th)
a   1808, officer
b   1793, private
c   1793, officer
d   1814, private
e   1814, officer
f   1826, officer
g   (c.1914) lieutenant service dress, mounted officer full dress
h   1832, officer
i   1852, private
j   1860, officer
k   1868, bandsman
l   1860, sergeant
m   1852, officer

a

b

c

d

e

f

g

PRINCESS VICTORIA'S ROYAL IRISH FUSILIERS

h

i

j

k

l

m

R. Simkin

Plate 67

PRINCE ALBERT'S SOMERSETSHIRE LIGHT INFANTRY

R.Simkin.

a

b

c

d

e

f

g

h

i

j

k

l

m

Plate 68

to show the colour of the lining which, when later these were turned back for ease of marching and fastened with hooks or buttons, allowed the facing colour to make a strong contrast. Originally collars were not worn, cravats or other neck cloths above the shirt being considered sufficient, but in the wars of Marlborough's time some troops did wear collars for a period. The two-coloured looping on the buttonholes was also a distinguishing feature in Marlborough's day. When the upper part of the coat was unbuttoned, the facing colour could be seen and by 1720–30 the fashion was to turn these fronts back to make lapels of the facing colour. The inadequacy of regimental distinctions being made by facing colour was highlighted when Colonel Hastings (later 13th) hoped that Beaumont's Regiment (later 8th) might be broke, so that he could acquire their uniforms with yellow facings, as they were the same as those of his regiment.

There were some coats in 1709 which were double-breasted down the front with yellow which may indicate that lapels were beginning to appear, but there must have been many varieties, for in 1720 patterns of clothing of all regiments were to be sealed but what degree of standardization was intended is not known. In 1727 George II ordered that there would be a fixed clothing and that all garments should differ in their facings 'or otherwise'. Once again, details are not available but obviously there were not enough different facing colours. The old coat was expected to be made into a waistcoat and worn under the new coat. In 1730 the pattern garment had wings or lacings on the sleeves which were to be removed and made plain.

By now many other regiments, other than royal regiments, had been raised with their own distinctive facings. Blue was reserved for royal regiments but any other colour was possible, even black as in the case of a colonel who was at that time in mourning for his mother. As the number of new regiments increased, the variety of colours for facings ran out, even though there may have been eleven shades of green, and even some of these were 'fugitive' and changed hues in the passage of time. Another method of distinction was needed and this was by varying the patterns of braid or lace on the soldier's coat – details of which are too complicated and changing to be covered in this work. Later the spacing of the buttonholes – regular or in pairs or even in threes – helped to create visible differences.

A *Representation of the Cloathing of His Majesty's Household and of all the Forces* dated 1742 gives the first full information on infantry uniforms by having a hand-coloured plate of every regiment of foot in being at that time. With each plate, the names of the colonels are quoted as are numbers but at that time indicating precedence and ranking rather than part of the regiment's title. It may be that the purpose of this work was to discover exactly what was being worn, with the intention of producing 'uniformity'. Most coats show the skirts being turned back but not all had the turned-back lapels, nor did all have patterned lace on the buttonholes, and the cuff patterns varied.

In 1747 a draft regulation was made regarding the uniform of infantry, including changes intended to improve the design and establish certain features. In 1749 it was ordered that all infantry coats were to be made with lapels but it was not until 1751 that the regulations were at last in print. A Royal Warrant regularized the 'fixed' clothing from which no change was to be made without authority. Each regiment was allocated a colour for the facings. But fashions and civilian clothing were changing as were the details of military dress, so that a new warrant was necessary in 1768 which gave a more military garment with narrow cuffs and long lapels. The colour of the facings with precise hue was laid down as was a description of the lace worn by each regiment, specified as white with the addition of coloured stripes. Examples of these laces or braids are still preserved and are in the special shape of the buttonhole loop (which was not mentioned in the warrant). A unique book of hand-coloured prints said to be made after the 1768 regulations shows a grenadier from each marching regiment, but as all the loops are set regular and it is known that some regiments had pairs, the work may be a reconstruction and not taken from life.

Before the end of the eighteenth century collars had evolved from the turned-down to those rising-up and eventually into the stiff standing collars. By 1796 some coats were buttoned over and soon all did so, fastening down to the waist and hiding the waistcoat. From the middle of the century the skirts had been permanently turned back and the fastening changed from hooks and eyes to sewn-down shapes with false pocket outline, with the genuine pockets underneath in the tails.

The shorter version of the infantry coat was the jacket established about 1797, worn at first by light companies and riflemen but it soon became popular for others, specially in the Peninsular War. The men's jackets continued to be single-breasted and the round cuffs were changed c. 1829 to those with flaps and buttons. In 1836 the stripes and patterns in the men's braid or lace were discontinued and they had plain white loops up to the Crimean War. In 1855 a double-breasted tunic was approved, but these had a short life and by 1857 single-breasted tunics were being worn. The flap on the cuff continued but in 1868 men had pointed cuffs. When the simplified facings were introduced in 1881 the cuff of the tunic was changed to a round or 'jam-pot' variety. In the reign of Edward VII, a pointed cuff was reintroduced and remained in being until the end of the men's full dress.

Waistcoats and nether-wear

The 'small-clothes' or 'under-garments' of a soldier were the waistcoat and breeches. Originally they were of various colours, frequently in the colour of the facings but not always: see the details 'Brief Descriptions'. But such colourful garments went out of fashion and in 1767 they were to be white (or buff, if the facings were buff). Red waistcoats became the mark of light infantry companies but when the coat closed down the front in 1796 the waistcoat was no longer seen – although it continued in wear as an undress item. In 1830 line infantrymen were given a red jacket for undress use but the Foot Guards and Highlanders continued the white jacket until the end of full dress.

Breeches were covered with overalls by the end of the eighteenth century. On active service in Europe overalls were most practical and varied in colour from white to various shades of grey. Eventually they became the trousers which then saw the abolition of white breeches and long black gaiters in 1823. White linen trousers continued to be worn in summer months or in hot weather, until they too were abolished in 1861. Various colours of trousers were worn at other times varying in colour from dark grey to blue-grey. The Oxford mixture (dark grey) of 1846 was worn until the dark blue trousers were introduced in 1855 (although the Oxford grey, the winter dress, continued until 1881). The dark blue trousers were worn in the last days of full dress.

Overleaf:
69.
13th Foot
a 1777, private light company
b 1812, pioneer

13ᵀᴴ REGIMENT OF FOOT – 1777.
(PRIVATE – PICQUET COMPANY)

a

13ᵀᴴ FIRST SOMERSETSHIRE REGᵗ
1812.

b

Plate 69

32ND CORNWALL LIGHT INFANTRY.
1864.

a

32ND CORNWALL LIGHT INFANTRY.
1870.

b

Plate 70

Gaiters

Gaiters or 'spatterdashes' were worn over hose early in the eighteenth century. White continued to be the full-dress colour for such occasions but black gaiters to the knee were worn on service. Half-gaiters were worn by light infantry. When overalls were introduced, small gaiters or 'spats' were worn in varying colours, grey, white or black. Infantry of the Line discontinued these but Highlanders wore them with their hose and still do.

Shoes

Shoes tied with bows had been worn in Charles I's army and continued in the Restoration. Buckles came in use before the end of the seventeenth century. Boots did not replace the infantryman's shoes until the nineteenth century, black always being the chosen colour until active service in the First World War brought in unpolished boots.

Neckwear

Before collars were added to coats, a neck cloth like a cravat was worn around the neck and tied in front. Later in the eighteenth century the stock was adopted from continental armies. This could be of leather or of a stiffened material. It continued to be worn under the standing collar and it was not until c. 1862 that the stock was replaced by a small black leather tab which covered the opening of the collar, this also disappearing early in the twentieth century.

Undress

Undress garments were many and varied, frequently of regimental fashion, and were partly paid for by the men. The caps were of changing patterns as were the lightweight jackets or frocks, mainly inspired during the service in India and the Far East.

Pikemen

The common soldier who fought on foot in the early days before the Standing Army was formed could be armed in more than one way. There were bows and arrows, sword, spear, long knife, staffed weapons, like a bill or a halbert, and eventually a firearm. By 1660 the arms of infantrymen had been simplified to those of a musketeer or a pikeman. The slow-moving pikemen, chosen from the tallest and strongest men, had a pike 12 to 16 feet long and were stationed in the middle of a regiment with the musketeers on either flank. For personal protection the pikemen had body armour and a sword, as well as a pot or helmet in action. The metal head-dress often had a feather but the broad-brimmed hat was often worn for comfort. The cuirass (front and back plates) had at the waist tasses or tassets, being overlapping plates on the thighs but they were later replaced by buff leather.

In William and Mary's reign it was ordered that there should be fourteen pikemen in each company of sixty men, except in fusilier regiments. When regiments were raised for sea-service, no pikemen were enlisted. The development of the bayonet, which extended the reach of the musket, made the pike obsolete even though this awkward weapon was the cheapest possible.

By the time of Queen Anne, pikemen were not considered practical

Preceding page:
70.
32nd Cornwall Light Infantry
a   1864, private
b   1870, officer

fighting men but continued as ceremonial troops, specially when captured French colours were to be paraded by them after the victories of Marlborough. But the armour and pikes were now being stored in the Tower of London and not issued, so these veterans gradually disappeared.

Grenadier Companies

Although the use of hand grenades had proved useful during the Civil War, England had been slow to employ men specially trained in the handling of this dangerous weapon. Grenades were in store at British forts on the Continent when Charles II returned to England but it was not until May 1677 that two soldiers were ordered from each company of infantry to undertake training in the Tower of London as grenadiers. These included men from the two regiments of Foot Guards, but in April 1678 a grenadier company was to be added to the eight oldest regiments of foot. It was not sufficient for the man to be trained to light the grenade, and to throw it at the right time and at the correct distance; he had also to beware of his explosive device. The normal infantryman had a musket which was discharged by a burning match. Such a fire-hazard had to be avoided and the match-lock was replaced by the fusil or flint-lock musket which did away with the burning match. The flint-lock was an expensive weapon and to preserve it, it was slung over the back before the grenade could be prepared for attack. This brought two innovations: first, the leather sling to hold the weapon close to the body thus leaving the hands free; and second, a head-dress which would not be knocked off in action. The hat was replaced by a low-fitting cap and the grenadier became an elite soldier, frequently in the fore of a battle and undertaking special engagements.

The diarist, John Evelyn, when at Hounslow Camp in June 1678 wrote of this 'new sort of soldier who with a pouch full of grenades was skilful in throwing them at the enemy'. He also noted their unusual head-dress which he colourfully described as 'furred caps with coped crowns like Janizaries which made them look very fierce, and some had long hoods hanging down behind as we picture fools. Their clothing being likewise, pyebald yellow and red.' Thus there were two versions of caps being worn by grenadier, the cloth cap which had fur all the way round and developed as such on the Continent, and the all-cloth version which had a little turned-up flap in front. It is the latter which appears in contemporary portraits, often elaborately embroidered for officers. The main body of the cap was stiffened later and led the way to the 'mitre-cap' so popular in England and Hanover. The cloth cap was able to carry many regimental distinctions like the Crown, royal or other cyphers, as well as other embroidered devices like muskets, leaves, etc. Grenadiers were considered so important that they were chosen from the tallest men in a regiment and encouraged to wear 'fearsome moustachios'. For a review they formed the position of honour on the right flank and were the leading company on the march.

Richard Simkin shows an officer of a grenadier company (22a) which is based on the reconstruction by Clifford Walton for the 11th Foot, 1686. The actual sources for the picture are mainly the colours noted at Hounslow 1686, but the costume is a reconstruction without firm evidence. The tawny lining, breeches, stockings and edge to the cap are said to have been the livery colour of the Duke of Beaufort, the first colonel. Elaborate loops were

Overleaf:
71.
Oxfordshire and Buckinghamshire Light Infantry (late 43rd and 52nd)
a   1741, private 43rd
b   1751, grenadier 43rd
c   1792, officer 43rd
d   1809, officer 43rd
e   1820, officer 43rd
f   1861, officer 43rd
g   (c.1906) officer, mounted and bugler both full dress
h   1755, private 52nd
i   1809, private 52nd
j   1832, officer 52nd
k   1852, private 52nd
l   1861, private 52nd
m   1875, officer 52nd

a

b
43RD FOOT.
GRENADIER, 1751.

c
43RD MONMOUTHSHIRE REGT.
OFFICER, 1792.

d
43RD MONMOUTHSHIRE LIGHT INFANTRY.
OFFICER, 1809.

COLONEL THOMAS FOWKE'S REGIMENT OF FOOT.
PRIVATE, 1741.

e
43RD
FIELD-OFFICER, 1820.

f
43RD
OFFICER, 1661.

g

R SIMKIN.

h
54TH FOOT.
PRIVATE, 1755.

OXFORDSHIRE AND BUCKINGHAMSHIRE LIGHT INFANTRY

i
52ND OXFORDSHIRE LIGHT INFANTRY.
PRIVATE, 1809.

j
52ND
OFFICER, 1832.

k
52ND
PRIVATE 1852.

l
52ND
PRIVATE, 1861.

m
52ND
OFFICER, 1876.

19.

Plate 71

51ST SECONDYORKSHIRE WEST RIDING,
THE KINGS' OWN LIGHT INFANTRY.
1830.

a

51ST SECOND YORKSHIRE, WEST RIDING.
THE KINGS OWN LIGHT INFANTRY.
1832.

b

Plate 72

no doubt worn but there is no evidence for this pattern nor for the shape of the grenadier cap. However, with the lack of any other evidence Simkin had to copy Walton very carefully. The 'looped' clothing for a grenadier is mentioned in a song and also in deserters' reports. Exactly how the loops were made up is not explained but they could be red and white, black and white or plain blue.

The cloth cap became the accepted head-dress for grenadiers and fusiliers, the fur-edged cap dropping out of favour in England. A clue regarding these caps is in a deserter's report of 1708 where one cap is described as being faced with 'bear's fur', but the new caps of the regiment were red cloth faced with yellow. The front of the cloth cap gradually became taller and the cap itself also finished with the threads at the top appearing upright like a pompon. Being of cloth it was possible to embroider devices on the fronts and on the band around the crown of the cap. It is known that colonels chose part of their coat-of-arms or their crest to be the main subject on the front, and in Georgian times the little flap carried the White Horse of Hanover. The surrounding band usually had leaves and a grenade, possibly also muskets. Royal regiments obviously had royal badges in front with a Crown or Coronet and cypher. When the 'Georges' were both Kings and Electors in Hanover, that nation had cloth caps with the Royal Arms including the Lion and the Unicorn.

Although the grenade was used up to the middle of the eighteenth century, it appears to have practically ceased use on the battlefield although the pouch and match-case continued to be worn. An order of 1730 ordered the wings to be removed from the sleeves but they soon came back again into fashion for grenadiers.

The complete series of oil-paintings made by David Morier *c.* 1751 (perhaps to illustrate the Royal Warrant of 1751 that did so much to regularize uniform) shows a grenadier of each line regiment. It will be seen that the cloth cap of the fusilier was similar to that of the grenadier. Richard Simkin shows his knowledge of these Windsor Castle paintings and frequently copies the same pose (see 5th Foot, 1751, 59c). The specially permitted badges are noted in the Brief Outlines but in most cases the crowned 'GR' cypher was sufficient in the British Army.

The uniform gradually altered and the 1768 warrant covered this. The main change was to the fur cap which Simkin depicts in another grenadier of the 5th Foot (59d) and this uniform is based on a unique hand-coloured book of prints in the Prince Consort's Library at Aldershot which Simkin could have easily visited. A single engraving served for all the seventy regiments of 1768 shown in this book, differing only in the colouring, even in the over-painting of the 42nd Highlander. As all the loops are shown as 'regular' it is possible that the result may not be strictly accurate. As early as 1763 fur caps had reappeared in the British Army and it was the 1768 Royal Warrant that made the cloth cap obsolete. The black fur cap was to have had a white feather or plume on the left and a universal plate but there were variations for specially favoured regiments.

In the early 1770s the waist-belt carrying the bayonet was being worn over the right shoulder. The pronged buckle gave place to a flat plate and in the early days some plates carried the word 'grenadier' or a grenade. The shoulder-belt was also used to carry the match-case, although possibly never used. In 1784 the sword which had earlier been abolished for other infantry became obsolete for grenadiers.

Preceding page:
72.
51st (2nd Yorkshire West Riding) King's Own Light Infantry
a 1830, bandsman
b 1832, officer

The use of match-cases was known after the turn of the century but the introduction of the shako made the grenadier fur cap an item for ceremonial duties. The 'stove-pipe' shako continued on service with the white plume now worn in front and the device of a flaming grenade might appear on the shako plate. Both officer and man are shown (59*f* and *h*) in 1814 service dress wearing the fur cap with the low brass or gilt plate in front, although this might have been at home only.

In 1824 the wearing of the bearskin cap was confined to Great Britain, Ireland and America and so the shako was the authorized head-dress for overseas service right up to the end of flank companies. The wings of grenadier company officers' coats became very elaborate including rows of chain. The new pattern coatee of 1829 with two close rows of buttons down the front continued to have the stiffened wings which could have up to three rows of chain.

When the 'Albert' shako was being worn in 1844, the bearskin caps of the grenadier companies were obsolete and were abolished although fusilier regiments were allowed to continue with their fur caps. In 1855 the tunic was introduced and this meant that both epaulettes and wings of grenadiers were abolished. The shako of the grenadier companies was now practically the only distinction left for these once-elite men with the white ball-tuft instead of the red and white. But in March 1856 all flank companies were to disappear and their distinctions only had a short life until they wore out; by 1858 all differences were forbidden.

Light Infantry Companies

It was during the fighting in North America against the Red Indians that battles fought in the solid parade formation used in Europe were found to be useless. The introduction of independent companies of rangers who dispersed to fight in the shelter of trees and elsewhere led to the formation of groups of 'picked' riflemen who became the first light infantry. General Wolfe in 1759 had his chosen men dressed in an appropriate uniform – the sleeves of the coat were put on the waistcoat and the altered coat had two large wings on the openings of these coats. Lace was removed and pockets were placed on the breast. The man's hat was altered into a cap, his leggings strapped underneath his shoes like spatterdashes and as an extra weapon he had a tomahawk hanging on his side. But in other regiments the light infantry companies were to be dressed like the others in the regiment unless orders were given to the contrary. These light infantrymen disappeared at the peace of 1763.

In 1770 it was decided that a tenth company of light infantry would be added to 'all Marching Regiments', the eighteen regiments in North America being the first to have them. A special light infantry cap was designed. It was black leather with three chains around the base, a piece of plate on the centre of the crown and on the front was placed a metal crown over 'GR' and the number of the regiment. Jackets were worn and a red waistcoat laced. White or buff breeches were worn and the black gaiters came no higher than the calf of the leg. An oil-painting of a Royal Review in 1778 shows the regulation cap worn by the 6th Foot but the caps of the 69th Foot were elaborate and made from altered hats. Plumes at this time were no fixed colour, sometimes red, or black and white, or other colours.

Overleaf:
73.
52nd Oxfordshire Light Infantry, 1812, officer

74.
90th Perthshire Volunteers Light Infantry, 1832, sergeant

52ᴺᴰ OXFORDSHIRE LIGHT INFANTRY
1812.

Plate 73

90ᵀᴴ PERTHSHIRE VOLUNTEERS LIGHT INFANTRY.
1832.

Plate 74

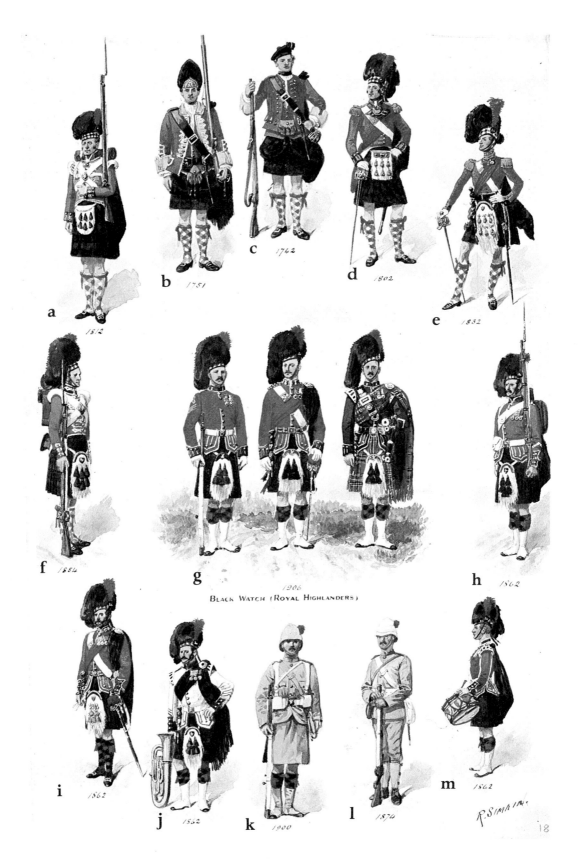

a

b *1751*

c *1742*

d *1802*

e *1832*

f *1854*

g *1906*

BLACK WATCH (ROYAL HIGHLANDERS)

h *1862*

i *1862*

j *1852*

k *1900*

l *1874*

m *1862*

R. SIMKIN.

18

Plate 75

In the Mediterranean garrisons, men of 'picket' companies wore the normal dress of the regiment but the head-dresses varied. That of the 11th Foot was the regulation cap with a black feather, the 13th had a distinctive upswept head-dress with an off-white or yellowish hair-tuft on top and the 25th (also called a Highland company) had a fur-edged front and a red plate in front including a thistle (97c).

The end of the war in America did not see the end of these light companies and in 1784 a committee went to some lengths to improve the light infantry dress and equipment. The old cap was considered 'very burdensome and totally useless to the soldiers'. The new cap was to be of black leather and apparently like that worn by the light dragoons. As signals in light companies were given by the means of the horn or bugle, the bugle-horn became the special badge for these men and part of their uniform. In 1791 the epaulettes of the officers were to have the addition of an embroidered bugle-horn.

In 1796 the lapels were closed down the front of the coat to the waist and they could be either buttoned over or closed with hooks and eyes. The pockets of light infantry were to be made oblique and slashed. About this time (1797) the feathers or plumes on head-dresses were standardized and were made white over red for the battalion companies, white for grenadiers, and green for the light companies. The helmet-cap was still in use, for officers with a dark green feather and a silver bugle and crown on the right side. The jacket of light infantry officers is described in tailors' books as 'short-skirted' and with oblique pocket flaps. In 1802 the scarlet wings had bullion and fringe when necessary and epaulettes according to rank. The embroidered bugle-horn was on the wings and the buttons were smaller than those worn on other company coats. The new cap or shako was expected to be worn by officers 'at all times' and made of the same material as the hat, with a dark green feather and a bugle horn in front. The wings of other ranks were laced all round and had a worsted fringe on the outer edge. The turn-backs of the skirts now carried a bugle on each side. When the great wars were over, the dress of the light infantry settled down and began to assimilate with that of the Infantry of the Line, with the exception of head-dress fittings, wings and the use of the bugle, specially as a badge.

Simkin depicts a light company officer of the 30th Foot, 1850 (35). His 'Albert' shako has a dark green ball-tuft (not black as used by riflemen). The elaborate gilt fittings had a bugle device on the central plate. The sword-belt not only carried the regimental plate but also had the whistle and chain so necessary for light company officers and sergeants who needed to signal to their men in action. The crimson waist-sash had hanging cords which were looped in varying fashions.

A light infantry print of the same period is that of the 46th Foot, 1854 (48) showing full fighting dress, a distinction being the all-red ball-tuft in his shako, an honorary distinction granted to the 46th Foot in 1833, commemorating their service in North America when for many years the light company wore red feathers in their head-dress.

The section on light infantry regiments (pp. 133–137) covers most facts on the uniforms but of course the upheaval at the time of the war with Russia saw not only the coatee and wings being replaced by the simple tunic but also the obsolescence of flank companies; by 1858 they were a matter of history.

Preceding page:
75.
Black Watch (Royal Highlanders) (late 42nd)
a   1812, private
b   1751, grenadier
c   1742, private
d   1802, officer
e   1832, officer
f   1854, private
g   1906, colour-sergeant, officer and piper all full dress
h   1862, private
i   1862, officer
j   1862, bandsman
k   1900, private service dress
l   1874, private service dress
m   1862, drummer full dress

Fusilier Regiments

Although there were grenadiers and grenadier companies, there had been no grenadier regiments or battalions in the British Army, although they were known on the Continent, until after Waterloo when the 1st Foot Guards were renamed the Grenadier Guards. The nearest British equivalent was to be made a fusilier regiment.

The cheapest firearm in the Restoration years was the match-lock, the powder of which was ignited by the burning end of a piece of match (an impregnated cord) by means of a descending cock into a 'flash-pan'. Obviously this weapon could be dangerous as was being in the vicinity of the gunpowder which the artillery then used from small barrels. So the production of the flint-lock or fusil which made a spark between flint and steel was much safer. However, at first this was thought to be an expensive weapon and thus was only issued to selected men or units.

One of the first to need this was the infantry which guarded the artillery train in 1685, who were at first known as the Ordnance Regiment and later as the English or Royal Fusiliers. In point of fact the Regiment of Scots Fuzileers had been raised in 1678 but not until they entered England in 1688 were they given the precedence of 21st whereas the English Fuzileers had been ranked as 7th. The Royal Welsh Fusiliers had been raised in 1688 but it was not until 1714 that they were named Fusiliers.

Hats were an incumbrance, especially if the flint-lock musket had to be slung over the shoulder to leave both hands free, so cloth caps were worn. The original red coat of the English fusiliers had red facings but changed later to the royal blue. Thus these three fusilier regiments all wore caps, emulating the grenadier fashion, and were also considered elite troops. Although Great Britain did not follow the European idea of grenadier regiments, late in the eighteenth century grenadier companies were detached from their regiments to form provisional grenadier battalions but later all returned to their original regiments.

Several regiments were honoured by conversion to fusiliers: there was the 5th Northumberland Regiment in 1836, and the 87th or Prince of Wales's Own Irish Regiment which was named fusiliers in 1827. Four regiments from India in 1861, the 101st (Royal Bengal Fusiliers), the 102nd (Royal Madras Fusiliers), the 103rd (Royal Bombay Fusiliers) and the 104th (Bengal Fusiliers), were all taken on the British establishment. In 1881 the 27th (Inniskilling) Regiment of Foot became the 1st Battalion of the Royal Inniskilling Fusiliers and the 20th (East Devon) Regiment of Foot became the Lancashire Fusiliers. All adopted a fusilier uniform with flaming grenade badges and fur caps. But grenadier companies continued to take pride of place in infantry regiments, despite the fact that all companies might have been equipped with flint-locks or fusils, and although the firearm was common enough for all regiments in the eighteenth century to have nothing but fusils, they were never called fusiliers except as an honorific title.

The Scots Fusiliers had red coats with red facings until 1714, it is said, when they became royal and took blue facings. When raised they had the nickname of the 'Earl of Mar's Grey-breeks', no doubt because their grey under-garments were distinctive at that time. When raised by Lord Herbert, the 23rd Foot-to-be wore blue coats faced with white but in 1714

Overleaf:
76.
42nd Royal Highland Regiment
a 1814, piper
b 1852, piper

42ND ROYAL HIGHLAND REGIMENT.
1814.

a

42ND ROYAL HIGHLAND REGIMENT.
(BLACK WATCH) 1852.

b

Plate 76

a   1802

b   1814

c   1814

d   1832

e

f   1832

1st Battn., Seaforth Highlanders
72nd Foot

K. Simkin.

g   1864

h   1882

i   1879

Plate 77

when they became royal, the royal blue would have been worn. Simkin gives a reconstruction of the dress in 1715 (65*a*) in which the red cap is turned up with blue, and has the Prince of Wales's Feathers on the red body and the White Horse on the turn-up (which may not be correct). The coat is based on that of the Queen's Regiment of Foot *c*. 1727 by which time the fully shaped lapels were in use, but evidence for 1715 is not so sure.

The 1742 *Cloathing* book shows the three regiments very clearly. The 7th Royal Fusiliers (62*a*) wears a uniform very like the other two fusilier regiments but it is the caps which show the difference. In the embroidery of the English regiment, there is a red cross within the Garter, set on silver rays and a Crown above. The 21st has the Scottish Star, no Crown above and on the small flap is the Thistle with 'Royal Fusiliers'. The 23rd has the Prince of Wales's Feathers on a star shape with the Crown above. Although the lace of all three regiments was white with blue lines, they varied regimentally.

The warrants of 1747 and 1751 give the grenadier badges on the front of the cap. The 7th had changed to the Rose within the Garter and had the Crown above. The 21st had the Thistle within the Circle and motto of St Andrew and Crown above it. The 23rd had the three Prince of Wales's Feathers and Coronet with the motto '*Ich Dien*'. Each little flap had the White Horse.

Simkin depicts the 21st (64) and the 23rd (65*c*) based on the David Morier paintings *c*. 1751. Morier shows that the new Rose of the 7th Fusiliers was 'slipped' with leaves on a stem. The dress is almost the same as in the 1742 *Cloathing* book but an extra pouch is being worn on the waist-belt. The next major change was made in 1768 when the cut was altered and became close-fitting. The cloth cap, which had been going out of fashion, was replaced by a black fur cap with a metal plate in front bearing the King's Crest and '*Nec Aspera Terrent*'. On the back of the cap was a grenade as a regulation device but some regiments were permitted to display their own badges: the 7th wore the Rose within the Garter with the Crown above, the 21st Fusiliers the Thistle within the Circle of St Andrew, and the 23rd Fusiliers the three Feathers issuing from the Prince of Wales's Coronet.

Simkin shows men from the 21st and 23rd Fusiliers (64*d*, 65*d*) as based on the unique book of '1768 Grenadiers' preserved at Aldershot. By 1784 it was realized that the normal soldier had little need for a sword and the last privates to have them, the fusiliers and the grenadiers, discontinued them. At the same time a new pattern of fur cap was authorized which now had more elaborate trimmings including a white plume on the left.

A magnificent series of water-colours of the various uniforms of the Royal Fusiliers was made at this time and Simkin gives examples of some of these (62*b*, *c*, *d* and *e*). The officer has much gold in his uniform – the cords on his cap, the lace on the coat and the epaulettes. He also wears the tie of his waist-sash on the right, normally a privilege for cavalry officers, but this is shown as so in the original painting. The pioneer demonstrates that the other ranks had wings. N.c.os had silver distinctions and the men white cords in their caps. Simkin shows officers and men of the 21st and 23rd Fusiliers (64*e*, 65*e*) dated 1792 which he has based on the carefully hand-coloured prints by E. Dayes. Here the officers carry their fusils as laid down for duty with the men and the sash is tied on the left in infantry style for the 7th Fusiliers.

The shako of 1800–12 was expected to be worn in action for fusiliers but the fur cap still remained in use (69*f*). The end of the eighteenth century saw the coat closed down to the waist and the fighting on the Continent brought overalls of white and other colours, these garments being worn over the breeches. The new shako of 1812–16 (62f) was now worn on service and the shorter jacket was a popular garment for active service.

In 1818 the three regiments of fusiliers were ordered to discontinue the jackets and to wear coats with long tails on all occasions. The officers' pattern had gold wings with grenades not only on the wings but also on the skirt turn-backs. In 1824 the wearing of bearskin caps was limited to Great Britain, Ireland and America and then in 1828 the fur cap was replaced by the shako elsewhere. Simkin shows an officer of the 21st Fusiliers, 1826 (64h) wearing the large bearskin cap with a grenade in front; this grenade badge or plate seems to have been introduced later, in 1831. The coat has the broad blue plastron front with gold-lace loops as worn up to 1829. He also shows an officer of the Royal Fusiliers (62h) similarly dressed but with the fur cap having a low plate in front (correct in this case) cords around the top, a white feather on the left and a black chin-strap. An officer of the 87th Fusiliers, 1826 (67f) also has the grenade badge on the fur cap.

By 1830 the double-breasted coatee with two rows of buttons was in use, and is shown for officers of the 87th (67h), but Simkin omits the peak and cords for the fur cap which are still quoted in detail in the 1834 Dress Regulations. A sergeant of the 23rd Royal Welsh Fusiliers (65h), which is based on Drahonet's oil-painting made for William IV, shows only the high plate on his fur cap, thought to forecast the discontinuance of the peak and tassels. It will be seen that the other rank has a single-breasted coatee. In 1835 the rudimentary peak and the tassels were officially discontinued and so the large grenade remained the main feature on the fur cap.

In 1836 the 5th Foot were made fusiliers and continued to wear their distinctive red-over-white feather in their head-dress. The officer of the 5th Foot, 1838 (59i) shows the dress of the period with the simplified fur cap and the regimental red-tipped white feather.

The introduction of the 'Albert' shako in 1843–4 made the fur cap obsolete for many years. A worsted ball-tuft was worn in front, white for most fusiliers but with the special red-over-white tuft for the 5th or Northumberland Fusiliers. The front carried the appropriate regimental grenade plate. An officer of the 7th Fusiliers (62j) and an officer of the 23rd (63i) show this dress, the Royal Welsh Fusiliers having the distinctive flash at the back of the collar. A man of the 21st (64), a man of the 23rd (65j) and of the 87th (67j) show the new shako, while a man of the 5th (59j) has the distinction of the red-tipped white ball.

In 1855, a new pattern shako was introduced, tapering towards the top, and now the fusilier regiments discontinued the ball-tuft and instead had a hanging hair plume of white hair, but with the privileged red-and-white for the Northumberland Fusiliers. The officer of the 23rd Fusiliers, 1856 (65k) shows the double-breasted tunic with the dark blue lapels turned down and the plain white ball still worn on the new shako. But the drooping white plume is shown for an officer and man of the 7th Fusiliers, 1860 (62), an officer and man of the 21st Fusiliers, 1859 (64l and j), an officer of the 23rd Fusiliers, 1862 (65l), and an officer and man of the 87th Fusiliers (67). The new pattern shako of 1861 continued the distinctive hair plumes. An officer of the 23rd Royal Welsh Fusiliers (65l) displays this head-dress. The four European battalions from India, the 101st, 102nd, 103rd and 104th, brought their own pattern of shako plates.

Overleaf:
78a
75th Foot, 1809, officer with Seringapatam medal

78b
The Gordon Highlanders (late 75th and 92nd) 1913, officer, full dress

75TH FOOT - 1809.
WITH H.E.I.C? SERINGAPATAM MEDAL.

a

THE GORDON HIGHLANDERS.
1913.

b

Plate 78

a   *1814*

b   *1809*

c   *1832*

d   *1858*

e

f   *1855*

R.Simkin.

1st Battn, Gordon Highlanders
75th Foot

g   *1864*

h   *1896*

i   *1879*

23

Plate 79

In 1865 a lambskin fur cap was recommended to be worn but later sealskin was also permitted for officers. By 1871 another fur cap was allocated to the fusiliers, this time the black racoon-skin type. The gilt grenade worn in front by officers had the regimental distinctions. Only the 5th Foot had the plume, their own distinctive red-and-white hackle. A man of the 23rd Royal Welsh Fusiliers, 1868 (65*m*) shows the new cap and it will be seen that he does not wear the black 'flash', as at that time it was a distinction for officers. A man of the 5th Fusiliers, 1878 (59*m*) displays the red-topped white feather on the left.

With the amalgamations and conversions of 1881, the 20th Foot became the Lancashire Fusiliers and the 27th Foot became the Inniskilling Fusiliers and these regiments wore their own pattern of grenade on their fur caps. In 1892 a new pattern fur cap was introduced, this time of bearskin. There was now some pressure to have special plumes for the fusiliers, and the Royal Irish Fusiliers were allowed to have one of dark green. Then in 1901 the Lancashire Fusiliers were permitted a primrose-yellow hackle. In 1903 the Royal Inniskilling Fusiliers acquired a grey plume. The 1904 Dress Regulations for officers quoted plumes for all – white for the Royal Fusiliers, the Royal Scots Fusiliers and the Royal Welsh Fusiliers worn on the right side. The Lancashire Fusiliers had primrose, the Inniskilling Fusiliers grey and the Royal Irish Fusiliers green, while the Royal Munster Fusiliers had white-over-green and the Royal Dublin Fusiliers blue-over-green, the green element indicating Ireland. These plumes continued until full dress became obsolete, only the white plumes being worn on the right and all others on the left.

Richard Simkin usually completed most of his historical sheets with a central group of officers and men from the period in which he was working, from 1905–15. The Northumberland Fusiliers (old 5th Foot) (59*g*) include an officer and a colour-sergeant in full dress with an officer in khaki. This latter has the distinctive red edge to the pugri, which could look like a 'V', thus representing the 'Fifth'. Another group of 1910 (60) shows not only the three men but also a mounted officer, another in the long blue frock and a drummer with the distinctive green-and-white triangles on the drum.

The Royal Fusiliers (the old 7th) have an officer in full dress (62*g*), another in khaki and two other ranks. The Lancashire Fusiliers (the old 20th Foot) have a plate of a second-lieutenant (63) dated 1913 holding his regimental Colour and wearing the yellow plume permitted in 1901. The Royal Scots Fusiliers (ancient 21st Foot) have a group of 1905 (64*g*) with an officer and a man in full dress plus a piper. The Royal Welsh Fusiliers (previously the 23rd) have a group (65) showing a mounted officer in full dress, a back view of the dismounted officer showing his 'flash' very clearly and a goat-major with the regimental goat. The goat does not wear the 'coat' as used in modern times but it does carry a leek behind the silver shield on the horns.

The Princess Victoria's Royal Irish Fusiliers (late 87th Foot) have a plate (67) showing a mounted officer with the green plume on the left, as granted in 1900, and an officer in khaki. The Inniskilling Fusiliers have no rendering of their full dress, only a piper of the 3rd Inniskilling Fusiliers, 1900 (66*a*). The regiment was permitted grey plumes on the left *c.* 1904. The Royal Munster Fusiliers (the old 101st and 104th) and the Royal Dublin Fusiliers (old 102nd and 103rd) were granted plumes *c.* 1904, both with green below to indicate Ireland and white or blue above being the facing

Preceding page:
79.
1st Battalion Gordon Highlanders (late 75th)
a 1814, officer and private
b 1809 officer
c 1832, private and officer
d 1858, private service dress India
e (c.1908) piper, officer and private in full dress
f 1858, officer service dress India
g 1864, sergeant and captain in marching order
h 1896, officer service dress Africa
i 1879, officer and private in marching order

colour of the earlier regiments. The Royal Fusiliers, the Royal Scots Fusiliers and the Royal Welsh Fusiliers were allowed to wear the white plume as in former days but now on the right side, thus avoiding any confusion of Foot Guards' plumes with those of the fusiliers.

Light Infantry Regiments

The creation of light infantry companies did occasionally lead to the removal of companies from regiments to form 'brigades', but only as a temporary measure. There were one or two light infantry regiments specially formed in time of war but these were disbanded when peace came.

The 80th Foot raised in North America in 1758 by Thomas Gage was also called 'Rangers' or 'Light Armed Foot'. They wore short jackets, following the fashion of the existing ranger companies. In 1758 another regiment of light infantry, the 85th or Royal Volunteers, was raised and David Morier painted pictures of the 119th (Prince's Own) Regiment of Foot who were raised in 1762 and wore a version of light infantry caps or helmets, shortened coats and long tight-fitting overalls which went into short gaiters. All these regiments were disbanded at the peace of Aix-la-Chapelle in 1763.

The first regiment to be raised as light infantry and to survive the coming of peace did not appear until the nineteenth century. It was the determination of Sir John Moore, who developed light infantry tactics in the Peninsula, which in 1803 saw the conversion of the 43rd and 52nd Regiments of Foot to light infantry. In 1808 the 68th and the 85th Regiments of Foot also became light infantry and the next year the 51st and the 71st (Glasgow Lowland) followed the new trend. The 90th Foot in 1815 were converted to light infantry, a change which seems to have been their destiny since formation when their light company was so prominent in battle, especially in Egypt. The 13th (Somerset) Regiment of Foot became light infantry in 1822 and in 1858 the 32nd became the Duke of Cornwall's Light Infantry. Then in 1881 the 53rd became light infantry as the 1st Battalion of the King's Shropshire Light Infantry because they had joined the 85th Foot who were already light infantry. The 2nd Madras (Light Infantry) Regiment, who in 1861 became the 105th (Madras Light Infantry) Regiment, joined in 1881 the 51st and became the 2nd Battalion of the King's Own Yorkshire Light Infantry while the 2nd Bombay (Light Infantry) Regiment, who became the 106th Bombay Light Infantry in 1861, joined the 68th and became the 2nd Battalion of the Durham Light Infantry.

Obviously the uniforms for the light infantry regiments were closely allied to those of light infantry companies which had existed for many years and had with hard experience developed their own specialities. The dress of the light infantry regiments in the Peninsular War was basically that of line infantry but all wore the felt cap or shako with the green plume of light infantry in front and with the metal bugle-horn badge instead of the normal large plate. The officers had feather plumes whereas the men had fabric tufts. The short jackets had wings on the shoulders. An officer of the 43rd, 1809 (71d) and another of the 52nd (73) show the bugle-horn badge on the front of the shako with the tassels on the green cords flying freely. Simkin also shows a private of the 52nd (71i) with the green-plumed shako but no cords. White tufting on the wings marks the light dress.

Overleaf:
80.
2nd Battalion Seaforth Highlanders (late 78th)
a	1793, sergeant
b	1793, officer
c	1806, officer
d	1806, private
e	1832, officer
f	1852, piper
g	1914, private, officer and piper all in full dress
h	1852, private
i	1864, private
j	1864, officer
k	1914, drummer
l	1915, officer service dress
m	1915, other rank service dress

a 1703

b 1793

c 1800

d 1801

e 1852

f 1852

g 1914

h 1852

SEAFORTH HIGHLANDERS
2ND BATTN · 78TH FOOT

i 1864

j 1864

k 1914

l 1915

m 1915

Plate 80

78TH HIGHLANDERS (ROSSHIRE BUFFS)
1793.

a

78TH HIGHLANDERS (ROSSHIRE BUFFS)
PIPE MAJOR - 1864.

b

Plate 81

The 'Waterloo' shako was not worn by light infantry regiments and the tapering shako with the metal bugle-horn in front and a regimental number, plus the green distinctions continued. After Waterloo the broad-topped shako was worn, in the case of the officers with silver or gold braid around the top (field officer, 1820, 71*e*). Field officers at this time also wore epaulettes over the wings.

Richard Simkin shows a detailed picture of an officer of the 51st (2nd West Yorks West Riding) (72*b*) which is based on the Dubois Drahonet oil-painting made for William IV. The shako (now without lace) has a gilt plate with a silver bugle-horn in the centre and a very dark green ball-tuft on top. The double-breasted coatee introduced in 1829 has small patches of embroidery on the collar and cuffs but the elaborate wings of gilt and silver now have three rows of interlocking rings instead of the two rows previously worn. Field officers who had worn epaulettes over their wings discontinued this practice in 1829. The sword-belt not only carried the regimental plate but also a whistle and chain hanging from a 'cross-patee' mounting. The crimson waist-sash had long cords and tassels looped up on the right side. An officer of the 52nd, 1832 (71*j*) is similar in detail but has buff facings and white trousers.

Another figure based on the Drahonet paintings is the sergeant of the 90th Perthshire Volunteers Light Infantry, *c.* 1832 (74). Here the other rank has a similar shako but with a brass plate and of course the dark green ball to distinguish light infantry. His coatee has light buff collar and cuffs with plain white braid or tape, a distinction of sergeants who did not have the braid with coloured distinctions like the privates. The wings for other ranks were red, laced and barred, with thick woollen tufts or fringes on the outside edge. His waist-sash is crimson with stripes of the facing colour. For nether-wear he has white overalls. As a sergeant he wears a sword, no longer a weapon for rank and file.

By 1844 the Albert shako was in wear as to be seen by the private of the 52nd, 1852 (71*k*). This man wears the single-breasted coatee with plain white loops, the coloured stripes having been discontinued in 1836. He still has the dark green ball-tuft and a simple plate which carries the regimental number and a bugle-horn. The day of the belt-plate was nearly over but they had become quite elaborate and included the bugle-horn plus other granted honours.

After the Crimean War the new tunic was in use, brick red for the men (52nd Private, 1861, 71*l*) and scarlet for the officer (43rd, 1861, 71*f*). The elaborate and expensive wings had disappeared and the rank badges for officers were now on the collar. The new tapering shako has a dark green hair plume and the tunic has flaps or slashes on the cuffs. The side view of a private of the 32nd Cornwall Light Infantry 1860 (70*a*) shows the cuff flaps and the outlines on the back of the skirts. The percussion cap pouch is to be observed high on the pouch-belt and this private has black leather gaiters, a feature of this period.

By 1867 it was decided that all light infantry regiments should have green cloth shakos instead of the common blue. In 1870 a new and slightly lower pattern of shako was introduced and worn up to the entry of the helmet. This was covered with a dark green cloth and this shako had a dark green horse-hair plume. The officers' tunics now had cuffs of a pointed pattern with cords and lace to indicate rank (see officer, 32nd Cornwall Light Infantry, 1870, 70*b*) and officer, 52nd, 1875 (71*m*). In 1874 the hair

Preceding page:
81.
78th Highlanders (Ross-shire Buffs)
a   1793, piper
b   1864, pipe-major

plume gave place to a black ball-tuft in a gilt socket for officers. In 1879 the helmet was being worn, in green cloth for light infantry instead of the blue of most Infantry of the Line. The regimental number was silver on the gilt plate but after 1881 the ancient numbers disappeared although the bugle plus permitted distinctions continued in use.

The light infantry dress had gone through the changes of the years and now was in the last stages of full dress. A mounted officer of the Oxfordshire and Buckinghamshire Light Infantry (71*g*) shows the pantaloons (breeches) and high boots. The gold lace down the trouser-seams had given way to a scarlet stripe. Buglers wore a drummer's uniform but had the badge of a bugle and carried a copper bugle with green cords. There is also the Scottish aspect to be considered and, that being different from normal infantry, such a unit like the Highland Light Infantry has to be covered elsewhere, in the Lowland section.

Highlanders

Originally the Black Watch was raised in the Highlands of Scotland where the inhabitants wore the kilt. The Scottish families in the Lowlands were not entitled to wear the kilt and so recruits from there normally dressed as Infantry of the Line, but sometimes sought Scottish distinctions. As may be expected in the British Army, the dividing line was confused with disbandments, reallocations and changing needs. This particular section is devoted to those Highlanders who wore the kilt in the days of Simkin's paintings for the convenience of giving here a simplified development of the kilt and its accessories. Other variations of Scottish dress are covered in the Rifle (pp. 165–173) and Lowland sections (pp. 156–165) without any disrespect to regimental origins, but for the clarity of describing uniforms as shown by Richard Simkin.

Early employment of soldiers wearing the Highland dress of plaid or kilt in the British Army is found in the six independent companies raised in 1725, who later in 1739 were to be formed into what became the 43rd and later the 42nd Regiment of Foot and became known as the Black Watch. It may be that the red coat was not worn until the regiment was formed but the tartan and style of dress worn before seem to have been continued. The earliest picture of another rank appears in the 1742 *Cloathing* book and this Simkin uses as the basis for his illustration (75*c*). There is a problem due to the fact that the original artist did not fully understand Scottish dress and the rendering of the tartan is dubious. Simkin shows what was known as the 'government tartan' which continued to be worn by the Black Watch. Needless to say, information on the subject of tartan has emerged slowly over the years because the precise evidence has been lacking or sparse. The 1742 picture showed the tartan as green and red dots and not in stripes or patterns. This has led the experts to say that the arbitrary colouring indicates that the basic tartan of blue and green (plus some black) indicated the government tartan plus red stripes, said to have been worn as a 'grenadiers'' tartan or officers' full dress. Simkin shows his 1754 grenadier with red stripes. As tartans at this time were produced in a haphazard proportion of pattern (long before the clan setts had been established) the colours of the threads were not the main distinction. The special distinction worn by Highlanders was the plaid instead of a coat and breeches.

Overleaf:
82.
Queens' Own Cameron
Highlanders (late 79th)
a 1815, private
b 1815, officer
c 1828, officer
d 1832, officer
e 1832, private
f 1854, bandsman
g (c.1914) private, officer and
     piper all full dress
h 1854, drummer
i 1864, private
j 1864, officer
k 1864, bandsman
l 1890, officer
m 1899, private service dress

a 1815

b 1815

c 1828

d 1832

e 1832

f 1854

g

h 1854

QUEEN'S OWN CAMERON HIGHLANDERS

i 1864

j 1864

k 1864

l 1890

m 1899

24

Plate 82

79TH CAMERON HIGHLANDERS
1884.

a

79TH CAMERON HIGHLANDERS
1884.

b

Plate 83

The belted plaid was a long rectangle of tartan approximately 12 to 16 feet long by 5 feet wide. The garment was worn by being wrapped around the body with many pleats and fastened at the waist by a belt, allowing the lower part to fall down to the knees. The upper part could be wrapped around the body to form a cloak or protection in bad weather, or it could be grouped so that part hung around the waist and the remainder held together and fastened behind the left shoulder. Being an admirable protection for a civilian, the bulk had some problems for an active fighting soldier. Later it was cut in two, producing a fixed and pleated kilt with the remainder being available for a shoulder plaid or shawl. Some early artists, perhaps not understanding the Highland dress, show the stripes on the bias and at other times with the stripes horizontal and vertical as now worn. In the beginning the plaid is shown overlapping in front but later the overlap was on the right thigh and the pleating of the voluminous plaid placed at the sides and rear.

The blue bonnet was an article of Highland dress and worn flat on the head. An account of 1707 said that they were made of blue cloth and a later account says that they were made of 'thrums without a brim'. The centre of the cap or bonnet usually is depicted with a short tail or 'toorie', frequently given as red for a soldier. Then a narrow rim of red was sewn around the brim of the bonnet where it rested on the head, a distinction continued up to the 1780s. As these Highlanders belonged to the Army, they were expected to wear the black cockade of the Hanoverians. Bonnie Prince Charlie's men wore a white cockade, like the French troops. The 1742 *Cloathing* book shows what looks like a piece of white tape with a red zig-zag line and the red toorie on top. During the '45 Rebellion a red saltire bow on the cockade also indicated the royal troops.

Because the upper part of the plaid was bulky, the red coats to be worn by the Highlanders had to be shortened and finished with small skirts all the way round. There was a row of buttons and stitched loops on each side and although the 1742 *Cloathing* book shows the buttons in pairs, this is not repeated in other contemporary illustrations. A feature of these 'jackets' was the cuff which opened to the elbow. The only places where the buff linings showed were on the small cuffs when turned back above the ample white shirt sleeves.

There was a long red waistcoat (said to have been made from the previous year's coat) which is shown longer than the jacket. At the waist is a soft leather pouch, similar to the black 'belly-box' later used for cartridges. No shoulder-belt for a cartridge pouch is shown and Simkin portrays the pouch as a sporran. The 1742 Scot carries a musket, a bayonet from the black leather shoulder-belt and an iron-hilted broadsword. This coloured print also showed the hose as 'speckled' like the kilt. Simkin has opted for the red-and-white hose as in other pictures of the period.

Pictures of 1743 show much the same dress but with a single-breasted jacket and white-metal buttons spaced regularly. The soldier's weapons are now increased to include a dirk and a pistol on a shoulder-strap. A sporran is now added to the pouch which is on the right hip, carrying the devices of a crown over 'GR'. It would appear that a cloth cap was worn by grenadiers but a ruling of 1747 quoted bearskin caps and this is what David Morier shows in his painting of the same period (75b). The red flap in front has an indented edge and the Crown over 'GR', though whether in metal or embroidered is not clear.

The Morier painting, which is c. 1750, has the short red coat with buff facings and a turn-down collar now carrying the facing colour. The jacket is single-breasted with pointed loops for the buttons. This lace which also goes around the collar, cuffs and pocket flaps is white with red stripes, something hinted at in the 1742 bonnet. The kilt and shoulder piece are in 'government tartan' with the red stripes said to be the mark of the grenadier company. The leather sporran has thongs ending in tassels, a forerunner of the later hair-bells. The red-and-white hose is almost correctly drawn by Morier, an aspect which Simkin could depict with authority. It will be seen that the cloth hose has no turn-over at the top and that the red tape was sufficient to keep it in place, although other paintings do show the tops turned over a little to make firmer fittings. The low shoes have brass buckles and as such continued in use for many years. The pistol is no longer shown, nor is the dirk, but the bayonet hangs from the waist-belt. The dirk was said to have been the privilege of officers and sergeants but it may have been a personal purchase.

Simkin's next picture in the large plate is dated 1802 but much happened to the Highland dress before then and must be mentioned here. The 42nd had been in Canada from 1756 to 1767 and being further away from official restrictions could assume variations of dress which might not be approved at home. When the men's bonnets were issued in 1761 officers were to provide their men with bearskin tufts to place in them and officers were to provide themselves with black feathers for their bonnets 'which were in future to be regimental'. The red band was still worn on the bonnet during the American Revolution.

In 1758 the 42nd were named the Royal Highland Regiment of Foot and the buff facings were changed to the royal blue but little else had to change. The Royal Warrant of 1768 consolidated certain changes in uniform generally. Buttons were now to have the regimental number, waistcoats were to be white and the coat was to be closer-fitting with small round cuffs. All the foregoing changes were carried out and confirmed by an inspection report made in May 1768 when the black ostrich feathers in the blue bonnets were also observed. The officers' coats had dark blue lapels and gold embroidered buttonholes and epaulettes. The gold embroidery was expensive, so in 1774 gold lace was placed on the buttonholes instead.

In America the hard campaigning played havoc with the Scottish dress, and by 1783 it had perished so much that the men now appeared dressed as British Infantry of the Line in short coats but retaining the bonnet. By this date the bonnet had received a diced brim and the black feathers on the officer's bonnet were more profuse, possibly because turkey feathers were available. The jackets were worn with wings in the flank companies and white under-clothing was worn, in the case of the men with 'white strong ticken trousers with short black cloth gaiters'.

Although other Highland regiments had been raised they were short-lived and disbanded. In 1778 the 78th Highland Regiment was formed and they continued to modern times, although changing their number to 72nd in 1786. This Earl of Seaforth's regiment wore the kilt and belted plaid in the normal government tartan with the red jacket. This garment had yellow (called 'orange' in an inspection report of 1779) for the collar, cuffs and lapels with silver lace for the officers. The men's lace was white, possibly with a green stripe and worn in bastion-shaped loops on the buttonholes. The bonnet was now cocked into a pill-box shape with a red-and-white

Overleaf:
84.
1st Battalion Princess Louise's Argyll and Sutherland Highlanders (late 91st)
a   1809 officer and private
b   1812, officer
c   1812, private and sergeant
d   1864, private
e   (c.1908), private, officer and piper all in full dress
f   1864, officer
g   1879, private and officer tropical dress
h   1874, bugler
i   1874, officer in full dress and officer in undress

a   *1809*

b   *1812*

c   *1812*

d   *1864*

e

R. SIMKIN.

f   *1850*

1st Battn., Princess Louise's Argyll and Sutherland Highlanders

91st Foot

g   *1879*

h   *1874*

i   *1874*

Plate 84

92ND GORDON HIGHLANDERS
1815.

a

92ND HIGHLANDERS.
1828.

b

Plate 85

diced border and a black feather on the left side. The 78th Highlanders went to India and there in 1786 became the 72nd Regiment. The hot weather there was not suitable for the thick plaid and so white cotton or linen pantaloons were worn. Another further indignity was the fact that the bonnet had to give place to a round hat because of the strong sunlight.

Other Highland regiments of the period included the 73rd, raised in 1777, which regiment became the 71st in 1786 and eventually the Highland Light Infantry; its uniform story is told in the Lowland section (pp. 156–165). The 72nd, 73rd, 74th and 75th Highlanders, all of whom were raised in 1786–7, wore Highland dress up to 1809 when for various reasons they became normal Infantry of the Line and lost their Highland dress. The 72nd became Highlanders again in 1829, the 73rd the Perthshire Regiment in 1862, the 74th became Highlanders in 1845 and the 75th the Stirlingshire Regiment in 1862, and their stories are dealt with elsewhere.

The 42nd Highlanders continued to represent the mainstream of the development of Highland dress. It was this regiment which discontinued the black cross belts in 1789 and took to buff leather or whitened equipment, other Highlanders not changing until 1798. Two water-colours by E. Dayes c. 1790 show this change, both officer and other ranks wearing the cocked bonnet with diced border and black feathers on the left side. The black rosette (larger for the officer) has a button in the centre. The red coat is still shorter than the normal infantry pattern and on the front has only two triangles of white lining turning back below the waist, while the back is cut square with two slits on each hip near the waist. The officer has two gold epaulettes and narrow buttonholes whereas the man has bastion-shaped loops. The turned-down blue collar links with the long narrow lapels. The single-breasted waistcoats were white, the officer having the buttons in pairs and also under the pocket flaps. The narrow white shoulder-belts have oval belt-plates. The hose is of the diagonal red-and-white pattern, the tops being slightly turned down over the red garter ribbons. The other ranks' dress agrees well with a water-colour made in Bruges 1793 which also indicates the red-striped bastion-loops worn in pairs and no sporran (as expected on active service). A Kay engraving dated 1791 shows an officer with many extra feathers in his bonnet, almost of modern style. He wears a large white feather and his epaulettes and wings indicate the grenadier company. Like other infantry, the Highlanders also had 'closed' coats at the end of the eighteenth century and the part of the skirts which turned back were of 'cashmere like light infantry' and they also had the sloping pockets.

Simkin shows the new pattern (75d) which he dates as 1802 but his source is from a print of 1808 by J. Smith. The feathered bonnet is now voluminous and has the red hackle feather which had been worn by the 42nd from the last years of the previous century. As the flank companies of infantry were distinguished by a white feather for grenadiers and green for light infantry, these variations were also used by the Black Watch, but for the tops only of their red plumes. Although the officer's jacket is not unusual, it will be noted that it fastens on the left side, for being double-breasted it could be fastened over on either side thus reducing wear on the front. The elaborate sporrans now worn by officers may be seen with the metal plate on the flap and the six gold tassels below indicating the ancient draw-strings of the purse. It will be noted that Highland officers now wore the sash over the shoulder. For many years other infantry officers had worn

Preceding page:
85.
92nd Gordon Highlanders
a   1815, drummer
b   1828, officer

the sash round the waist but the complications of the bulky plaid especially round the waist made it better that the shoulder position be retained and this remains so up to the present day.

A new 78th Highlanders was raised in 1793, known as the Ross-shire Buffs. The feathered bonnet was an impressive article as worn by the officer and sergeant 1793 (80*a* and *h*). The red jacket had buff facings with silver buttons and lace for the officers. The tartan was the dark government pattern with the addition of red-and-white stripes, which became known as the Mackenzie tartan. Simkin shows the sergeant (70*a*) carrying the halbert, a sign of his rank, and he has the red waist-sash with a central stripe of the facing colour, buff. The sergeant also wears a broadsword following the style of the officer, but with a brass hilt. Simkin shows the officer with silver lace, which seems to have changed to gold by 1802. There is also an officer and a man of 1806 (80*c* and *d*) wearing the closed coat introduced about 1796. The officer wears his sash over the left shoulder. The private no longer has lapels and his single-breasted coat has bastion-loops on the central row of pewter buttons.

The year 1812 saw changes for many British uniforms but the Highland dress retained its character. The Black Watch private (75*a*) shows the full dress of 1812 but the officer and private of the 79th Highlanders (82*a* and *b*) show the service dress, both wearing the added peak to the feather bonnet, the white-over-red feather indicating the battalion companies. The officer wears grey overalls and the other rank has his pack as well as his sporran, the latter usually omitted for service in the field. The 79th Highlanders have green facings and gold lace and buttons for the officers. The tartan of the 79th or Cameron of Erracht was not derived from the government tartan but is said to have been designed by Mrs Marjory Cameron, being blue and green with red and yellow over-stripes.

Other regiments of this period were the 92nd Gordon Highlanders who acquired this number in 1798 after having been raised the 100th. They wore the full Highland dress and as the red coat had yellow facings, over-stripes of yellow were added to the government tartan to produce the Gordon sett. The 93rd, raised in 1800 as the Sutherland Highlanders had been sent to the Cape of Good Hope and later in 1814 to America. In America circumstances made the kilt redundant and they wore trews of the regimental tartan, the old government tartan. The feathered bonnet also gave place in battle to the blue 'hummel' bonnet, cocked up and with a broad border of red-and-white-only squares, a distinction carried on to the present day. The facings were yellow.

The officer's jacket after 1815 frequently displayed the broad plastron front in the colour of the facings (see the Cameron Highlanders, 82*c* and also the Sutherland Highlanders, 88*c*). There was little change from the previous dress but the sporran was very ornate. Highlanders took the change of jacket *c*. 1829 when the double-breasted coat came in fashion with the two close rows of buttons down the front, the buttons of which became gilt for all officers in 1830. This new pattern is to be seen for the Black Watch, 1832 (75*e*), the Cameron Highlanders, 1832 (82*d*) and the Sutherland High-landers, 1852 (88*e*). Up to 1830 silver lace had been worn by officers of the 92nd and the 93rd; the rest wore gold. The jacket of other ranks was single-breasted with lace or braid loops on both sides of the buttonholes, and in 1822 all men including battalion companies wore wings like the flank companies instead of the shoulder-straps with tufts at the ends.

Overleaf:
86.
92nd Gordon Highlanders
a   1838, colour-sergeant, light company
b   1838, bandsman

92ⁿᵈ HIGHLANDERS ~ 1838.
(COLOUR SERGEANT, LIGHT COY)

a

92ⁿᵈ HIGHLANDERS.
1838.

b

Plate 86

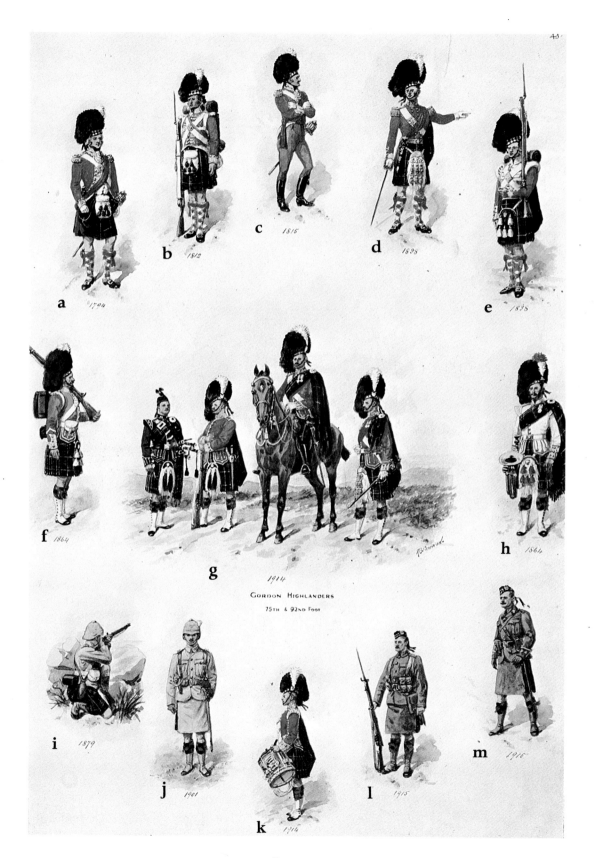

a 1794
b 1812
c 1815
d 1838
e 1838
f 1864
g 1914
GORDON HIGHLANDERS
75TH & 92ND FOOT
h 1864
i 1879
j 1901
k 1914
l 1915
m 1915

Plate 87

In 1830 the rank and file of Highlanders wore a new pattern jacket similar to that of Infantry of the Line with flaps on the cuffs. The change by officers to gold trimmings made no difference to the other ranks who continued to wear pewter buttons up to the Crimean War. The feathered bonnet was built up with two types of feathers, fox-tails (curled types) and flats, all of which went on a frame over the knitted cap. Those which hung down the right side made the tails and a hackle feather was worn on the left side to indicate the regiment or company. For a time the Black Watch favoured a low version of the feather bonnet.

The 1822 Dress Regulations for Officers only quoted one feather, which must have been intended for the 42nd alone as it was to be 'red vulture'. As the 42nd claimed exclusive use of the red hackle, the 1826 Dress Regulations then quoted that the hackle feather was to be white (and red only for the Black Watch). This indicated that the coloured feathers for flank companies were not recognized and that white was the distinction for all.

In 1836 a new pattern Highland jacket was introduced, each skirt to be nine inches long with the turn-backs and buttons not to be seen from the front. The stripes in the men's lace were to be discontinued but to be worn in the same fashion and shapes as before but plain white. In the same year the sergeants were ordered to wear double-breasted jackets with round brass buttons and no tape on the front buttonholes.

When the tunic was introduced for infantry at the time of the Crimean War a new garment was chosen for Highlanders as the kilt was not compatible with the long double-breasted tunic. The new 'jacket' was what is known as a doublet (but not like the ancient garment) with four pieces instead of skirts which were called 'Inverness flaps'. The first doublet was double-breasted but it soon became single-breasted like the later infantry tunic. The officers' jacket (as it was called in the Dress Regulations) was scarlet with collar, cuffs and lapels of regimental facings. The lapels were buttoned up to the fifth and then could be turned down above. There were nine buttons in each row on the front. The gilt buttons were diamond-shaped with the regimental number under a crown.

The replacement garment of 1857 was single-breasted with eight buttons at equal distances and the buttons were now round. The three-buttoned flap on the cuff was the colour of the facings. The double Inverness flaps were six-and-a-half inches deep with three buttons and loops on each flap, the loops being gold braid. Simkin shows a soldier of the 93rd Highlanders, 1860 (88*i*) in the new garment and it will be noted that his sporran has six white bells or tassels.

Military Scottish hose had been made of red-and-white patterns, sometimes with a narrow black edge to the stripes, but about 1856 the 42nd and the 92nd adopted black-and-red hose and the 79th red-and-green, possibly because the hose with the white base showed both wear and dirt. Although the skean dhu, the shoulder brooch and the dirk plate may have been in use many years for civil and unofficial purposes, it was not until the 1864 Dress Regulations for Officers appeared that they were approved and quoted. Then in 1868 the normal infantry cuff with the three-buttoned flap was changed to a gauntlet cuff, four inches deep in front and six behind, still with three buttons and with lines of braid set vertically.

Simkin's water-colours cover most Highland regiments in 1864, perhaps because they could be easily checked against the Dress Regulations for

Officers of that year. The officer and private of the 42nd Highlanders (75*i* and *j*) show the doublet with the flap on the sleeves, the officer's sporran with five gilt tassels and the men with five black tassels on their sporrans. They now wear the red and black hose. An officer and man of the 72nd Highlanders (77*g*) display the same doublet and both wear trews of the Royal Stuart pattern. An officer and a man of the 78th Highlanders show the doublet with buff facings, the Mackenzie tartan, the ancient red-and-white striped hose, while the officer's full-dress sporran has eight gold tassels and the man has six black ones.

A similar pair for the 79th Highlanders show the doublet with dark green facings, the red-and-green hose, with the officer's sporran having six gold tassels on the grey fur and the man five white on black. The officer and man of the 91st Highlanders (84*d* and *f*) do not have the feather bonnet but rather the shako with the diced border. The doublet however is Scottish and the trews and shoulder-plaid are in the regimental tartan. A private of the 92nd Gordon Highlanders (87*f*) has yellow facings to his doublet, with the Gordon tartan for the kilt, red and black hose, and five white tails to the black sporran.

The undress head-dress had been the 'hummel/humble' bonnet, later of woollen weave, which could be stretched or pulled into many shapes. One of the shapes was the 'glengarry', which was at first practically a civilian shape and worn by pipers, but in 1851 it was authorized for men wearing the kilt in Highland regiments with a border as on the feather bonnet. By 1868 it was deemed a 'universal' pattern for all Infantry of the Line.

The hard-wearing and thin texture of the kilt acquired a sharp edge in wet weather and when at a parade in 1870 Queen Victoria noted blood at the back of Highlanders' legs she was prompted to order that the old tartan should be replaced by a softer and kinder texture.

In 1873 when the brick-red cloth of the infantry tunic was replaced by scarlet the same change took place for the Highland doublet. An officer of the 91st Foot (84*i*) dated 1874 wears the doublet with the gauntlet cuff, the lower pattern shako, trews and shoulder-plaid of regimental tartan.

In 1880 the officers' badges of rank which had been on the collar were ordered to be removed and placed on gold shoulder-cords. The rank badges were to be of silver for the Star and Crown although the latter had a crimson inset. A sub-lieutenant (previously ensign) had no badge of rank, the lieutenant one Star, the captain two while the major had a Crown, a lieutenant-colonel a Star and Crown and a full colonel two Stars and a Crown. Field officers continued the second line of lace on the cuffs and other cuff distinctions remained in use.

In 1881 the 'territorial' amalgamations took place, often linking two regular regiments together and having militia regiments added as extra battalions. Thus the 42nd and the 73rd became the 1st and 2nd battalions of the Black Watch (Royal Highlanders), the 71st and 74th became the Highland Light Infantry, the 72nd and 78th became the Seaforth Highlanders, the 75th and 92nd the Gordon Highlanders, the 79th became the single battalion (unique example) of the Queen's Own Cameron Highlanders and the 91st and 93rd as the Argyll and Sutherland Highlanders.

At the same time all infantry uniforms were to follow a simplified system of facing colours – blue for royal regiments, white for English and Welsh, yellow for Scottish, green for Irish, and variations for the Rifle corps. This meant that in some cases the ancient buff facings had to disappear, but

Overleaf:
88.
2nd Battalion Princess Louise's Argyll and Sutherland Highlanders (late 93rd)
a 1814, sergeant
b 1814, officer
c 1820, officer
d 1832, private
e 1852, officer
f 1852, piper
g 1914, sergeant, private, officer
     and piper all full dress
h 1852, bandsman
i 1860, private
j 1873, sergeant undress
k 1893, drum-major
l 1914, private service dress
m 1914, officer service dress

a *1814*

b *1814*

c *1820*

d *1832*

e *1852*

f *1852*

g *1914*

h *1852*

PRINCESS LOUISE'S ARGYLL AND SUTHERLAND HIGHLANDERS
2ND BATTN - 93RD FOOT

i *1860*

j *1875*

k *1893*

l *1914*

m *1914*

Plate 88

93RD SUTHERLAND HIGHLANDERS.
CORPORAL — LUCKNOW. 1857.

Plate 89

93RD SUTHERLAND HIGHLANDERS
Lance Corporal (Marching Order) 1882.
Showing Oilskin Cover on Bonnet.

Donor — Major G.F. Watson - 1930.

2ND BATTN. ARGYLL & SUTHERLAND HIGHLANDERS
PIPE MAJOR — 1889.

Plate 90 a   **Plate 90 b**

patience and persistence in the case of the Seaforth Highlanders and the Highland Light Infantry saw the buff facings restored in 1899.

The 72nd Highlanders had served in India after the Afghan War and did not return home until 1882 still wearing their 'Prince Charlie' version of the Royal Stuart tartan. Simkin shows an officer of this date (77b) still in the regimental tartan and the white helmet as worn in India but of course on amalgamation both battalions were to wear the 'Ross-shire Military' of the old 78th.

The final Highland full dress had developed before the First World War and did not return to the ordinary soldier, although officers still had a need for full dress at levées and such special occasions until the Second World War saw the end of full dress in service use (although it might be retained for bands and tattoos).

In most of Simkin's large plates, the central group is of the last full-dress period. For example, the Black Watch (75g) shows the officer wearing his crimson sash over the left shoulder, but the sergeant with his over the right. Both have five black tassels on the white sporran, but the officer has a gilt ornamental top. The Highland Light Infantry is covered in the Lowland section. The Seaforth Highlanders (77 and 80) show the officers in the regimental tartan and the full-dress sporran with the gold tassels whereas the men have two black tails. The Gordon Highlanders (87g) show a mounted and a dismounted officer, the former wearing tartan trews and the plaid across his chest. The dismounted officer has a fly-plaid and a full-dress sporran with gold top and tassels.

The Queen's Own Cameron Highlanders (87g) show an officer and a man more or less in their previous dress but now with the royal facings of blue. The officer's sporran has six gold tassels on grey while the man has two long white tails on black (instead of the five white tassels formerly worn). The 1st Battalion of the Princess Louise's Argyll and Sutherland Highlanders (84e) shows the Highland dress adopted since 1881, the officer's sporran has the badger's head over the white tassels, the head not being worn by the privates. Simkin shows the same uniforms for the 2nd battalion (88g).

Scottish Drummers

Drummers and bandsmen are dealt with in special sections (pp. 180–189) but the dress of these musicians is so different that they are dealt with separately here and associated with the Highlanders.

Drummers and buglers of infantry regiments were part of the fighting troops and their uniforms in early days differed by the 'reversed facings' (see p. 180). The 42nd, being Royal Highlanders and having blue facings, had no need to 'reverse' their facings and so their red coats had to be distinguished by suitable lace and braid. Towards the end of the eighteenth century those new regiments of Highlanders had drummers with coats of the facing colour and favoured the bonnets, as worn by the privates. Unfortunately Simkin illustrates only one Highland drummer pre-1850 and he is of the 92nd Gordon Highlanders, 1815 (85a) and, although splendid in appearance, the portrait is not entirely trustworthy. There exists a contemporary painting by Fischer which shows such a drummer in undress. He wears a 'hummel' bonnet (without feathers) with a white hackle, red-tipped. This colouring for a plume is known for those of the musicians of the period but the parti-coloured garment which Simkin shows as red with yellow sleeves is not backed by any known evidence.

Preceding page:
89.
93rd Sutherland Highlanders,
1857, corporal at Lucknow

90*a*
93rd Sutherland Highlanders,
1862, lance-corporal, marching order

90*b*
2nd Battalion Argyll and Sutherland Highlanders (late 93rd), 1889, pipe-major

The yellow jacket with red collar, cuffs and wings was known and was regulation. The tartan, no sporran and the half-gaiters are as expected for service conditions. The red and yellow diagonal stripes on the drum-hoops, although possible, are not in contemporary evidence and should be all red.

By 1831 the red coat or jacket was to be worn instead of the vulnerable facing colour which made the drummers so obvious in battle, but the drummers' lace continued as before. Simkin had shown two drummers dated 1852, those of the 78th Highlanders and of the 93rd Highlanders (89b). They wear the feather bonnet with white hackle and black chin-strap and ribbons. The 93rd has the regimental distinction of the red-and-white diced band. The red jackets had collars and cuffs of the facing colours and drummers' lace was on the seams and buttonholes. The 93rd drummer had chevron patterns on the sleeves as worn formerly but the drummer of the 78th had the simplified version with lace only on the seams of the sleeve without chevrons. Drum-hoops were now combining red with the colour of the facings. However, the blue, red and white hoops shown by Simkin for the 92nd are those of a royal regiment and not for the Gordons. The drummer of the 79th Highlanders, 1854 (82h) still has the coatee with the regimental lace of the distinctive thistle pattern worn since 1826 and the wings with tufts of white, yellow, black and sky blue.

The new double-breasted doublet of 1855 was white for drummers but soon gave place to the single-breasted pattern of red. The drummer of the 42nd Highlanders, 1862 (75m) has no unusual features and carries a half or 'cheese' drum, popular at that time. The worsted fringe on the wings was not continued on the new doublet and in 1866 the individual drummers' laces were abolished (although they did continue for a time, no doubt to use up existing stocks) and they were replaced by a single universal pattern of white with red crowns.

Drummers were expected to be competent on the bugle as shown for the 91st, 1874 (84h), where the man has the new lace on his doublet, also with the new gauntlet cuff. Simkin shows a drum-major of the 2nd Battalion Argyll and Sutherland Highlanders, 1893 (88k) who wears the drum-belt and doublet with yellow facings plus all the other ornaments needed.

The last full dress of Scottish drummers is to be seen on the Seaforth plate (80k), where an accurate representation also includes the drum badge on the upper right arm, and on the Gordon Highlanders plate (87k) which shows the left side of a drummer in the shoulder-plaid and gives a careful rendering of the garter flashes.

Scottish Bandsmen

Highland regiments had musicians as well as drummers and pipers but the earliest picture by Simkin is that of a bandsman of the 92nd Highlanders (86b) of the 1838 period which, although including the customary feathered bonnet, kilt and sporran and hose, shows how different and exotic such a dress could be. White garments had been worn by bands in the eighteenth century and as the regiments paid for these, they could vary considerably in detail. In fact an official letter to the Colonel of the 92nd in 1832 said that the coatees prescribed for the Bands of Infantry were not intended to apply to Highland regiments. Regiments of this description were allowed to provide jackets for these bands corresponding in shape and make with the jackets of the rank and file and to be in colour and quality up to the pattern presented for bands generally. A contemporary water-colour exists showing the precise details which Simkin portrays and it may be this dress which the War Office letter called for, as the coatee seems to be of an earlier pattern still in wear. The red tip to the white hackle indicates the band and the profusion of red cord on the coat is definitely for musicians. The red tassels on the sporran are also band distinctions, as are the puffed-up shoulder-pieces.

Another variety of Scottish dress is that of the bandsman of the 71st Highland Light Infantry (99d), dated by Simkin as 1849. This shows the white coatee with very light buff collar and cuffs, cut as the normal pattern but with full wings. The trews and shoulder-plaid are of the regimental tartan. The broad-topped shako also should have been obsolete in 1844 when the Albert shako was being worn but it is covered with the blue bonnet, showing the red toorie and the diced border. Simkin gives this musician a sword and a black waist-belt, on the right side of which is a pouch bearing a bugle-horn and '71', all of which looks regulation but does not agree with other known facts. As early as 1837, M. A. Hayes depicted the band in a large feathered bonnet with a large red feather on the left side and A. N. E. Brown, in his comprehensive work on the Highland Light Infantry uniform, shows nothing but the feather bonnet for the bandsmen and comments on the dirk being on the right hip. The white coatee of the band in Hayes's water-colour has red epaulettes but these changed to wings in 1849, so Simkin is correct on this point.

A bandsman of the 79th Highlanders (82f) wears the feather bonnet with a white hackle. His double-breasted jacket is white with a green collar, cuffs and wings, the latter having thick white tufting; otherwise his dress is normal. The bandsman of the 93rd Highlanders, 1852 (88h) has a red hackle in his feather bonnet. His white jacket with yellow collar and cuffs is double-breasted, but that was only worn by the band-sergeant and no such chevrons are indicated. The jacket was single-breasted for members of the band. The red tartan no doubt indicates the Prince Charles Edward sett, which was introduced for the band in 1850. The sporran has six black tassels on white, as was favoured by the band.

The doublet was introduced in 1855 and soon changed from the double-breasted version to the single-breasted. The bandsman of the 42nd Highlanders, 1860 (75j) has a white doublet with blue cuffs, collar and wings, with all piping and edging in red. The plaid was worn across the chest and all the rest of the dress followed regimental practice. A bandsman of the 71st Highland Light Infantry, 1866 (99f) has a similar doublet but with red facings and his feather bonnet seems to have a red feather hackle like that of the 42nd. His shoulder-plaid and trews are of the Mackenzie tartan. The bandsman of the 74th Highlanders, 1864 (100h) is similar to that just described, except that the tartan is Lamont or the government pattern with added white stripes. The bandsman of the 79th Highlanders, 1864 (82k) also has a similar doublet but with dark green collar, cuffs and wings, plus the red trimmings. The feather bonnet has a white hackle and a shoulder-plaid is worn, the other articles of dress following regimental practice. A bandsman of the 92nd Gordon Highlanders, 1864 (87h) has the white doublet with yellow facings and red trimmings. His feather bonnet has the white hackle tipped with red. His sporran has five red tassels on the white fur. The shoulder-plaid and kilt are of Gordon tartan and the rest of the uniform is regimental.

The gauntlet cuff was introduced in 1868. However, on the white undress jacket (100*i*) there are red pointed cuffs which match the collar. The full-dress shoulder-plaid and trews were worn here with a plain glengarry cap. In 1871 the white coat of the bandsmen was changed to red but Simkin does not depict any of these uniforms. The red doublets had the collar, cuffs, shoulder-straps and wings in the colour of the facings. Shoulder-plaids were also worn. To distinguish further the red doublet, which was similar to that of the rank and file, an elaborate band badge was worn on the right arm.

Pipers

It was the tradition for a captain of a Scottish company to have his own piper, not only for his services in the field but also to play music for him at other times, just as though he might have been in his own home. In the beginning bagpipers were not part of an Army establishment but they were in evidence on active service, as may be noticed in the contemporary painting of the evacuation of the Mole at Tangiers *c.* 1683, where a small figure of a piper is outlined against the water.

When the Black Watch became a regiment there were many prints of the pipers, who seem to wear the normal Highland uniform. As a royal regiment any service musician would wear the normal red coat or jacket. The 78th Highlanders of 1793 would have their drummer wearing a coat of reversed facings, i.e. buff with red collar and cuffs. Simkin shows an all-buff coat for his musician (81*a*) which has neither the reversed facings nor the expected white for a bandsman. The rest of the uniform is as expected for a man of the Ross-shire Buffs. The hackle on the left side could be the white of the grenadier company or the white-over-red of a battalion company, as the lower portion is hidden. Simkin does not indicate any special lace.

The jacket was made to button-over soon after this dress and the piper of the 42nd Highlanders, 1814 (76*a*) shows the jacket of a private with white tufts on the shoulders and the red top gives no clue to the type of company. The black shoulder-belt, which later was a distinction for pipers, is shown although by this time the equipment of the Highland soldier had changed to white. By this period there had been many Highland regiments raised and disbanded, specially in the case of the Fencible infantry.

When George IV went to Scotland in 1820 there was a great upsurge in interest in things Scottish and in the development of Scottish dress and later in 1837 Queen Victoria appointed Angus Mackay to be her own piper. The dress of the piper was now undergoing many variations. That of the piper of the 42nd Highlanders in 1852 (76*b*) begins to follow that of the regiment including the feather bonnet, but the jacket or coatee is in government tartan and the kilt and shoulder-plaid are in Royal Stuart. Simkin shows a piper of the 78th Highlanders of the same date (80*f*) with a double-breasted jacket in white like the bandsman, with green worsted shoulder-tufts.

The doublet with the 'Inverness' flaps was now beginning to appear in the Army as a print of January 1854 shows for a piper of the 93rd. Simkin (88*f*) displays this new garment, as in the print under the date of 1855. The doublet is all red without any facing colour. The full wings on the shoulders have indented edges and the garment is single-breasted. A return is made to the wide flat blue bonnet with a red toorie and a single long feather on the left side. The strings and ribbons on the bagpipes are light yellow and blue. The hose, instead of being the expected red-and-white tartan, are in black-and-red.

The piper of the 74th Highlanders wore a jacket of regimental tartan cut on the bias and hose of red and black. In 1854 pipers were allowed on the establishment of the Army, one pipe-major and five pipers for each regiment but also up to six 'acting-pipers' would be allowed if maintained by the officers. In 1855 the doublet was taken into wear by Highland regiments, so the pipers were no longer unique in the wearing of the 'four-flapped' garment. Plain green was to be the colour for pipers and the plain glengarry was to be their head-dress. The 42nd Highlanders, however, retained their feather bonnet after 1860 when other pipers had taken the glengarry.

Simkin shows a piper of the 71st Highland Light Infantry dated 1866 (99*h*) where the collar and flapped cuff is buff on the dark green doublet. Other pipers are shown with the gauntlet cuff long before the rank and file adopted it, and they also have the diamond-shaped buttons of brass metal which they retained for many years. The piper of the 78th Ross-shire Buffs, 1864 (81*b*) seems to be based on a photograph and is a most accurate rendering. A piper of the 74th, 1880 (100*i*) is in undress, which is much the same as full dress, with the exception of the white jacket with the green collar and cuffs.

The territorial amalgamations of 1881 brought pipers the dress which they continued until the last days of full dress, and even beyond. The 1st and 2nd battalions of a regiment frequently had minor variations of dress and badges. The pipe-major of the 2nd Argyll and Sutherland Highlanders, 1889 (90*b*) shows the glengarry with the added feathers of the black-cock and a large regimental badge. His green doublet has regimental collar badges and as a pipe-major much gold lace and trimming to distinguish him from the ordinary pipers (it changed from silver lace in 1865).

Simkin covers the dress of pipers up to the outbreak of the First World War as follows. The Black Watch (old 42nd) (75*g*) with the feather bonnet and red hackle and Royal Stuart tartan. The 1st Battalion Highland Light Infantry (old 71st) (99*e*) with the glengarry and the Mackenzie tartan, sporran three black tails on white. The 1st Seaforth Highlanders (old 72nd) (77*e*) with the glengarry and Mackenzie tartan, sporran two black tails on white. The 2nd Battalion Highland Light Infantry (old 74th) (100*e*) Mackenzie tartan, sporran three black tails on white. The 1st Battalion Gordon Highlanders (old 75th) (87*g*) glengarry and Gordon tartan, sporran two black tails on white. The 2nd Battalion Seaforth Highlanders (old 78th) glengarry and Mackenzie tartan, sporran two black tails on brownish grey. Queen's Own Cameron Highlanders (old 79th) (82*g*) glengarry with single eagle feather, Cameron of Erracht tartan, sporran two white tails on black. The 1st Battalion (old 91st) and 2nd Battalion (old 93rd) of the Princess Louise's Argyll and Sutherland Highlanders (84*e* and 88*g*), both battalions wear the glengarry, the government tartan and three black tails on the grey sporran.

Lowland Regiments

There were no problems in the early days of the British Army when English or Irish regiments were raised, for they all wore a similar uniform. When the Highland regiments were raised, the Highland dress was distinctive and permitted. But difficulties arose later when Highland regiments were reduced or converted and also when Lowland troops proved to be good fighting men and worthy of special distinctions. The restoration of earlier Highland articles or the production of new ideas began to confuse the development of Scottish uniforms. Those who retained the full Highland dress have been discussed on pp. 137–156. This section covers all Scottish troops not included in the Highland section, and as many variations occurred, each regiment is dealt with from its own point of view.

The Royal Scots who had been numbered the 1st Regiment of Foot (see also the Brief Outlines) and were known as the Royal Regiment wore the normal infantry dress for many years. At the beginning they wore red coats with white facings (at that time a known Scottish facing colour) and carried regimental flags (colours) with St Andrew's saltire (not the Cross of St George). It is known that they had pipers in the seventeenth century as they appear in a contemporary painting of the evacuation from Tangier.

An acknowledgement of their Scottish origin was in the eighteenth-century warrant which noted the 'ancient badge' which was to be carried, including the Circle and Motto of St Andrew. The Scottish thistle from the Order of St Andrew appeared on belt-plates, head-dress and coats. Unofficially, pipers were with the regiment in the eighteenth century and in 1801 their colonel, the Duke of Kent, applied to have the regiment clothed in Highland uniform. However, this was disallowed as the Royals had always been a Lowland regiment. As a slight compensation, officers were permitted to have their buttonhole loops embroidered through the cloth instead of surface lace.

It was the amalgamations of 1881 that brought a change of uniform to the Royal Scots. The previous year they had adopted a glengarry with a diced border but now a Scottish doublet was to be worn with thistle lace instead of 'royal' lace for the officers. The thistle was now adopted as a collar badge. The tartan trews had a sett like that worn by the Black Watch. The head-dress continued to be the blue helmet as worn by the Infantry of the Line but with a Royal Scots plate. This was not considered very Scottish and in 1904 permission was given to wear a dark blue Kilmarnock bonnet with a diced regimental band and a scarlet toorie, and on the black cockade on the left side was the regimental badge of St Andrew's Star and an ornamental black-cock feather, as seen in the Simkin painting of an officer, 1913 (86) based on a photograph by Messrs Gale and Polden.

The 21st or Royal Scots Fusiliers were a Lowland regiment but as their dress was mainly fusiliers, it is covered in the fusilier section.

The 25th Regiment of Foot, raised in Edinburgh, was definitely a Lowland regiment. At the beginning their dress was that of normal infantry, but Lord George Henry Lennox, colonel from 1762 to 1805, created certain Scottish elements when the regiment was stationed in Minorca. He had a piper in full Highland dress – blue bonnet with black feather, kilt and shoulder-plain as well as red-and-white hose. One speciality was the 'Scottish' company, a 'picked' body of men who were a type of light infantry, dressed in a shortened coat and with half-gaiters. Most distinctive was a low cap, fur-edged, bearing in front a small red plate with lettering and what appears to be a thistle. In 1782 the 25th were named the 'Sussex' Regiment which tended to obscure any Scottish connection. In 1805 there was a new colonel and a new name – the King's Own Borderers. In 1858 the regiment was permitted to continue to have pipers but at no

Overleaf:
91.
The King's Royal Rifle Corps (late 60th)
a   1759, officer
b   1814, rifleman
c   1814, officer
d   1826, sergeant
e   1832, officer
f   1850, officer
g   (c.1915) rifleman, mounted officer and officer all full dress
h   1850, bugler
i   1857, rifleman in India
j   1864, rifleman
k   1864, officer
l   1915, rifleman service dress
m   1915, officer service dress

a 1759

b 1814

c 1814

d 1826

e 1832

f 850

g 1814

h 1850

King's Royal Rifle Corps

i 1857

j 1864

k 1864

l 185

m 1915

Plate 91

60ᵀᴴ THE KING'S ROYAL RIFLE CORPS
1854.

a

60ᵀᴴ KING'S ROYAL RIFLE CORPS.
1854.

b

Plate 92

expense to the public. Then in 1869 the new shako plate carried the Castle
of Edinburgh and the motto 'Nisi Dominus Frustra'.

But it was not until 1881 that a Scottish dress was approved with the
Scottish doublet and trews of the government tartan. In 1898 the regiment
was permitted to wear Leslie tartan instead and the pipers gained the
privilege of wearing the Royal Stuart tartan. The red doublet with blue
collar and cuffs plus the blue helmet as worn may be seen on the officer,
1885 (97) who also wears the government tartan trews. In July 1903 this
regiment, like the Royal Scots, changed the foreign-looking helmet for the
diced Kilmarnock with black-cock feathers (97g), and the Leslie tartan with
the red-and-white over-stripes can also be seen on plate 97. The glengarry
with the diced border is shown worn with the service drab of 1914 but later
the khaki tam o'shanter was worn in action.

The 26th or Cameronian Regiment of Foot was raised in 1689 and was
clothed as a line regiment until 1881 when it became a rifle regiment.
Simkin shows the various basic uniforms (98), the development of which is
covered in the infantry uniform section. The white facings worn in the
beginning indicate a Scottish connection. After Waterloo, Scottish emblems
and devices appeared on the cross belt-plates and head-dress – the thistle
and the 'Scottish' star. When the diced border was first worn on the
undress cap is not known but it was to be seen worn by officers in 1826 and
by the 1840s the other ranks' undress cap or bonnet had dicing of red,
yellow and white. By 1854 pipers of the 26th Foot appear in Highland dress,
feather bonnet, kilt and shoulder-plaid. The distinctive diced border was
worn until the last days of the red coat, not only on the glengarry but also as
peaked 'cheese-cutter' of officers and senior n.c.os. In 1881 the uniform
became that of the Scottish Rifles and is covered in the section on Rifle
uniforms.

There is a problem as to where to place the Highland Light Infantry – in
the section on Highland dress or in the section on Light Infantry dress – it
does not fit in exactly with either. However, because it was known as the
City of Glasgow Regiment this makes it Lowland, and so it is better dealt
with here. The problem of dress has an ancient origin, because the five
Highland regiments numbered from 71 to 75 which had been raised in
1786–7 had problems in recruiting, and in 1809 they were ordered to be
converted to ordinary regiments of Infantry of the Line.

The 71st Regiment did not give in easily and, in the year that they lost the
kilt, took on light infantry distinctions keeping Highland in the name and
eventually being allowed pipers. Other ranks were able to retain the
Highland bonnet because they wore the approved infantry shako but with
the woollen bonnet stretched over it including the diced border (99a). The
jacket was now of light infantry pattern with wings, and grey trousers
which had been worn on active service since 1808 had gaiters or spats. It
will be noted that the officers did not have the diced border on the tapering
cap, only the metal bugle badge.

Simkin shows an officer of 1828 (99b) wearing the plastron-fronted coat
and the large green cock's feather plume, but Marcuard's plate of 1819
shows that it had changed to the dark green ball-tuft. The officer and man of
1832 (99c) show the new pattern coatee as double-breasted for the officer
but single-breasted for the man. The lace or braid on the soldier's coatee is
plain white but that was not ordered until 1836; before then plain white
was the mark of a sergeant. White trousers are shown, no doubt to show

Preceding page:
92.
60th The King's Royal Rifle Corps
a   1854, sergeant-major
b   1854, bandsman

that the regiment was then stationed in Bermuda. In 1834 the tartan plaid scarf had been restored for officers and worn over the left shoulder. The 71st were also permitted to wear the Highland jacket instead of the coatee (which meant little more than that the tails were shortened). The officer and soldier, 1849 (99g) show the same coatee and shakos as before, trews of the government tartan with the thin lines of white and red added, making a new tartan. It may also be noted that the 71st did not wear the straight up-and-down 'Albert' shako but one with a slightly wider top, the red toorie being much in evidence and worn up to the Crimean War.

The facings on the earlier white band-jacket may have been red, but by 1849, as Simkin shows, they were buff. With the advent of the tunic, Scottish regiments had their own new pattern doublet, double-breasted at first but soon changed to the single-breasted pattern. The bonnet-covered shako now disappeared and the normal infantry pattern was worn with a diced border and the dark green ball of light infantry. The officer and man of 1866 (99i) show the small shako of that period and the man's doublet with the upright cuff flaps which continued until 1868.

The bandsman of 1866 (99f) shows the white coat with red facings and the large red plume in the feather bonnet, a colour favoured by bandsmen as well as the Black Watch. The piper of 1866 (99h) wears the feather bonnet also with a dark green doublet and a three-tailed sporran. The glengarry could be expected to be worn from 1856 onwards but there were six feather bonnets that were issued later, drawn and worn by the band. The gauntlet-cuff was added to the doublet in 1868 which brought the basic uniform of both officer and man to its last pattern (99e). The piper is seen in the dress which came in 1868 plus the changes of badges and devices.

The 72nd Highland Regiment in 1809 lost its right to wear Highland dress, so the normal infantry dress was worn until 1824, although pipers were still maintained. This regiment did not become Lowland and thus their later uniform is dealt with in the Highland section. In 1823 the regiment was honoured by being named the Duke of Albany's Own Highlanders and as soon as possible reassumed the kilt.

In 1809 the 73rd Highland Regiment also lost the right to wear Highland dress despite the fact that it had been raised in Perth in 1780 and had been a 2nd Battalion of the Black Watch. Thus the normal infantry uniforms had to be worn and it was not until 1862 that the title was changed to the 73rd (Perthshire) Regiment. The men were now able to wear the 'hummel' bonnet with a diced border and the badges could include the Scottish thistle. In 1881 the 73rd became the 2nd Battalion of the Black Watch and their story is continued in the Highland section.

The 74th Highland Regiment, which lost its right to Highland connections and became Infantry of the Line (officer and man, 1809, 100a) had to wait until 1845 when they were permitted again to be called Highland. Even this did not see the restoration of the kilt, although the regiment was allowed a 'plaid cap', shoulder-plaid as worn by the 71st, and tartan trews, as long as the Scottish recruits were sufficient in number. Thus they became the second regiment to wear tartan trews, the other being the 71st. A magnificent painting by D. Cunliffe, 1846, shows many of the variations of the new dress. Simkin shows an officer and another rank of 1845 (100d and f) which in the main agrees with the contemporary painting, except that the officer did not have the dicing on the shako until 1850 and the dark cords and tassels have been omitted. It will be noted that the shako is not the

Overleaf:
93.
The Rifle Brigade (Prince Consort's Own)
a   1801, rifleman
b   1806, officer
c   1814, officer
d   1814, rifleman
e   1828, officer
f   1832, sergeant
g   1914, officer service dress, mounted officer and bugler both full dress
h   1852, officer
i   1864, officer
j   1864, rifleman
k   1875, rifleman
l   1882, officer
m   1914, rifleman service dress

a
1801

b
1806

c
1814

d
1814

e
1828

f
1832

g
1914

RIFLE BRIGADE
PRINCE CONSORT'S OWN

h
1852

i
1814

j
1814

k
1875

l
1852

m
1914

Plate 93

a 83RD FOOT. OFFICER 1793.

b 83RD PRIVATE, 1804

c 83RD OFFICER, 1812.

d 83RD OFFICER, 1826.

e 83RD PRIVATE, 1832

f 88TH OFFICER 1852.

g ROYAL IRISH RIFLES

R SIMKIN.

h 86TH Shropshire Volunteers. PRIVATE 1793.

i 86TH (ROYAL COUNTY DOWN. PRIVATE 1812.

j 86TH OFFICER, 1832.

k 86TH OFFICER 1856.

l 86TH PRIVATE, 1804.

m 86TH OFFICER, 1872.

25

Plate 94

common 'Albert'. The authorized tartan was to be the government tartan as worn by the 42nd and 93rd, but with the addition of a white line and called Lamont. The officer's shoulder-plaid shows this distinctly as do the other examples of trews up to 1881, when it was replaced by the Mackenzie tartan.

In 1855 the new doublet was being worn and the new small version of the shako had the diced border. Simkin's picture of an officer, soldier and bandsman depicts the doublet with the flap as worn in 1864. The bandsman (100h) wears the feather bonnet with the red feather beloved by bandsmen. A bandsman and piper of 1880 shown by Simkin wear the glengarry and the white shell jackets. This was the last year for the regiment to wear the old tartan and the special hose top. In 1881 the 74th became the 2nd Battalion of the Highland Light Infantry, and wore the altered dress shown in the centre of the plate (100e).

The 75th Highland Regiment lost its special distinctions in 1809 and had a long battle to regain them. The portrait of an officer in 1809 (78a and 79e) shows the normal infantry dress but with the addition of a thistle badge on the shako. The infantry dress was worn with at least one Scottish distinction, the thistle on the button and later a glengarry with a diced border. In 1862 the regiment was given the title of Stirlingshire but the kilt did not return until 1881, when the 75th became the 2nd Battalion of the Gordon Highlanders.

The 90th Regiment of Foot had been raised in 1794 as the Perthshire Volunteers, but despite the Scottish origin the dress remained that of line regiments or light infantry, although an officer may have dared to wear an undress cap with a diced border. Even when linked with the 26th as the 2nd Battalion of the Scottish Rifles, the uniform was now that of Rifles but with Scottish additions and entirely new (see also the Rifle uniform section).

The 91st Foot had been Highlanders until 1809 when they were another regiment to be deprived of the kilt. As in the case of other 'de-kilted' regiments of that date, Simkin does not show the early Scottish dress and begins with the infantry dress of 1809 (84a). The officer and private have no special features, nor has the change to the next uniform of 1812 for officer, sergeant and private. However, it is known that officers of the light company wore the tapering shako with a green tuft and the thistle badge in front. The officers' coatee later had skirt ornaments of gold thistles embroidered on scarlet.

In 1864 the 91st were allowed to be named the 91st Argyllshire Highlanders but equipped and clothed as a non-kilted Highland corps. The change took place in April 1865. The shako was to be of blue cloth, with diced band and black braid, a white-and-red pompon, the tunic as worn in Highland regiments (a doublet), trews of Campbell tartan and officers to wear 'plaids and claymores'. Simkin shows an officer and a soldier in this new dress dated 1864 (84).

In 1868 the slashed cuff was changed to a gauntlet one now generally adopted by Highland regiments. Trews were now worn in the 71st, 72nd and 74th Regiments of Foot and leather leggings as worn by Infantry of the Line were worn with the trews of the 91st as well. The regimental piper wore full Highland costume including a feather bonnet with a white hackle. The officer's full dress in 1874 (84) showed the accepted dress with the new lower shako.

In 1881 the 91st joined the 93rd as the Argyll and Sutherland

Highlanders when they again wore the kilt and up to 1883 in the old 91st tartan with the red stripe. The dress is of course covered in the section on Highland uniform, and the dress is shown in the centre of the large plate (84). It may be mentioned that the officer and firing soldier of 1879 show the dress as worn on active service in Zululand.

Rifle Regiments

The rifle was a musket with a rifled barrel, that is to say the interior was made with gradually twisting grooves that forced the soft bullet to spin and make a determined effort to reach the target. This being a more expensive weapon than the smooth-bore musket, it was only available to a few soldiers in the eighteenth century. Normally the smooth-bore musket was fired in platoons so that at least some of the random bullets reached the target, but the rifleman was expected to hit a selected target with a minimum of shots. On the Continent the German *Jaegers* – the huntsmen of the rich nobility – were specially trained and wore the green costume expected for woodsmen.

In December 1797 a fifth battalion had been raised and added to the 60th Royal American Regiment, comprised of about 400 men from 'Hompesch's Mounted Riflemen' and later with the addition of 500 men from 'Lowenstein's Chasseurs'. For the first time a green uniform was worn in the British Army. It proved a success, and this colour was then also worn by the riflemen in the otherwise red-coated 1st, 2nd, 3rd, 4th and 6th battalions. The 5th battalion jacket had short skirts and was lined with green serge, and the collar and cuffs were red, as were the featherings or piping on the front and shoulder-straps. The jackets of the rifle companies were feathered with red cloth as were the cuffs, shoulder-straps and collar of green cloth. The 5th battalion had blue cloth pantaloons and the rifle companies green cloth breeches. It is said that blue or white pantaloons were worn in the West Indies and that the green ones were for home service. Officers had their own different and elaborate uniforms. C. H. Smith made a print in 1813 which seems to be the inspiration for the Simkin plate '1814' (91). The shako should be the tall tapering type with green cords and tuft and not the 1812–16 shako which Simkin gives to the officer.

In 1815 it was decided that the battalions dressed in red should change to green and be called 'light infantry', which change took place the next year. The new jacket for officers had lapels lined with scarlet, and scarlet collar and cuffs. The wings were made of gold chains and bullion and the pantaloons were green 'with a figure for dress' (an ornamental pattern). The new cap or shako was broad-topped with a tall green feather and gold cap-lines. It was trimmed with black lace and had a gilt bugle in front, which device was also on the wings and jacket skirts.

In 1818 the battalions were reduced to four, the 2nd being the rifle battalion and the others light infantry and further reductions in 1819 saw the rifle battalion becoming the 1st and the light infantry the 2nd. The 1822 Dress Regulations note the shako with a new type of decoration in front with black lines and a round black ball-tuft. The jacket and pelisse were dark green, the latter with black astrakhan fur. A sergeant is shown (91) dated 1826 but he is actually based on the E. Hull print of 1829 showing the new drooping black plume adopted *c.* 1824. The dark green uniform is relieved by the red collar, cuffs and edging and backing to the chevrons.

Overleaf:
95.
Royal Irish Rifles, 1913, officer full dress

96.
The Royal Scots (The Lothian Regiment) (late 1st), 1913, officer full dress

ROYAL IRISH RIFLES.
1913.

Plate 95

THE ROYAL SCOTS (LOTHIAN REGIMENT)
1913.

Plate 96

a 1742
b 1751
c 1715
d 1742
e 1814
f 1826
g 1914
h 1840

KING'S OWN SCOTTISH BORDERERS

i
j 1806
k 1876
l 1883
m 1914

Plate 97

Black braid is used for the chevrons and for trimming the jacket. But in 1830 the plume in the shako is discontinued and the black ball-tuft was being worn again. In the same year when the title the King's Royal Rifle Corps was authorized, the white-metal buttons gave place to black composition (or brass painted black). The new dress is shown on the officers of 1832 (91*e*) based on a Mansion and Eschauzier print.

By 1844 the new 'Albert' shako was being worn and this is shown on an officer (91), the rest of the uniform following accepted patterns and taken from a painting by Michael Angelo Hayes made in 1850. A bugler of this period is shown also (91*h*) but differs from the contemporary picture in the pattern of the elaborate red and black braid which covered the chest between the three rows of black buttons. A rifleman of 1857 (91) shows the slight concession made when fighting in India – the forage cap has a white cover and curtain, known as a 'Havelock' after the General who made it famous. The King's Royal Rifle Corps had adopted a tunic of green when that garment came into general wear, the collar and cuffs were red, and the cuffs had a red scalloped flap carrying three buttons. The new pattern shakos of both 1857 and 1861 had the round ball-tuft. In 1868 pointed cuffs were worn on the officers' tunic with appropriate braid above to indicate rank. The riflemen had no cuffs as such but a red braid marked the place and had a single eye or loop at the top.

In 1873 busbies were thought to be more fitting for rifle corps than the shako; the new head-dress for an officer being in black lambskin and those for the men in sealskin. When the new infantry helmet was introduced for line regiments in 1878, the busby went out of use but in 1890 it was reintroduced, of the same material but slightly different in shape. The officers wore a black egret plume with a base of scarlet vulture feathers. Men wore a black-over-red hair plume. When the officers adopted a scarlet ostrich plume with a black base (91*g*) the men did not change their plumes, and thus Simkin depicts the wrong combination of colours.

The mounted officer shows the horse furniture worn up to 1914, black sheepskin with scarlet edging, black-over-red throat plume and a red backing to the black bridle. The back view of the standing officer shows the simple black pouch with a silver bugle-horn. The men in khaki show black buttons and badges (red backing for some) and in the case of the officer a red boss should be shown on the forage cap in 1903.

The success of riflemen in the 60th Regiment must have inspired the authorities to find a British corps of riflemen instead of those paid foreign marksmen of the Royal Americans (many of whom had no connection with that continent). Thus in January 1800 it was decided to form a corps of detachments from different regiments of the line for the purpose of being instructed in the use of the rifle. Some 448 men were sought from fifteen regiments of foot plus officers and sergeants as well as drummers who were to be able to play on bugle-horns. In August 1800 while still training, this 'experimental Corps of Riflemen' went into action at Ferrol. This new regiment now of ten companies had 'a green coat without lace' and a 'pair of green pantaloons', a kersey waistcoat and a cap of felt with a brass plate as well as green tuft and cords (93*a*).

The uniform coat of the officers in the new Rifle Corps was to be dark green cloth lined with 'white shalloon'. The collar, cuffs, lapels and wings were of black velvet embroidered with silver. The officers' head-dress had been a 'helmet with hair cockade and green feather and a silver crown and bugle ensigned on the right side of the helmet'. Contemporary pictures of officers of these Rifles 1801–4 show the light dragoon helmet with the black fur crest, green plume and turban. Simkin has an officer dated 1806 (93b) based on the pencil sketch by Captain A. D. Cameron made in March 1804. The officers had a dark green jacket and tight-fitting pantaloons as well as a dark green pelisse trimmed with black fur. In fact officers of Rifles (including those of the 60th Rifles Battalion) seemed to favour a dress based on that of light dragoons, even to the crimson girdle around the waist. The helmet must have been unwieldy for active campaigning and officers appeared in a tubular shako with a rectangular peak turned up in front, plus the green plume and cords. Simkin shows such a uniform with the officer wearing dark green overalls strapped with black leather as might be expected on campaign in the Peninsular War (93c).

Our artist also shows a careful rendering of a rifleman dated 1806 (93a) which is based on an Atkinson plate of 1807. The jacket and pantaloons are dark green with black collar, cuffs and skirt turn-backs. The original print shows white piping to the collar, cuffs and skirts and unusually a white piping down the pantaloons, these details being carefully shown by Simkin. The Rifle Brigade Chronicle when dealing with uniform does not refute this, but the white does not appear in other pictures. The regulations for clothing in 1802 say that 'corporals and privates of a Rifle corps serving in Europe and North America are to be provided with green cloth pantaloons in lieu of breeches'. An interesting feature of buglers in the Rifle Corps is that they did not wear jackets of the 'reversed facings' but jackets of dark green cloth with the number of buttons and setting thereon similar to the rank and file with the collar, cuffs, shoulder-straps and wings of black cloth, and the seams feathered with white and a black-and-white worsted fringe on each wing.

In 1803 the Rifle Corps had been numbered 95th or the Rifle Regiment and in 1816 they were privileged to be removed from Infantry of the Line and called the Rifle Brigade, thereafter taking their position on the left of all infantry. The dress continued with the tapering shako until 1816 (although French pictures of bandsmen give the 1812–16 shako, a fact not confirmed by other sources). Thus the rifleman dated 1814 (93d) does not wear the correct head-dress. By 1816 a broad-topped shako was being worn and the style of succeeding head-dresses followed the infantry changes. The men had single-breasted jackets until 1832 when they became double-breasted with black-horn buttons instead of white metal. Instead of the plain round cuffs, these were now made with an upright flap or slash with four buttons.

The officers' dress became very elaborate and Simkin shows an officer of 1828 (93e) which is based on the colour plate in the *Gentlemen's Magazine of Fashion* of that year. The enormous plume of dark green feathers was hardly the best aid for a fighting man and a War Office direction of 1831 said that these plumes were to be discontinued and a black ball-tuft was to be adopted instead. The drooping horse-hair plume of the other ranks would also have been discontinued at the same time. Simkin's picture of a sergeant, 1832 (93f) shows the new ball-tuft in wear with the red sash with two red lines as depicted in Dubois Drahonet's oil-painting of that period. The introduction of the new Albert shako in 1844 saw no change in the ball-tuft and in fact it continued in use until the last days of the shako. The fittings were bronze including the large plate in front (the 60th had a large Maltese-cross cap plate bearing the number and the bugle) as on the officer

Overleaf:
98.
**1st Battalion Cameronians
(Scottish Rifles) (late 26th)**
a   1688, officer
b   1742, private
c   1751, grenadier
d   1768, grenadier
e   1792, officer
f   1812, officer
g   1914, piper and officer in full dress, officer in service dress
h   1832, private
i   1852, officer
j   1860, officer
k   1880, officer
l   1884, officer
m   1884, piper

a 1688
b 1742
c 1751
d 1768
e 1792

f 1812
g 1914
h 1852

CAMERONIANS (SCOTTISH RIFLES)
1st BATTN. – 26TH FOOT

i 1852
j 1860
k 1880
l 1884
m 1884

Plate 98

a   1815

b   1828

c   1832

d   1849

e

1st Battn. Highland Light Infantry
71st Foot

f   1866

g   1849

h   1866

i   1866

20.

Plate 99

of 1852 (93g). The men dressed similarly to the officer but with a single row of buttons on the jacket whereas the officers had three rows. Men had tufts at the end of their shoulder-straps and of course the pelisse was confined to officers. The introduction of the tunic soon gave the officer simplified looping on the jacket, with five loops of black cord with netted caps and drops, fastening with black olivets. Besides the rank badges on the collar, field officers, captains and subalterns all had their own version of braid and cord on the sleeves and collar. Buttons were now restricted to small ones on shoulder-cords and of course the pelisse was obsolete (93i and j).

In 1872 the shako was changed to a fur busby with a bag or cloth top and a stiff upright brush of green hair in front, see the rifleman, 1875 (93k). In 1878 the new helmet was introduced and that for the Rifle Brigade was dark green with bronze fittings (see the officer, 1882, 93l). In 1881 the officers' badges of rank were moved from the collar to the shoulder-cords.

In the 1890s, the busby was reintroduced, the officers having black lambskin with a bronze bugle below the black cord boss, and the plume was all black. The mounted officer of 1914 (93g) shows the later pattern of plume and the bugler has the black hair plume on his sealskin cap. The green and black wings indicate his profession and the bugle has plain dark green cords. The officer in khaki service dress (93g) has black leather gloves, belts and boots, although it is considered by some that by 1914 all should have been in brown leather.

Two other regiments became 'Rifles', but only in 1881 – the 26th and 90th who converted to the Scottish Rifles, and the 83rd and 86th which became the Royal Irish Rifles. Thus the rifle dress for these regiments only dates from 1881. The helmet was in vogue when the conversions took place. The Cameronian Scottish Rifles had a green helmet with silver fittings for the officer and brass for the men. They wore Scottish doublets in green with black braid as trimmings, the officers having the bronze badges of rank on black chain-gimp shoulder-cords. The trews in the beginning were of the government or Black Watch tartan as shown on the officer, 1884 (98l) but after 1891 the tartan was of the Douglas sett. Two years later the green helmet gave place to a green cloth shako of the earlier 1869 pattern.

Simkin gives a very interesting picture of a piper, 1884 (98m) wearing a doublet, trews and shoulder-plaid of government tartan, and with a dark green bonnet or Balmoral. Later the dress became the full Highland dress with kilt, hose, sporran and glengarry as seen for 1914 (98g). It is known that the bandsmen also wore the dark green balmoral with toorie and ribbons at the back. The officer in khaki service dress, 1914 (98g) wears a glengarry and has black belts and gloves as favoured by rifle regiments. Some years earlier the tartan trews had been worn on service.

The 83rd and 86th Regiments of Foot became the Royal Irish Rifles in 1881 and had been dressed as Infantry of the Line up to that date. The new rifle uniform began with the helmet, officially green (although the *History of the Royal Irish Rifles* quotes black) with bronze, almost black, fittings. The tunic was dark green with similar facings, which indicated their Irish origin. In 1891 the helmet was discontinued for the busby, black lambskin with a crown of rifle green cloth, black cords and a green cord boss in front and bronze fittings. The officers' plumes were of black egret feathers over a dark green vulture-feather base; later ostrich-feather plumes presented a more imposing feature (94g). The horse furniture of the officer includes a green throat plume, green edging to the black sheepskin and green backing to the bridle. The bugler has a dark green tunic with dark green facings and black braid while his black busby has the stiff brush of black out of green. An officer of 1913 (95) shows the distinction of the facings from the tunic and the white metal or silver ornaments on the pouch-belt may be clearly seen.

Officers' Uniforms and Distinctions

Although one might expect the uniforms of officers to be somewhat like those of their men, this was not so in the earliest days. As officers had to purchase their own uniforms there obviously was latitude as to quality and ornamentation, especially as uniform itself was just beginning to evolve. The lack of money in the case of junior officers would be obvious when compared with the coat of a colonel who as a member of the gentry or nobility might favour the most expensive embroidery. It seems that almost any colour could be chosen as a basic: scarlet was popular, but so was blue and even 'coats of cloth of gold' are mentioned. Later, staff officers are noted with crimson coats which with the blue of other staff officers could be worn when the officers moved from one duty to another, without trouble. Regimentally it seems possible that higher officers for a period had gold trimming and junior officers silver, but later the choice of metal, gold or silver became the distinction of a regiment. The main mark of an officer in the English Army since early in the seventeenth century had been his red silk scarf which followed the Continental use of a national colour, in this case the red from the Cross of St George. The voluminous red scarf, usually of silk or some rich material, was edged with a metallic fringe and could be worn over the shoulder or around the waist. All officers had swords chosen for their own taste and according to their pocket. Regimental officers also carried staved weapons which indicated rank. In early days the leading staff, something in the nature of an ornamented stick, was held in the hand but this gave way to the pike which captains carried, sometimes over the shoulder. This had a spear-head with a tassel below and was changed about 1710 for a spontoon, which by 1786 had been replaced by the sword. A lieutenant had a partisan, the metal head of which was flat and it had a pointed top with projections either side. This was replaced by the spontoon in 1710. The ensign, when not carrying his ensign or colour, had a half-pike until 1710 when he too had the spontoon; all officers after 1786 no longer carried a staff weapon and the sword was deemed sufficient. Grenadier officers were in a different category and at times had the flint-lock or fusil.

In 1692 some officers were wearing blue coats lined with blue (no doubt after the Netherlands fashion introduced by William of Orange) or plain red or crimson without regimental distinctions. This would be of value when a regiment might be disbanded after a year, and the officer would find employment in a new regiment. But when regiments began to attain a permanence, then the regimental facings became a necessity.

Gorgets were another mark for officers. This piece of armour was the first to be put on the neck and the last to be taken off when armour was worn. When armour was giving way to the power of gunpowder in the seventeenth century, many knights and noblemen contented themselves by wearing only a gorget or a 'pot' (helmet). The first gorgets were iron or

Overleaf:
100.
2nd Battalion Highland Light Infantry (late 74th)
a   1809, officer and sergeant
b   1812, private
c   1832, private and officer
d   1845, officer
e   (c.1910) private, officer and piper in full dress
f   1845, private
g   1864, private and officer
h   1864, bandsman
i   piper and bandsman in drill jackets

a *1809*

b *1812*

c *1832*

d *1845*

e

f *1845*

2ND BATTN. HIGHLAND LIGHT INFANTRY
74TH FOOT

R SIMKIN

g *1864*

h *1864*

i *1880*

22

Plate 100

TRAIN OF ARTILLERY.
MATROSS.
1685.   1710.

Plate 101

steel, sometimes ornamented with engraving. In the late seventeenth century, officers were expected to wear their gorgets in camp and on duty. It seems that captains wore gilt gorgets, lieutenants blackened metal with gilt studs and the ensigns a silver colour. When gold and silver became regimental distinctions, the gorgets followed the regimental metal. It was not until the end of the eighteenth century that all gorgets were ordered to be gilt with the Sovereign's cypher.

About 1710 the Duke of Marlborough ordered that all officers in the army should be clothed in 'red plain or uniform' and that no officer was to be on duty without his regimental scarf and spontoon. Officers usually had waistcoats the colour of the facings and sometimes the breeches might also be so. But it was usual for the breeches to be either in red or perhaps blue when the facings were royal. Later the gold or silver on garments made a regimental distinction for officers. The hat had the appropriate metal around the brim. The coat might have the embroidery, not only around the buttonholes but also on the edges of the coat, the cuffs and the pocket flap. About 1759 officers were discontinuing the fashion of coloured waistcoats and wore either white or buff.

The introduction of silver or gold lace which could be sewn on made a saving, for it was cheaper than embroidery although the latter continued among some infantry officers into the nineteenth century. Officers in the eighteenth century had worn shoulder-knots in the regimental metal behind the right shoulder, but in the 1760s the epaulette was beginning to be worn by some officers. Finally in 1768 epaulettes were to be worn by infantry officers, one in the case of most officers but two for grenadier companies. But later it was not unusual for all officers in a regiment to wear one on each shoulder. The use of a staff or staved weapons for officers declined and by 1786 a sword was sufficient for most, although grenadier officers were known to carry the fusil occasionally. The epaulette at first appeared to be a combination of the shoulder-cord and the shoulder-knot. This might look like a knotted cord or strap going from the collar to the edge of the shoulder, with the ends hanging down, soon to be converted into a fringe and later still bullion, i.e. hollow spirals of metal wire. At first these epaulettes were little more than a regimental distinction for an officer within a regiment but later they developed aspects of ranks, either by the thickness of the bullion and by the relegation of fringe to the junior ranks. At this time an embroidered badge, like a thistle or the Prince of Wales's Feathers, might be worn but this was regimental and not of rank.

Infantry officers had worn their crimson sashes over the right shoulder but in 1768 they were ordered to wear it around the waist, possibly because there was a difficulty in having it under the epaulette strap. The wearing of silver gorgets was forbidden in 1796 when all were to wear the gilt gorget with the Crown over 'GR' within branches of laurel. The old and ancient badges were now to be found on the horns or corners as the King stressed that he was in command and that his commission was to be noted.

It was not until 1810 that the practice of wearing badges of rank on the officers' epaulettes was adopted in Great Britain though it appears to have developed a few years before in India. Distinctions were made in other ways: the subalterns had only fringe on their epaulettes and captains had bullion but no badge of rank. Field officers had bullion at the ends, frequently of a larger dimension, a major an embroidered Star, a lieutenant-colonel a Crown and a full colonel both the Crown and the Star.

Preceding page:
101.
Train of Artillery, 1685, officer and matross; 1710, officer

In 1830 the gorget was made obsolete and it was decided that all regular officers should have gold lace and distinctions, thus indicating the royal connection of their commission. Silver was to be the distinction of militia officers.

In 1855 the officers were ordered to wear their sashes over the shoulder, again with the instructions that the fringes were not to hang below the coat. In 1880 the badges of rank were transferred from the collar back to the shoulder and this time they were to be on twisted gold cords. The system of denoting rank changed again. The sub-lieutenant had no badge, the lieutenant had a silver Star, the captain two Stars, the major a silver Crown, the lieutenant-colonel a Crown and a Star, while the full colonel had a Crown and two Stars. In 1902 the most junior subaltern was at last given a Star, which meant that the lieutenant was now expected to have two Stars and the captain three. Once again the officers had to wear their sashes around the waist in 1902, but Highland officers continued to wear them over their shoulders.

With khaki in 1902 the ranks were placed on the cuffs where a system of lines and loops soon gave place to a combination of naval rings and 'Crown and/or Star' on a patch denoted the rank. In the trenches the sleeve markings were not always easily seen and the practice of wearing the Crown and Star badges on the khaki shoulder-strap was condoned on active service but not fully approved for home wear until 1920 when the cuff rank markings were abolished.

Non-commissioned officers' Distinctions

The distinctions for non-commissioned officers of infantry developed gradually. In the beginning there was the rank of sergeant to take the commands of an officer to submit to the rank and file and the most obvious of their visual distinctions was the halbert, a long, staved weapon with a hatchet-like head. He wore a red or crimson sash following the example of the officer although not of silk but of worsted or other poor material. By the end of the seventeenth century there was a difference in their coats from that of the men and they now wore extra lace on the seams. Sometimes the lace was a galloon or imitation of gold; later it acquired the silver or gold as permitted.

In 1769 sergeants of grenadier companies, and presumably of fusiliers, discontinued the halbert and carried a fusil instead. About the same time sergeants tied their sashes around their waists following the example of the officers and to make their sashes distinctive had a central stripe of the facing colour added. In the last years of the eighteenth century the halbert was changed to a spontoon, another pole or staved weapon but with a simple point and a cross-bar just below the spike-end. Corporals were now wearing a distinction, a shoulder-knot or type of shoulder-strap, and some pictures show that sergeants had their own versions of this strap.

It was not until 1802 that a General Order stated that chevrons were to be worn as a distinction. There had been unofficial use of chevrons before this date but in 1802 it was ruled that 'epaulettes and shoulder-knots' of n.c.os were to be replaced by chevrons. This meant that corporals now had two chevrons on the right arm, sergeants had three and sergeant-majors and

Overleaf:
102.
Royal Artillery, 1743, 1760 and 1815, officers

ROYAL ARTILLERY.

1743.   1760.   1815.

Plate 102

ROYAL ARTILLERY.

1794.   1799   1820.

Plate 103

quarter-master-sergeants had four. When colour-sergeants were introduced in 1813, they wore a Crown over a Union flag with a single chevron
below on the right arm. For some occasions three chevrons were also worn
on the left sleeve. By this time sergeants were wearing silver lace as a
distinction round the collar and elsewhere.

In 1845 the stripes in the sashes of sergeants were discontinued, leaving a
plain all-crimson woollen sash. These were worn around the waist but in
1855 when officers began to wear the sash over the shoulder again, their
sash was over the left shoulder but those of the sergeants were expected to
be worn over the right shoulder to avoid any possible confusion. The other
ranks had worn a dull red or brick-red tunic but the sergeants were
distinctive in having scarlet (like the officers). The other rank distinction
ceased in 1871 when all were given scarlet tunics.

By now there were many duties for n.c.os to undertake and so the senior
ones had to acquire fresh distinctions, like the sergeant-major who now had
a Crown over his four chevrons. Then in 1882 the Crown alone was the
badge of rank for Class B warrant officers and worn on the cuff. The Crown
within a wreath was introduced in 1901 for warrant officers, first class.
Their present badge of the complete Royal Arms was introduced in 1915 for
most warrant officers class one, but there are many ranks and changes
which cannot be covered by this work.

Drummers and Fifers

The use of drummers in the army has an ancient lineage going back to
Ancient Egypt where the wall-carvings show men tapping their long skin-
covered drums with the armed soldiers all keeping step. The rhythmic
sound was a decided aid to marching and no doubt helped to occupy the
soldiers' minds when keeping step. It is known that conches and horns
could give signals and commands, so possibly a drummer could even in
those days tap a message and in consequence each company had its own
drummer to transmit the captain's orders. In the companies of the early
seventeenth century each company also had a fifer, but Oliver Cromwell
soon dismissed such 'flippant' sounds of music. The Restoration brought
the fifer back but in an unofficial capacity, for he had to be supported and
paid any extras by the captain of the company. This was also the practice on
the Continent where the captain had to pay for the clothing of a drummer or
fifer and thus they often appeared dressed in the livery of the captain
instead of the regimental coat.

In the Foot Guards the dress of the drummer was red and blue similar to
that of the infantryman because this was the livery of the commanding
officer – the King. But 'livery' was not utilized in the British Isles, as it was
in France and elsewhere; the system of 'reversed facings' was chosen. That
is to say, the drummer's coat was to be of the facing colour and the collar
and cuffs to be red (which was the colour of the basic coat). An early
example may be quoted, that of a drummer (the regiment being an ancestor
of the 13th Foot) who wore a 'yellow faced coat, lined with red' being the
reversal of the regimental coat, red faced yellow.

The style of the original drummer's coat was much different from that of
the fighting man and somewhat after the fashion of the mediaeval doublet
which had hanging sleeves (as worn by Henry VIII) so, apart from the

Preceding page:
103.
Royal Artillery, 1794, 1799 and
1820, officers

elaborate lacing and braid, an empty sleeve hung from each shoulder at the back of the garment. This may also have a bearing on the origin of the 'wings' on the shoulders which served to cover the holes left for the arms to come through. This dress also emphasizes the civilian nature of a drummer, who on the field of battle might be called upon to contact the enemy at the time of an armistice or similar occasion. Vestigial 'hanging sleeves' may be seen on the modern State clothing worn by the bandsmen of the Household Cavalry, where these narrow strips hang from the back of the shoulder and are looped up into the waist-belt.

Royal troops also carried a large Royal Cypher on the chest when the drummers were wearing the red coat and it was possible for other commanders of infantry regiments also to have a cypher of their initials with appropriate crown or coronet. At first a hat possibly with feathers was worn by drummers but when the grenadier companies were created, their cloth caps were soon adopted for the two grenadier company drummers (one of whom was later trained as a fifer). It was always possible that other companies took into wear a cloth cap.

Towards the middle of the eighteenth century when the fighting soldiers' uniforms were being regularized, drummers were not overlooked and the draft warrant of 1747 stated that the drummers of all Royal Regiments were allowed to wear the royal livery, 'viz, red, lined, faced and lapelled on the breast with blue'. The drummers of all other regiments were to be clothed with 'the colour of the facing of the regiment, lined, faced and lapelled with red and laced in such manner as the Colonel shall think fit for distinction's sake, however being of the colours of that on the soldiers coats'. These regulations appeared in the 1751 printed version. An amendment of that year also ordered that the drummers of foot were to have 'hanging sleeves as the Foot Guards have, and they are to have caps'. The front was to be the colour of the facings but the little flap was to be red (as was the back of the cap). The front was embroidered with the badge of the regiment or a trophy of flags and drums, while the little flap had the White Horse of Hanover and the motto 'Nec Aspera Terrent'. On the back of the turn-up of the cap was embroidered a drum and the number of the regiment. The badges of regiments are quoted in the section on the grenadier dress.

David Morier painted a drummer of the 18th Royal Irish Regiment which had the royal livery and Simkin uses this a basis for his version of a 'reversed facings' regiment, the 5th Foot who had gosling-green facings (67a). The inner red lining of the hanging sleeves may be observed. The lace of the 5th was white with two red stripes and this the artist shows. Although the lace was to be in the colours of that worn by the soldier, it is probable that in some cases the pattern varied, although the colours were the same. The drum-hoops in 1751 were plain red and the triangular pattern depicted by Simkin was a later Victorian innovation.

The 1768 warrant repeated much of the 1751 regulations but had extra regulations. The coats of drummers and fifers whose regiment had red facings were to have white coats faced, lapelled and lined with red. Those who wore white or buff coats were to have red waistcoats, breeches and linings, while all others were to have the same colour as ordered for the men. Hanging sleeves were now forbidden. The cloth cap was also obsolete and the new black bearskin cap had a metal plate in front with trophies of colours and drums, white metal on black. Badges, if permitted, were also

Overleaf:
104.
Royal Artillery
a 1794, gunner
b 1799, gunner

ROYAL ARTILLERY.
GUNNER-1794.

a

ROYAL ARTILLERY.
GUNNER-1799.

b

Plate 104

ROYAL ARTILLERY.

1825.   1840.

Plate 105

worn. All drummers and fifers had a short sword with a scimitar blade.

In December 1795 the drummers and fifers of the 58th Regiment were permitted to change the colour of their coats from black to white and in January of the next year an order to the 50th, 58th, 64th, 70th and 80th Foot was for the coats of the drummers and fifers to be made of white cloth (instead of the black) and to have black cuffs, collars and facings. The waistcoats and breeches were to be white. In 1796 it was decided to alter the cut of the coat and eventually the coat was closed across the front, keeping the arrangement of buttons and loops as before.

A new cap or the shako was now being worn and in 1802 the clothing regulations from 1768 onwards were revised and brought up to date. The changes mentioned above were included and further the coats were to be short-skirted and lined throughout. Those with white, red, black or buff were to have red linings. The collar, cuffs, wings and shoulder-straps for Royal Regiments were to be of dark blue cloth and for others to be of scarlet cloth. The cuffs were to be round and without slits. The lace of Royal Regiments was called royal lace and could be blue and white, or blue, white and yellow worsted 'considerably raised above the common lace'. Other drummers had lace which was 'raised' and in a variety of worsted approaching nearly the colour of the lace of the rank and file but the patterns of same were varied and to be at the option of the colonel.

For full dress the caps of drummers and fifers were black bearskin with a black front plate bearing the King's Crest and trophies of colours and drums, plus the number of the regiment and any badge, if so entitled, on the back. In 1811 the gosling-green coats of the 5th Foot were changed to white with scarlet collar and cuffs. In September 1811 it was thought that buglers and trumpeters on active service were exposed to enemy fire as their coats were so distinctive and in future they were to wear coats the same colour as those of the privates. But as drummers had not been mentioned in the order, they continued to wear clothing of 'reversed facings'. The new shako of 1812–16 was also worn by drummers in battle, although the fur cap was available for ceremonial duties.

White breeches and black gaiters were worn as were overalls at the time of the Peninsular War but it was not until 1823 that trousers won the day. In 1831 all drummers were ordered to wear red coats instead of those of the facing colour but with the drummers' lace on it as before. With the change to the new pattern double-breasted coatee, the round cuffs now had an upright slash or flap with a thick padding of wool or a fringe on the wings in the colours of the drummers' lace. The lace went round the edges of the coatee and down the seams but the darts or chevrons on the sleeves were not always worn. The broad-topped shakos gave place to the 'Albert' cap or chaco about 1844 and this saw the end of the fur cap for company drummers of the line.

The introduction of the double-breasted tunic in 1855 brought about a short-lived white tunic or doublet for drummers. All the seams were covered with the regimental drummers' lace but the elaborate wool or tufting on the wings was discontinued. However, a small coloured fringe was worn in the small of the back, a feature not seen before. In 1857 the new single-breasted tunic was introduced and the impractical white garment was replaced by a red item as worn by the rank and file. The Scottish doublet of a Black Watch drummer of 1862 (75m) should still show the special lace but in 1866 the many patterns were replaced by a single simple

Preceding page:
105.
Royal Artillery, 1825 and 1840, officers

white braid with red crowns for all infantry of the line.

About 1880 the last of the shakos gave place to the helmet and on the tunic the 'jam-pot' or round cuff was in fashion. By 1899 an Austrian knot in braid above the cuff was worn by some, but in 1901 following the general change in fashion the pointed cuff was adopted with a narrow edging of white and red tape. Richard Simkin portrays several drummers of the period of Edward VII and George V, including the Buffs (late 3rd) (15*g*) with thickly fringed wings; the 2nd Seaforth Highlanders (late 78th) (80*k*) in doublet and the shoulder-plaid hanging from the left shoulder; the Hampshire Regiment (late 37th) (41*g*) similar to the Buffs and neither wearing knee-aprons; and the 1st Battalion Gordon Highlanders (late 75th) (87*k*) wearing doublet and shoulder-plaid.

Buglers

In the eighteenth century, the light infantrymen were not grouped together in action but were dispersed over a wide area. The drum was not considered to have sufficient carrying power and so the hunting horn was pressed into service. When light infantry regiments were being formed early in the nineteenth century, buglers were added to each company and wore the uniform equivalent for drummers. But any special head-dress worn by the men might be worn by the buglers or 'hornist'.

Even in Victorian times the light infantry influence was not eliminated and the spiked helmet of 1878 and later was covered with green cloth to indicate light infantry. The cords to the bugles were green, except in the case of Royal Regiments when the cords were red, yellow and blue, thus presenting a speckled appearance to the tassels. Simkin shows buglers of the Prince Albert's Somerset Light Infantry (late 13th Foot) (68*g*) and of the 1st Battalion Oxfordshire Light Infantry (late 43rd) (71*g*) where the green cords may be seen and the full red and white wings.

Of course, rifle corps had their own version of dress for their buglers, usually the green jacket of the rifleman with special cord. A bugler of the King's Rifle Corps (or 60th) (91*h*) has a red collar and piping down the front and on the cuffs with black braid around the edges, while the bugler of the Rifle Brigade, 1914 (93*g*) has green and black cord on his tunic and the cords on his bugle are green.

Drum-Majors

Drum-majors were known before the Restoration but were important after 1661 because they were not only responsible for the training of young drummers but they also had other regimental duties such as recruiting and punishment. As might be expected, a drum-major wore more expensive clothing, and carried a cane or a walking-stick. On the Continent this stick was actively used for punishment but in England it developed into the long staff or mace still to be seen leading modern bands. By the middle of the eighteenth century, his coat was elaborate with silver lace, as also was his cocked hat. As he no longer beat a drum on parade, his sticks were carried on a shoulder-belt.

As he was not a 'bandsman' he wore the 'reversed facings' of drummers in non-royal regiments although there are examples of a white coat in the late eighteenth century. When the shako became a common head-dress, he continued to wear a cocked hat to signify that he was a 'non-fighting' man. An example may be seen in a print by C. H. Smith from his work 'according to the latest regulations, 1814' and here the hat is much feathered around the brim. So grandiose was his appearance during the Peninsular War, that Portuguese natives are known to have considered this uniform to be that of a high-ranking officer and treated as such. Thus the picture by Richard Simkin (55), which is a reconstruction, shows the 1812–16 shako being worn, perhaps as on active service. The coat is the colour of the regimental facings and has red lapels, cuffs, collar and wings. The overalls Simkin makes green to match the coat (which may be 'an educated guess') present a problem as to whether they are genuine, although the 24th Foot may be suggested.

By 1828 the cocked hat was out of fashion and following the practice of the drummer the drum-major wore a bearskin cap with a long hackle feather. When the 'Albert' shako was taken into wear c. 1844 the infantry drum-majors seem to have taken a large fur cap with a red plume. As befits a senior n.c.o. the coatee had much silver lace. The change to a red coatee followed that of the drummer. When, in 1865, embroidered badges were introduced to distinguish some of the red coats, the rank of a drum-major was signified by a drum and four chevrons on the right arm and in 1871 his tunic was made of scarlet cloth of officers' quality instead of the dull red. He had ranked as a Class 2 Staff Sergeant but in 1881 was downgraded in the infantry to a sergeant-drummer, although keeping the same rank marking, perhaps because the drum-major was no longer responsible for corporal punishment and the flogging of regimental culprits. At this time his tunic and wings had half-inch gold lace. In 1926 the title of drum-major was restored, perhaps because it had been found that the reintroduction of full dress for bands was a great help to recruiting. The sash of the drum-majors, which originally had two drum-sticks, later small token versions, became most elaborate with Crowns, Cyphers, regimental badges and battle honours, far too complex a subject to be covered here.

Regimental Bands

It may not be realized that regimental bands were not formed in the early days of infantry. In fact, it was very many years before bands received official recognition as they have today. It was not until the middle of the eighteenth century that infantry bands were formed and even then they were very limited in number, eight men being the total on many occasions. As the regiments and the officers were expected to find, pay and clothe these individuals, there were no rigid regulations as to dress in the early days. But a preference for white dress soon developed with many ornate additions and trimmings. Very little written evidence of this period is available regarding band uniforms and so it is the pictorial evidence towards the end of the eighteenth century that proves that white coats were being worn by the infantry of the line, although red coats were to be seen, as might be expected, for royal regiments, including the Foot Guards.

Simkin shows two plates of 1815 (56 and 57) both based on contemporary French pictures and perhaps slightly fanciful, although based on seen figures. The musicians have white coats and are given green collars and cuffs by Simkin. The green cording across the front appears in the French pictures, as does the red, white and green/black fringe on the wings, but Simkin makes the wings themselves rather puffed-up articles which may not be intended by N. Finart. The shakos have the white-over-red plumes which the original artist must have observed on most of the British troops. The grey overalls were well known but the white side-stripes, especially in twos, are unusual though not impossible, and indicative of coming fashions.

The original drawing of the negro drummer (57) was named '*musicien nègre. Chasseur de pied Anglaise. Paris 1814*' and shows a drummer of what might be intended as the Rifle Brigade. He wears the 1812–16 shako with a white metal bugle-horn in front and the normal plume of the left with white cords, not particularly 'musical'. The jacket, or perhaps pelisse for it has bands of black fur on the sleeves (and above the cuffs in the original), Simkin shows with green braid linking three rows of buttons on the front. The original has five rows of buttons with what may be black braid. The green trousers with two side-stripes of white may be reminiscent of the original rifle pantaloons. The long drum is typical of the period and the original picture shows a green disk in the centre without any expected device, while the light yellow and green triangles are unusual. Whether the white and red hackles of the line were worn by musicians is not known. There is no doubt that when the French artists produced the many paintings and prints of British musicians they were more concerned with impressions rather than accuracy, although they were based on what they saw during the occupation of Paris.

The War Office in London eventually had to concede that bands formed part of a regiment and it organized band funds to support them, the money being found by the regimental officers. In 1811 bands were officially limited to one sergeant (as master) and one musician for each company, plus a few men taken from the ranks, but the total number was not to exceed one sergeant and ten musicians. By 1823 the number was increased to one sergeant and fourteen musicians, once again a number not to be exceeded; which makes one think that with the various amendments, the number was often exceeded.

After Waterloo the broad-topped shako was taken into wear and the large hackle plume was worn in front and musicians are usually depicted having red or crimson as their distinctive colour, as this was not used by other troops. As expected in time of peace, elaborations took place. The men's blue-grey or white overalls were not very striking and so one saw the musicians of the 17th Foot (28*b*) in 1828 wearing deep pink or red trousers of an ample cut as well as an ornamental sword. The band sword was a long thin weapon which would not have been the slightest value in a fight. The hilt and cross quillons were cast in one piece and sometimes with no more than a narrow chain to act as a knuckle guard. The white coatee has a profusion of red braid on the front (not black as Simkin shows) and on the shoulders are the metal scales, popular at that period. They could be brass or gilt with often a trophy design within the crescent. Simkin shows a white-over-red plume whereas the original is a bushy feather affair, all red, as expected for bandsmen. The musical instrument which he carries is a serpent, also favoured in churches.

In 1830 an official order (somewhat retrospective) stated that all infantry bands should be clothed in white. This meant that the new pattern coatee approved in the previous year would be worn with two rows of buttons down the front and with flaps or slashes added to the cuffs. In January of 1831 a further directive said that a pattern coat for bandsmen had been 'sealed' and that the facings in all cases were to correspond with those of the regiment. The trousers and caps (shakos) were also to be conformable in every respect to 'the patterns for the regiment at large'.

Richard Simkin shows a bandmaster of the 51st Foot (later the King's Own Yorkshire Light Infantry) wearing this dress (72a). The white coatee has a dark green collar, cuffs and backing to the chevrons. The epaulettes, buttons and four large chevrons are silver. The plain black shako has green plaited cords, a large dropping hair plume and heavy 'swags' across the chest in the same colour. A crimson sash around his waist also indicates his rank. In most contemporary illustrations the white sword-belt is shown on top of this red sash. The trousers are dark green matching the facings, and he also appears to have silver lace down the side seams.

By 1848 there is evidence that some bandsmen were wearing the red hair plume on the Albert shako. There must have been unofficial variations in the colour of the wings and shoulder-straps as in 1851 these were ordered to be the colour of the facings. The long band swords were still carried with the solid 'Roman' hilts and no cutting edge to the blades. The dress of this period is shown for a trombone-player of the 6th (Royal 1st Warwickshire) Regiment 1852 (17). The plain black tubular shako has the circular plate of the other ranks with the number '6' in the centre and the long hanging plume is red horse-hair. The simple coatee is white with dark blue collar and cuffs. The metal shoulder-scales are worn and besides the white waist-belt there is another white belt over the left shoulder, no doubt · holding a pouch for sheet music. The brass scabbard for the sword may be clearly seen. The trousers with the dark Oxford colour have red welts down the sides. The Scottish musicians have their dress described in their national section (pp. 152–156) where it will be seen that the bandsmen of the 79th wear wings and not the brass shoulder-scales favoured by infantry of the line. The 60th King's Rifle Corps being rifles had their own version of a bandsman's uniform (92b)). The shako is like that of the rifleman with a simple dark ball-tuft and the black chin-strap worn under the chin. His uniform appears almost black (in fact the official description at one time for the rifleman's dress was 'invisible green') but is relieved by a scarlet collar and mixed red-and-black cord and tracing across the chest and on the sleeves. He wears thick black tufting to his shoulder-straps and not the metal shoulder-scale. His sword has a steel hilt and the scabbard is dark to match the sword-belt around his waist, which is on the right side and carries a black music-pouch. His waist-belt is fastened by the traditional snake-hook of riflemen.

When the new double-breasted tunic was introduced in 1855, infantry of the line continued to wear the white garment with the two rows of widely spaced buttons. The collar, cuffs and wings were in the facing colour. Around the top of the collar, the cuffs, the cuff-flaps and down the opening of the tunic was piping of red cloth. The white waist-belt had a brass locket-fastening and the long scabbards are shown as black with brass fittings. The shako continued to have the ball-tuft, dark green in the case of light infantry regiments, but many pictures show the bands wearing undress caps.

By 1857 the replacement tunic, the single-breasted garment, was being

worn, still white with the facing colour being used for the collar, cuffs, flaps
on the sleeves, shoulder-straps and wings. Red piping continued to be on
the edge of the wings, the cuffs and flaps and down the front of the tunic.
There was white tape on the wings and on the three-buttoned cuff flap.
Simkin depicts the bass-drummer of the 5th Northumberland Fusiliers,
1858 (50k) but his big drum obscures his tunic, although the white arms
with gosling-green cuffs appear either side. He wears the new tapering
shako with the drooping hair plume of fusiliers in the white, tipped red,
distinction of that regiment. The front of the shako has the large metal
grenade that distinguished fusiliers. Below his drum may be seen the white
apron worn by such drummers. His drum carried on the hoops the triangles
of white and gosling green, a style well known in the Crimean campaign and
brought to the United Kingdom on captured Russian side-drums.

The change in 1861 to a lower shako saw the ball-tuft still worn, white-
over-red for most regiments (15k) but light infantry had the dark green hair
plume. The normal dark trousers of the infantry man were worn. Simkin
shows three examples of this period all dated 1864, the 3rd Foot (15k), the
11th Foot (22l) and the 67th (Hampshire) Foot (41k). All three men look very
similar except for the facings, the Buffs have red, the 11th dark green and
the 67th yellow. The short sword with black scabbard and the all-brass hilt
is worn by all three men, being the new government issue for bandsmen
(drummers having slightly shorter types).

By 1865 the flapped cuff had changed to the pointed type and this
pattern of tunic is shown on the bandsman of the 21st Royal Scots Fusiliers,
1868 (64k) and another of the 87th Royal Irish Fusiliers, also 1868 (67k)
where both fusilier regiments wear the fur cap with the large grenade badge
in front. The pointed blue cuff has a white braid or tape going to the point
with a blue light before the narrow edging of white finishes off the
decoration.

But the days of the white band tunic were numbered. In 1871 it was
noted that these white garments needed special treatment to make them
clean and that left them damp and unhealthy to the wearer. It was
suggested that they be discontinued although it was not until 1873 that an
order was made. The new tunic was to be scarlet with the cloth of the
regimental facing on the collar and cuffs. Wings were still to be worn with
white tape, and white piping was on the back and sleeve seams. Bandsmen's
wings were made with a plain edge, thus differing from drummers and
buglers who had a fringed edge. To make a further distinction, bandsmen
were given an arm badge to be worn on the right sleeve above the elbow,
which had an embroidered device of trumpets and lyre. Many years later
this badge was changed to one of a lyre with a crown over it. When the
shako was changed to a helmet, there was no special 'band' feature,
although some bands did loop the chain up to the top, a feature carelessly
continued in modern bands who also have an extra chin-chain worn under
the chin.

Overleaf:
106.
Royal Artillery
a   1839, trumpeter
b   1840, drum-major

Pioneers

The use of pioneers with military forces in the field goes back to the days of
antiquity because there was so much that a fighting man could not
undertake. Trenches could be dug by the fighting man but then he would
not have been available for action; roads may need to have been cleared;

ROYAL ARTILLERY.
1839.

a

ROYAL REGIMENT OF ARTILLERY
1840

b

Plate 106

ROYAL ARTILLERY.
GUNNER -1840.

Plate 107 a

ROYAL ARTILLERY.
GUNNER -1850.

Plate 107 b

ROYAL ARTILLERY.
GUNNER -1858.

Plate 108 a

ROYAL ARTILLERY.
OFFICER - FIELD BATTERY -1864.

Plate 108 b

bridges made or restored; and many tasks were necessary with fortifications. So labouring and skilled artisans were sought outside the ranks of the armed men. Unfortunately, early pioneers were treated with scant regard and at times considered very lowly. Even the origin of the word suggests this, for one derivation gives 'pawn', the lowest piece on a chess board, or 'peon', meaning a peasant or labourer. But the pioneer soon proved his worth and advanced to a post of importance and need in warfare.

When on the march with infantry, the pioneers were in front and had the task of making sure that the way was cleared from natural or unnatural obstacles. A warrant of 1683 said that pioneers attached to regiments would carry both hatchet and hanger (sword). A contemporary painting of Marlborough's troops c. 1709 shows the pioneers moving tree trunks out of the way of advancing troops. Their clothing was distinctive, for they were dressed in dark blue coats instead of the normal red, a colour which would be much better for the rough work in which they were engaged. Also distinctive were the fur caps which would have stood up to the hard conditions and the wearing of voluminous whiskers indicated that little time was to be wasted on shaving and this gave them a fearsome and aggressive appearance. Large axes were conspicuous in the picture to show the method of man-handling the obstructions.

Later in the century pioneers appeared in red coats, so perhaps the blue coats were intended for off-duty or dirty work. In the case of farriers in cavalry regiments, the blue coat continued as a sign of their trade. A report of 1783 speaks of runaway pioneers wearing blue jackets but as these men were negroes, they might have been worn for another reason.

Regulations speak of the pioneer cap being of leather with a black bearskin and that the plate in front was to have a red ground with the King's Arms in white and the depiction of a saw and an axe, while the regimental number was on the back of the cap. Pioneers were to parade on the right of the grenadiers and precede them on the march. The large aprons were of leather, as were the slings and cases for carrying axes and saws. In 1778 it was noted that the tools of pioneers also included spades and pickaxes. Contemporary pictures show the cap as described, the dark leather apron and the long-handled axe as the popular tool, with a musket slung over the shoulder.

A print of 1815 by C. H. Smith shows a pioneer with his axe over his shoulder and this is Simkin's basis for his pioneer of the 13th Foot (69b) where he keeps the same pose but changes the green collar and cuffs to yellow. However, instead of showing the new pattern plate of brass, Simkin shows a red plate with two axes. He also changes the white tufted wings to short tufts on the shoulder-straps. The holder for the axe head can be seen on the left thigh and the musket is slung over the shoulder with invisible supports. The ancient fur cap continued in wear but eventually lost the brass plate in front and the introduction of the 'Albert' shako saw the end of the fur cap, except in fusilier regiments.

By now the apron was made of white leather, or buckskin it is said, and had extended above the belt in a bib-like fashion. Large white leather gauntlets were also to be seen. But in the nineteenth century in some regiments there were no pioneers and indeed frequently no pioneer equipment in store. In 1856 the pioneer was no longer armed with a musket but was given a saw-backed bayonet which 'will serve both as a weapon and a tool'! In 1866 the pioneer who looked like an ordinary soldier on

Preceding page:
107.
Royal Artillery
a 1840, gunner
b 1850, gunner

108.
Royal Artillery
a 1856, gunner
b 1864, officer

many occasions was given a special badge of distinction, crossed axes which were to be worn on the upper arm. Thankfully, the fearsome saw-backed sword was obsolete by 1903 but apron and gauntlets did reappear to be worn with the axe over the shoulder on parades.

The pioneers of the Royal Welsh Fusiliers appear today with all these special features – fur cap, apron, gauntlets, axe and fearsome whiskers – but the trade of the pioneer in the modern army has taken on special features with modern methods of warfare.

Khaki and Service Dress

The word 'khaki' stems from a Persian or Urdu word meaning 'dust' and originated in India when local cotton garments were dyed or stained *c.* 1846 into a hue which acted as a kind of camouflage in that country where the 'red-coat' was only too visible to the enemy snipers. Drab smocks were worn by the 74th Foot, 1851–3, in Africa with their tartan trews. The tunic worn by the 93rd Highlanders in Lucknow, 1857 (89) is a light khaki colour with red collar and cuffs as well as a red-edged cuff-flap. The rest of the corporal's uniform is as for full dress and is taken from a painting by Skeoch Cumming.

The 42nd Highlanders when in Ashanti, 1874 (75*l*) wore light brown jackets and trousers (looking like khaki) with long naval-type canvas gaiters, but retaining the distinctive red hackle in the tropical helmet. The 72nd Highlanders when fighting in India, 1879 (77*i*) wear khaki jackets with loops on the chest to take cartridges. The nether-wear was tartan trews and hose. Officers of the Gordon Highlanders in India, 1896 (79*h*) wear a khaki jacket, cut away in the front in a Highland fashion and wear a khaki helmet and spats. The kilt, sporran and hose are Highland and so is the sword which has a service cross hilt with attached red tuft. A private of the Queen's Own Cameron Highlanders in the Sudan, 1899 (79*l*) wears a similar dress with the cutaway jacket, helmet and spats, but kilt, sporran and hose as full dress. A private of the Black Watch in South Africa, 1900 (75*k*) wears a khaki apron over his kilt and his white equipment is toned down to the buff leather. The rest of his dress is khaki and only the red hackle and the hose give spots of colour.

The officer of the Northumberland Fusiliers, 1901 (59*g*) has a complete khaki uniform with brown equipment and boots but the regimental distinction is the V-shaped red stripe on the pugri, signifying '5', the old regimental number. In 1902 'universal drab' was ordered for wear at home. An officer of the Royal Irish Fusiliers (67*g*) wears this service drab, as for home use, with peaked cap but breeches of a regimental shade and puttees.

The First World War was fought completely in khaki uniforms; the private of the King's Own Scottish Borderers (97*m*) wears a glengarry as the only Scottish token in a service dress. An officer of the same regiment on the same plate does have a cutaway jacket as well as the glengarry. He wears his badges of rank on his gauntlet cuffs. The officer of the Cameronian (Scottish Rifles) (98*g*) wears his glengarry and black equipment as may be expected for a rifle regiment. Officers and men of the Seaforths, the Gordons and the Argyll and Sutherland Highlanders (80, 87, 88) all show the khaki Scottish 'doublet' and aprons, the glengarries and hose being the only regimental distinctions to show.

The officer of the South Wales Borderers (32g) shows the accepted dress with rank markings on the sleeves, as does that of the officer of the Devonshire Regiment (22g), while the officer of The King's Royal Rifle Corps, 1915 (91m) shows the khaki dress with the black buttons and equipment. It is said that the officer's black equipment had changed about 1908 to brown and that the private should have red backing to his cap badge. It will be noticed that the officer has a red cord boss on his cap. The officer of the Rifle Brigade (93) is also said to have had brown boots after 1908.

The Royal Artillery

In ancient times the artillery was stored in the Tower of London and looked after by the Master Gunner of the Ordnance whose post went back to the Middle Ages. But there was no organized body of artillerymen. In fact the men who fired the cannon were employed on a different footing and were not in the regular army but were part of the Board of Ordnance. When Charles II finally returned to England in 1660, cannon and other types of artillery were still stored in the Tower as well as in forts around England and Wales, with the men in charge being little more than custodians. In 1661 the number of gunners was 48 but this number gradually increased until in 1670 there were 103 fee'd gunners. Scotland also had a few gunners for its artillery. Documents of the period of Charles II and James II note that the gunners wore red coats guarded with black velvet 'as the Yeomen of the Guard at London'. A portrait by Godfrey Kneller depicts Anthony Payne as such a gunner with a dull red garment guarded with black but no crown, letters or device as worn by the Yeomen.

Richard Simkin did not illustrate this dress, possibly because he took most of his illustrations from the *Dress of the Royal Artillery* by R. J. Macdonald covering the period of 1625 1897 and did little research elsewhere. Thus the officer which Simkin depicts for 1685 (101a) is based on one which Macdonald dates as 1660 1702, where our artist gives red cuffs when the original had orange cuffs, and based on the information 'coats of blue with brass buttons and lined with orange bayes and hatts with orange silk galore'. This being the dress of the Netherlands artillery as is that of the matross in the same plate. By the end of William's reign the English gunners were wearing red or crimson coats faced with blue, following the normal infantry dress and into Queen Anne's time still with the scarlet and blue as expected for Royal troops. But by 1714 the House of Stuart had given place to the Hanoverians and George I brought to Great Britain his own ideas. Thus when the Royal Regiment of Artillery was formed in 1716, the gunners wore blue coats faced with scarlet. On the same plate Simkin shows an officer (101c) of 1710, based on Macdonald's officer 1702–14, but there is no doubt that scarlet cloth with blue for facings was being worn in 1713 and the sources for Macdonald include at least two officers' portraits known to be engineers.

The 1742 *Cloathing* book produced for the Duke of Cumberland brought for the first time a series of coloured plates showing the different uniforms of infantry privates. There was no original print for the artillery but the copy once preserved at Woolwich had two additional water-colours showing a gunner with a field-stave and an officer with a fusil. The gunner has the dark blue coat, waistcoat and breeches with red cuffs, lapels and turn-backed skirts. The officer (102a) has blue lapels and his waistcoat and breeches are scarlet, and he has gold buttons and gilt lace on the edge of his waistcoat. As his weapon was a flint-lock musket he keeps his ammunition in the white pouch on his white waist-belt. There is a gilt crown on his pouch. Officers in 1750 were ordered to mount guards in their regimentals with their 'fusees and cartouch boxes'. White spatterdashes (or long gaiters) were worn to protect the legs from mud and splashes, but officers were expected to provide their men with a pair of white stockings in which they were to parade at all times when not under arms. Black spatterdashes were also supplied and these showed the dirt less than the white ones.

Normally cavalry officers wore the crimson sash over the left shoulder so that the ends did not interfere with drawing of swords, but the artillery changed to the right shoulder (102b). As a help, an order of 1751 stated that when on duty officers were to wear the knots of their sashes in the left pocket with the ends hanging out, in the hope of leaving the sword-hilt free. This officer is based on three portraits by Macdonald, one of which is a later date and none showed the heavy boots. The officer's coat now had gold lace around the lapels, the turned-down collar and the frame of the slashed cuff. A Master-General's order of May 1758 stated that the uniform waistcoats were to be of plain scarlet cloth without lace but by 1760 buff waistcoats and breeches were being worn in the army. Officers also had a gold shoulder-knot on the right but this was changed in 1770 to a fringed epaulette on the right. Also the plain red lapels took on many gold-edged buttonholes as did the cuffs and collar.

The buff waistcoats and breeches were ordered to be changed to white in 1768 but officers do not seem to have obeyed this order, as it was repeated in 1772 when white did become the rule. In 1770 the awkward shoulder-sash of officers was changed to a neat crimson waist-sash. In 1772 it was ordered that as black stocks were not a uniform part of the dress of the Royal Artillery, officers were to provide their men with white ones. No doubt this looked more elegant, but they presumably did not serve the correct purpose and in 1788 all artillerymen were ordered to have stocks of black leather 'instead of tape'. The officer's coat which had gold lace loops was to be made plain in 1782 (103a).

An interesting head-dress was adopted by artillery officers for service in the Low Countries in 1794. This was a hat, the brim of which turned up at the sides, which had three gilt chains around the crown with a rosette on the left and a fur crest over the top (103a). The coat on campaign had the lapels loose and casually fastened at the third and fourth button down. The gunner at this time also wore a kind of top hat (104a) not only in Europe but also in America. General A. C. Mercer describes it as of 'the true Mother Shipton breed'. There was a yellow band round the crown as well as a yellow edge and a loop up to the black cockade with a scarlet tuft rising in front. Men wore white breeches and black gaiters to the knee but loose white trousers were also worn. These hats were replaced later by the cocked hat of the 'bicorn' type (104b) and by the end of the eighteenth century the coat was closed across the front, hiding the waistcoat. The double-breasted garment could have the top buttons undone and the scarlet lining turned down to make two small triangles (103b). The officer depicted here is based on the colour print of 1799 from the *British Military Library*. The gunner of the period (104b) is from a contemporary print by Edward Scott and shows the bicorn hat with the plain white feather of the

artillery. The white belt over the left shoulder has a red cord which held a
small powder horn and the two brass pickers for plugging the touch-hole of
cannon can be seen on the chest.

The 'stove-pipe' shako introduced into the British Army c. 1800 was
worn by the Royal Artillery and the yellow braid of the loops on the single-
breasted jacket was shaped as 'bastion' or 'spear-headed'. The red
shoulder-straps and cuffs also had the yellow braid. Men's nether-wear
could be white breeches and black gaiters or the all-white trousers worn in
the Peninsular War. Officers continued to have the cocked hat worn 'fore
and aft' but on service after 1812 had the 'Belgic' cap, the high false-fronted
shako, now also worn by the men. The new pattern had plaited cords across
the front and hanging tassels on the right, which were gold for officers and
yellow for the men. The officers had a white feather hackle on the left and
the men a white tuft (102b). The officer's full dress now had many gold lace
buttonholes on the chest, collar, cuffs and pockets. They also had white
breeches and hessian boots but for service and similar conditions there
were light blue or blue-grey overalls or trousers.

After Waterloo a new broad-topped shako was taken into wear, a style
possibly inspired by the French or German patterns. Simkin shows a
circular gilt plate for an officer with three cannon on it (103c) but this does
not agree with known shakos and badges which carry the 'GR' cypher
within a Garter bearing 'Royal Regiment of Artillery', all under a crown.
The short jacket had red lapels shaped like a lancer's plastron front with
gold-wire-embroidered loops to the buttons. Junior officers had but one
epaulette on the right but field officers had one on each shoulder. The back
of this jacket had a 'tommy back', a triangle of lace between two buttons in
the small of the back. A portrait of Lieutenant-Colonel Debrisay shows the
white waist-belt being worn over the crimson waist-sash. The same jacket
could be worn buttoned over with the tops turned down showing the red,
as in a portrait of Lieutenant-Colonel Henry Shrapnel who invented that
type of ammunition.

Up to 1827 the Royal Artillery full dress, dress and undress coatee were
single-breasted with red collar and cuffs (white skirt turn-backs) with
pointed lace loops on the collar, round cuffs and pocket flaps. The trousers
were sky blue with gold lace side seams for full dress but with two-inch
scarlet stripes for undress. In September 1827 the lace on the coat was
changed to oakleaf and acorn embroidery and the skirts were now lined
with red. Blue cloth was used for the trousers. Prints and pictures c. 1828
show the three-button flap on the cuff (105a), Simkin using here a Hull
print for guidance. This shows the new fringeless epaulette on the left
shoulder as worn by a company officer, an innovation which was
discontinued in November 1830. Once again in 1830 the officer's dress coat
was changed and the expensive embroidery gave place to gold lace with
rectangular loops $1\frac{1}{2}$ inches broad. Captains and below were now allowed to
wear an epaulette on each shoulder, now 'boxed' – that is to say, with
hanging bullion fixed and not in loose pieces. The grenade was worn on the
strap of the epaulette.

When Queen Victoria came to the throne she permitted in 1838 a change
back to the gold embroidery and this ornamentation was reduced on the
officers' garments (105b). The plain skirts had an embroidered grenade at
the bottom where the linings turned back. White trousers had been worn in
the summer months but in 1841 they were no longer to be worn on home

stations. The dress of the gunner (107*a*) had hardly changed from William IV's day and in fact Simkin/Macdonald seem to have based this uniform on an 1828 print but showing the red skirts. The white pouch at the back carries a gilt or yellow-metal crown which was seen as early as 1742 (the pouch was later moved to the centre of the back) but the shape of the shako had altered slightly with the period. The white gloves worn by staff-sergeants were of white leather but those of lower rank were of white worsted. The other ranks' coat or coatee in its last days had an embroidered grenade on each side of the collar and a small button at the meeting of each skirt lining.

A new pattern cap with brass chin-scales was introduced in 1844 — the 'Albert' shako (107*b*) with a special plate in front as well as a white hair brush. The double-breasted coatee with grenades on the collar continued in wear and the dark blue trousers had broad red side-stripes. The small white pouch on the right side of the waist-belt held percussion caps, which indicate that a new pattern firearm had replaced the flint-lock.

At the time of the Crimean War there were many changes in the uniforms throughout the British Army, an important one being the abolition of the expensive coatee and epaulettes of an officer and the introduction of the tunic in 1855. At the same time the fragile shako was changed to a fur busby. This cap was basically the same as that worn by the Royal Horse Artillery, black sable for officers with a scarlet bag on the right side of the cap, but what did differ was the position of the white goat-hair plume which was worn on the left side by the Foot Artillery (108*a* and *b*). The new tunic was of dark blue cloth with a scarlet collar and edgings. The gold cord and tracing on the cuffs of officers indicated certain rankings, but the badges on the collar indicated precise ranks. This uniform was well depicted in contemporary publications and the officer shown by Simkin is after a large print by W. Jones & Co., well-known tailors of the period. The gunner (108*a*) has a simplified version of the officers' uniform but with yellow worsted instead of gold for the Austrian knot on the sleeves, the collar and shoulder-straps (except in the case of sergeants and above, who were allowed gold lace). The small white pouch for percussion caps had now moved from the waist-belt to the centre of the shoulder-belt. It will be seen that now the grenades are not on the collar but they were embroidered on the shoulder-straps with a regimental number.

Basically these uniforms remained the same up to the days of Richard Simkin, with the exception of the head-dress which changed to the helmet in 1878. This helmet covered with blue cloth had gilt fittings, brass for the men, with a spike on top, a large regimental plate in front and a chin-chain. By 1881 the spike was replaced by a ball, a much more convenient ornament when dealing with horses. The Crown of Queen Victoria was changed in 1902 for a Tudor Crown. When badges of rank were moved from the officers' collar to their shoulder-cords *c.* 1881, silver grenades were placed on the collar and other ranks had brass grenades on both sides of their collar.

As all fighting troops had to employ a person to transmit messages over a distance, as in the case of infantry where the drummer had a beat which carried to the furthest ranks or the trumpeter of cavalry whose sound reached the extent of the mounted squadron, so the artillery had the need of such 'music' (not a band) to transmit understood calls or signals. Thus the

Overleaf:
109.
Engineer officer, 1710

110.
Royal Engineers, 1790, officer

ENGINEER OFFICER.
1710.

Plate 109

ROYAL ENGINEERS.
1790.

Plate 110

ROYAL ENGINEERS.
1846.

Plate 111

ROYAL ENGINEERS.
1860.

Plate 112

artillery at St Quentin, 1557, paid a shilling a day to the 'drumme' and 'phife' for their services. Much later the kettledrum carriage was favoured by artillery trains, not only to convey the beat but also to sound 'tattoo' at the end of the day in camp. When the Royal Regiment of Artillery was formed, two drummers were sanctioned for each company, over and above the kettledrummer and trumpeters.

An oil-painting by John Wootton in the Royal Collection shows a drummer and fifer c. 1756. Following the infantry practice these 'musicians' wear a type of grenadier cap — an all-red mitre cap with a shield bearing the Ordnance Arms (three black canon-balls on a white 'chief' and three gold cannon on blue) on the main front of the cap, and on the small red turned-up flap a mortar surrounded by weapons or rays. The coat is red with blue facings — following the normal 'reversed' facings for drummers. The blue lapels, sleeves and seams have a complicated blue lace which has yellow edges with red and yellow dots. The back view of the fifer shows the short hanging sleeves as worn by musicians at that time, the ends finishing with yellow tassels. The drummer has a blue waistcoat with much yellow trimming and blue breeches but the fifer has red breeches (the waistcoat is not visible) and long black gaiters.

By 1788 the drummers were wearing white waistcoats and breeches, while the head-dress had changed to a fur cap. In 1795 a contemporary writer noted that the drummers had grenadier fur caps which means that the tradition of such head-dresses was continued, having possibly changed in 1768 when infantry drummers made the change. Little information is available at this time but it is possible that artillery drummers continued to wear the red coats in changing style of fashion, and then adopted the various shakos as they appeared. A band had been raised for the artillery and they may have had red plumes in their head-dress, but the drummers would be expected to have the white plumes like the gunners.

Drummers and boys were expected to augment the Royal Artillery Band and it is not surprising when a water-colour by George Scharf of 1825 shows a red-coated boy among the white-coated bandsmen. The trumpeter depicted by Simkin (106a) shows the normal shako with the long white feather plume and the double-breasted scarlet coatee with epaulettes. There were mounted trumpeters who accompanied the senior officers, and in prints of the 1840s their red coats stand out. A French general sketched a trumpeter of the Royal Artillery in marching order when in Gibraltar in 1847. The double-breasted scarlet coatee had blue collar, cuffs, flaps and striped wings edged yellow with grenades on the collar. He wore the 'Albert' shako and his dark blue trousers had stripes of red cloth.

Preceding page:
111.
Royal Engineers, 1846, officer
112.
Royal Engineers, 1860, officer

The system of 'reversed facings' for infantry drummers had ceased in 1831 and drummers' lace (varying for each regiment) was thought to be sufficient as a distinction, but the Royal Artillery continued to wear the red coat until a letter from the Deputy Adjutant General, Royal Artillery in July 1849 stated 'that the artillery is the only exception wherein drummers and trumpeters clothes are a different colour to that of the men and it is desirable that the appearance of all ranks in the field should be assimilated. I would beg to recommend that they may be clothed in all respects as the men with the exception of the wings as at present, the only alteration of which will be a strap of scarlet cloth instead of the blue and this may be carried into effect in nine days.'

One of the most striking uniforms, in the Royal Artillery at least, was that of the drum-major in the 1840s after he had acquired a most imposing bearskin cap. This (106b) is based on a contemporary print by A. Comer and follows its colouring carefully. The full bearskin cap has an enormous crimson feather plume which begins on the right side, continues across the top and finishes half-way down on the left side. The drum-major wears the scarlet coat with blue collar and cuffs, a plastron-like pair of lapels heavily ornamented with gold lace. His two epaulettes have deep bullion, and the light blue trousers (which changed to dark blue cloth in 1847) have gold lace and much embroidery on the thighs. He carries a sword with a white belt over the right shoulder, a crimson waist-sash and the blue drum-major's sash over the left shoulder, this having the Ordnance badge under the Crown with other distinctions as well as the two token drum-sticks. With his white gloves, the silver-and-gilt-topped staff and his curling moustache and beard, he was an impressive figure when leading the drums and the band.

Drums and fifes as duty instruments were abolished in 1848, although four drummers and eight fifers plus three trumpeters were retained on the Headquarters staff. The drum-major was allowed to hold his appointment in the drum and fife band until 1856 when it was abolished.

Royal Engineers

As the artillery men were more than occupied with the movement and firing of guns, the task of erecting platforms, siege positions, places of fortification and aspects of mining was given to a small group of qualified men – the engineers. They were an important section of the Board of Ordnance and as they acted as officers, the actual labouring and work was undertaken by the infantry or any able-bodied men who could be pressed into service. Many officers in the army at the beginning of the eighteenth century wore their own version of a military dress, blue coats being favoured as workmanlike. A portrait of Captain John Romer, an engineer, c. 1710, depicts him in a dark blue coat with cuffs and lining of red with gold buttons. He also wore a cuirass beneath his coat, a popular article worn by engineer officers who were much exposed to enemy fire. This portrait has served as inspiration to Richard Simkin who has created a full-length figure (109) from a bust, which, although possible, is not borne out by fact.

However, by 1757 engineer officers were given military rank and their own uniform. As a contemporary account states, 'their uniform is red, lapelled with black velvet, with buff waistcoat and breeches, richly laced'. Portraits show that the lace was gold as were the buttons. There was no special gold lace but the epaulettes were gold and the buttons eventually carried the Ordnance Arms. The crimson silk sash was now worn around the waist.

In December 1782 it was directed that in future the uniform of engineers was to be a blue coat faced with black velvet, lined with white and with white waistcoat and breeches. Portraits show that the coat was worn open, and the Ordnance pattern of buttons was worn. Simkin's picture (110) is dated 1790, but it must be of a later date as the coat is buttoned down to the waist. Simkin's source seems to be the half-length picture of Captain W. Fyers, but he served until 1799 and so the added details are suspect. In Flanders officers wore a round hat with a bearskin over the top, no doubt

Overleaf:
113.
Artificer company, Gibraltar, 1786, sergeant

114.
Royal Military Artificers
a 1787, sergeant-major
b 1787, drummer

SOLDIER ARTIFICER COMPANY.
(GIBRALTAR)
SERGEANT-1786.

Plate 113

ROYAL MILITARY ARTIFICERS.
(SERGEANT MAJOR-1787.

ROYAL MILITARY ARTIFICERS.
1787.

Plate 114 a   **Plate 114 b**

ROYAL MILITARY ARTIFICERS.
1793.

Plate 115

ROYAL MILITARY ARTIFICERS
SERGEANT-1808.

Plate 116

similar to that worn by artillery officers in the same campaign. This dress was worn after the turn of the century with a slight alteration in the cut of the coat and a flatter cock to the hat, which had a white feather plume over the left eye. White breeches and black boots to below the knee were worn.

In 1812 the blue coat was changed to a double-breasted one of scarlet, now with garter-blue velvet and gold embroidery – much more expensive than the older coat. The gilt buttons now carried the 'GR' cypher within the Garter. The officers who had to serve with the Sappers and Miners did not wear the cocked hat but the false-fronted shako as worn by the men, though with a gilt plate, gold cords and a white feather hackle. The coat was usually buttoned over with the top of the lapels being turned down to form triangles. However, for full dress the blue lapels could be fastened back to form a plastron. The zigzag design on the lace made a striking pattern. After Waterloo a single-breasted coatee was worn with no lace down the front but loops on the collar and round cuffs. The cocked hat was still high with a large white feather plume.

By 1830 the pattern of the coatee had changed again to a double-breasted garment with three-buttoned flaps on the cuffs. The collar had four-sided gold loops set on a blue patch but the three gold patches on the cuff flap were set on red. The skirt ornament was a gold exploding grenade on dark blue. The uniform was now more or less formalized until the Crimean War, but there were minor changes like the white feather plume being made mushroom-shaped in 1845. Once again, officers serving with the Sappers and Miners wore the men's head-dress, the 'Albert' shako. White overalls were worn in summer. Simkin depicts an officer of 1846 (111) based on the portrait of Whitworth Porter which appears in his *History of the Corps of the Royal Engineers*. At this time both the Royal Artillery and the Royal Engineers were granted the single battle honour '*Ubique*' and the Royal Arms.

In 1856 the Royal Engineer officers and the Royal Sappers and Miners were formed into one unit and known as the Royal Engineers. Now with the sweeping changes in British uniform, the corps also changed the coatee for the tunic and in 1857, to conform with the men, officers serving with them wore their fur busby. The officers' version was in sealskin eight inches high in front and nine-and-a-half behind. On the right side hung a bright blue cloth bag, and on the left a gilt grenade held a six-inch plume of white goat's hair. The single-breasted tunic was scarlet with blue velvet collar and cuffs as well as edgings. Senior officers had flat gold lace and braid on the collar and the Austrian knot on the sleeve (112). Junior officers had less gold braid on the collar where a combination of Stars and/or Crowns served to distinguish the various ranks.

Other ranks had red tunics with blue worsted plush facings and yellow lace on cuffs and elsewhere. Sergeants were allowed blue velvet facings and gold lace. The 'Albert' shako had been worn for a short time after the Crimean War but the fur busby soon took over. Trousers were of the dark Oxford mixture, almost black, and officers had side-stripes of gold lace for full dress and scarlet for undress. Abroad, white linen trousers were permitted in warm weather.

In 1878 the helmet was taken into wear – dark blue with gilt fittings. Originally, there was a spike on the top, but it was found not to be desirable when working close to horses and was changed to a ball-fitting. The Royal Arms helmet plate was like that of the Royal Artillery but without the

Preceding page:
115.
Royal Military Artificers, 1793, private

116.
Royal Military Artificers, 1808, sergeant

'gun'. This dress is what the Royal Engineers would have worn at the time when Simkin made his paintings.

Military Artificers

Although the officers of the Royal Engineers were responsible for fortifications, bridging and many tasks needed to assist the fighting forces, they had no workmen of their own and had to employ whatever troops or civilians were available. However, when abroad, especially in Gibraltar, strictly controlled workmen were needed and companies of soldier-artificers were formed as early as 1772.

The earliest information on these uniforms seems to be that of 1786 and in fact comes from T. Connolly's *History of the Royal Sappers and Miners* (1855). The writer was a quarter-master-sergeant who researched into regimental orders and the official papers in the Public Records Office and his results cannot be bettered. It is true that his colour plates contain some reconstituted material but they are a firm basis for Richard Simkin's water-colours which are copied most carefully for both the artificers and the men of the Sappers and Miners.

The soldier artificer of 1786 had a red coat with the collar turned down and round cuffs of yellow-orange laced all round with narrow red ferreting. The flat brass buttons are said to have borne the Ordnance device of three guns and three cannon balls. The waistcoat was white laced with yellow ferreting, and the breeches blue at first, then changed to white. The long black gaiters had small brass buttons as on the waistcoat. Above the black cockade on the hat was a black feather. Sergeants had clothing of a better quality with gold lace and a crimson waist-sash under the coat (113).

In 1787 a corps of Royal Military Artificers and Labourers was raised in England and they wore blue coats with black cloth facings (thus following the black velvet facings already established by the Royal Engineer officers). The double-breasted coat had yellow braid, following the Board of Ordnance practice, set in 'bastion loops' for the buttons (114a). The cocked hat had a short red feather. The sergeants wore gold lace and the crimson-waist-sash as before. The drummer (114b) dressed as the artificers but had his coat covered in special livery braid as Ordnance men, appearing as yellow with red and blue devices. The laced wings had a yellow fringe.

The Gibraltar company was absorbed in 1797 but it is not known whether they wore their red coats to this date or changed earlier to the blue. In 1792 the cocked hat had been changed to a black felt round hat (similar to that worn by the Royal Artillery) with a yellow band round the crown and as a loop up to the black cockade, above which was a scarlet plume (115). A similar top hat without the loop or plume had been worn for working craftsmen. The Ordnance lace of drummers was simplified to a mixed lace of black, red, and yellow worsted.

In 1797 a new pattern of cocked hat was taken into wear; this was with black binding around the edge but the cockade and loop were retained. The short red feather was now changed to a white hackle plume eight inches long. The long-skirted coat was changed to a jacket and as the front was closed, the waistcoat was not seen and lapels discontinued. The single-breasted garment had yellow frogging or loops, and for the first time the drummer wore a scarlet coat or jacket.

Overleaf:
117.
Royal Sappers and Miners
a　1813, sapper
b　1823, bugle-major

118.
Royal Sappers and Miners, 1854, bugle-major

119.
Royal Engineers, 1860, bandsman

ROYAL SAPPERS & MINERS
SAPPER – 1813.

Plate 117 a

ROYAL SAPPERS & MINERS.
BUGLE MAJOR – 1823.

Plate 117 b

ROYAL SAPPERS & MINERS.
BUGLE MAJOR – 1854.

Plate 118

ROYAL ENGINEERS.
1860.

Plate 119

a ROYAL WAGGON TRAIN, 1812.

b MILITARY TRAIN, PRIVATE, 1864.

c ARMY SERVICE CORPS. OFFICER. WAGGON and TEAM.

d MILITARY TRAIN, SERJEANT, 1864.

e MILITARY TRAIN. OFFICER, 1864.

f ARMY SERVICE CORPS. DRIVER, 1874.

g CONTROL DEPARTMENT, ARMY SERVICE CORPS. OFFICER, 1874.

Plate 120

When the British infantry adopted the stove-pipe shako the artificers were not far behind and took it into wear in 1802, still with the white feather or tuft in front (116). In 1806 three artificer companies were formed in Malta and they wore a very similar uniform but made of cotton manufactured on the island, which was not only better suited to the local weather but cheaper than the cloth version. Queues were cut off *c.* 1808 and hairstyles made more modern.

Sappers and Miners

In March 1813 the title was changed from Royal Military Artificers, or Sappers and Miners as they were occasionally named, to the Royal Sappers and Miners, which brought a change of dress. During the Peninsular War the blue coats of the artificers stood out among the red-coated infantry, even sometimes being taken for French, so it was decided to give the new body red coats with blue facings. The new shako with the false front generally introduced in 1812 was now taken into wear with a white feather or tuft on the left side (117*a*). The red coat had a blue collar, cuffs and shoulder-straps edged with yellow braid or tape for the men, gold for sergeants and above. The bastion-ended loops continued. White breeches and knee gaiters may have been worn for full dress but in the field overalls of grey or white were worn with short gaiters.

After taking part in the Occupation of Paris the Sappers and Miners acquired in 1817 a new shako somewhat of the French pattern with the white plume now rising from the front. Drums were abolished in the corps and replaced by bugles. The 1823 illustration of the bugle-major (117*b*) shows him in a cocked hat with the normal white feather and the scarlet coat with the broad blue plastron.

In 1818 the companies in France substituted yellow woollen epaulettes for the plain shoulder-straps, but at the expense of the men themselves. In 1823 the brass buckles which had been worn for many years on their belts were replaced by proper belt-plates bearing the Crown over a Garter with the name of the corps enclosing the Royal Cypher. Early in 1825 the white breeches, long gaiters and low shoes still worn occasionally under overalls were now replaced by light blue trousers with scarlet side-stripes and short Wellington boots. The elaborate loops on the front of the coatee were discontinued and white turn-backs were added to the skirts of the coatee but the pointed loops continued on the collar and cuffs.

A new pattern shako was now ten-and-a-half inches high with a goose feather a foot long coming from an 'exploded grenade' holder and the gold or yellow bands around the top were replaced with black. In 1830 yet another shako appeared, one of a much reduced form and with yellow lines and tassels which were looped up on the chest. Scales for the first time were worn under the chin. In July 1832 the motto '*UBIQUE*' and '*Quo fas et gloria ducunt*' was granted to the Corps (as it was to the Artillery and the Engineers) and new cap and breast plates were made. The cap-lines of 1830 were now abolished.

In 1833 men's coatees were changed from scarlet to the red of infantrymen but the buglers were allowed to retain the scarlet with the lace of the privates. The coatee now had two rows of buttons down the front and the cuffs now had upright flaps. There were also imitation epaulettes made of stamped brass. Trousers now became dark Oxford mixture instead of light blue but still with the red stripes down the side seams. In 1837 the scarlet of the coatee was restored and later in the year the shoulder-belt of staff-sergeants was changed to a waist-belt.

The 'Albert' shako was introduced about 1844, as may be seen on the bugle-major (118), who continued to wear the coatee with the broad blue plastron front with the long pointed gold loops above his white waist-belt. Underneath the belt he has a crimson sash with long tassels on the left thigh. The small blocked epaulettes were changed in April 1846 for loose twisted cords three inches long from a raised corded crescent, and the shoulder-straps were of blue cloth. The coatee collar for all ranks which had a three-sided piece of scarlet cloth at the back was now made all blue with rectangular loops. This was the dress until 1856 when the Royal Sappers and Miners became part of the Corps of Royal Engineers.

There had been buglers in the Royal Sappers and Miners who in 1836 formed into a Depot Brass Band, and when the Corps of Royal Engineers was formed at Chatham it was converted into a Regimental Band as from August 1856. The uniform of the band was very distinctive (119). They all wore large plain black bearskin caps with gilt chin-chains. They had white tunics with bright blue collars, cuffs and edgings with much gold lace and embroidery, especially down the front and on the two back seams. White waist-belts were worn, except by the bandmaster who had one of officers' pattern. The red or crimson trousers had gold lace side-stripes. These striking tunics and trousers were replaced in 1866 by scarlet trousers and dark trousers although the tall fur caps continued in wear for many more years. In 1928 when bands were regaining their full dress, an Army Order stated that the busby would be worn instead of the fur bearskin.

Military Train and Army Service Corps

It is so easy to think of an army as fighting troops that one is liable to overlook the fact that a successful fighting force needs an efficient supply source and services like medical staff, food and its delivery, weapons and ammunition and so on. This was the task of the Army Service Corps, later made Royal and today the Royal Corps of Transport, who catered for all these needs.

In the days when transport was commandeered locally or paid for by civilian drivers, no reliance could be placed on adequate delivery in the time and place of war. The Georgian kings were also closely connected with the Hanoverian Army and this Continental force in the third quarter of the eighteenth century had a military train for its technical troops authorized by George III. Thus when a Corps of Waggoners was to be established in Britain, experience was available to Captain James Poole in 1794 who took his men to the Netherlands to serve under the Duke of York. But as the campaign was short and disastrous, the Corps of Waggoners was disbanded within the year. The men had a red jacket closed in front, with blue collar and yellow cuffs. The buttons had a Crown over 'GR' and on the upper arm was a blue cloth badge with a red number, ranging from 1 to 100. The Hanoverian waggoners had armlets with initials of a different colour which

may have been the inspiration. The British corps also had long blue woollen
trousers, blue woollen stockings, either very strong boots or high-
quartered shoes with a leather cap, possibly turning up in front with a
leather peak and folding, as was popular then.

August 1799 saw another Corps of Waggoners being raised under
Lieutenant-Colonel Digby Hamilton. It was then named the Royal Waggon
Corps and expected to rank in the Army on the continent of Europe only,
following the West India Regiment. In 1803 it was reranked as a mounted
corps immediately after the 29th Dragoons. Once again the Netherlands was
to be the battlefield, and the corps continued to serve not only in the
Peninsula but at Waterloo, gaining these battle honours.

There were several changes in uniform until their disbandment in 1833
but there is little documentation for the first dress. Charles Hamilton Smith
made a rough sketch of the Royal Waggon Corps c. 1800 showing a short
blue jacket with white lace. The facings appear as either black or dark blue,
perhaps indicating a connection with the Commissariat at that time. By the
time that they had moved into the 'cavalry' precedence, the blue jacket was
noted as faced with red and silver lace for the officers, white for the men.
The breeches were blue and the helmet the light dragoon pattern.

In 1811 the uniform was changed to red jackets with blue facings and the
best-known print of this new uniform is the early 1812 print by C. H. Smith.
R. Simkin follows the original print very closely, but there are doubts about
Smith's original drawing although he is supposed to have worked 'after the
regulation'. The new shako is drawn somewhat like that of the infantry but
has the plume centre front as expected for cavalry and not at the side as the
infantry placed the plume on the new shako. As the waggoners were still in
the cavalry precedence, it would seem that they should have been wearing
the light dragoon shako. Later pictures do show this light dragoon type
with white cords. The officer wore a cocked hat as did 'non-fighting'
officers like the Medical Staff and Engineers. His jacket is very similar to
that of the men, showing little evidence of elaborate lace. The men's jacket
had three rows of white-metal buttons down the front. A lace-maker of the
period says 'no wings or epaulettes' and this agrees with C. H. Smith. The
skirt ornaments were of 'silver double crowsfoot' on blue.

After Waterloo the coatee is known to have had much silver lace on the
front for officers and on the sleeves as well but still no epaulettes. The three
rows of buttons had so much silver lace linking them that it made a solid
front. The officers' undress sabretache had silver mounts of crown over the
Royal Cypher with the battle honours on scrolls below. By 1828 silver
epaulettes were at last being worn by officers on their single-breasted
jacket.

In 1830 the officers' silver lace changed to gold as in the case of all regular
officers in the Army and a new double-breasted coatee was worn with a
single gold loop on each side of the collar and one on each cuff. The broad-
topped shako was worn until 1833 with either the upright white-and-red
plume or the drooping red-and-white horse-hair type. The 'target'
ornament on the early shako changed to a gilt 'Maltese Cross' plate in the
reign of William IV.

When the Royal Waggon Train was disbanded in 1833, there was no
pressing need for such a corps until the Crimean War and it was in January
1855 that the new Land Transport Corps was formed. It was to be a military
corps (not civilian like the Commissariat), the officers being classed as

cavalry and the men issued with carbine, bayonet and revolver. Colonel McMurdo formed the corps in the field and in September 1855 it was split into two battalions, which by March 1856 consisted of six infantry divisions and one for cavalry.

The Land Transport Corps wore a distinctive uniform, of which Richard Simkin did make a painting but it is not included in this plate (120). A dark blue double-breasted tunic was worn by the men and the six infantry battalions wore the distinguishing colours of their facings, 1st light blue, 2nd red, 3rd yellow, 4th white, 5th grey and the 6th green. The head-dress was a broad-brimmed slouch hat which turned up at the side where a rosette of the divisional colour was worn. The waist-belt with the snake-hook fastening and the other leather equipment was light tan, as were the high boots. Obviously footwear varied under the service conditions. The dark blue trousers had broad side-stripes. Undress caps were worn, peaked for officers but apparently with no badge, although the men had 'L.T.C.' on their peakless forage caps.

As the Land Transport Corps had been formed in the Crimea, it was decided in August 1856 to raise a body for the Army at home, to be named the Military Train. Colonel McMurdo was given this task and took over the Land Transport Corps, which withered away. Eventually the new body was in 1869 placed under the Control Department. The battalions served on many foreign stations – Canada, India and China. In fact, the active service of the 2nd Battalion won them two Victoria Crosses while the 1st Battalion in China gained them the battle honours of 'Taku Forts' and 'Pekin'. Then in 1863 the whole of the Military Train was authorized to bear 'Lucknow' on appointments, while in 1865–7 the Military Train impressed the Maoris of New Zealand when they made a successful cavalry charge. There had been three battalions, later increased to six, with a depot at Bristol.

The uniform of the Military Train had a blue tunic edged with white. The collar and shoulder-straps were also white but the cuffs were blue. The leather equipment was light brown and the waist-belts had snake-hook fastenings. The black shako had a falling black horse-hair plume and the cap lines were also black. In front was a metal (gilt or brass) plate with the words MILITARY TRAIN and having the number of the battalion pierced in the middle. When changes were made from a battalion basis to those of troops, the number was discontinued and replaced by the Royal Crest – the Lion on the Crown.

Simkin shows the uniforms of this period with great accuracy. At this time official photographs had been made of the Military Train which left little doubt as to what was worn. The men's trousers were dark blue with broad white stripes down the sides (120b). The sergeant (120b) has a similar uniform but of better quality with gold chevrons and a steel sword and scabbard with a knot of light brown leather. It will be noted that his trouser stripes do not reach the ankle because at that time black leather bootings were worn. The mounted officer (120) also has the leather bootings and white stripes but on nether-wear in full dress the side-stripes were of gold lace. The gold-edged pouch-belt had a backing of pale Russia leather.

By 1874 the leather booting had been discontinued for black high boots and pantaloons. A reorganization scheme from 1868 onwards saw the creation of a Control Department which, among other branches, covered supply and transport, now to be called the Army Service Corps. So in December 1869 a new corps, the Army Service Corps was to be created with volunteers from the Military Train, the Commissariat and the Staff Corps, as well as others. The new companies not only saw service at home but went to Canada and the Ashanti War.

The blue tunic was now simplified with a blue collar for the men (velvet for the officers who also had gold lace and embroidery on the collar and cuffs). Some officers had cocked hats, but those serving with the men of the Army Service Corps had an infantry type of shako with a blue and white ball (120g). The men or drivers had a blue tunic trimmed with white edging and braid (120e) and the breeches now had two narrow white stripes down the side seams. The waist-belt was still brown leather and the collar badge was a simple brass crown.

Once again in 1880 there was a change when the Commissariat and Transport Staff and Corps was organized to take over the Army Service Corps but in 1888 the Army Service Corps regained independence. The Commissariat and Transport of 1881 took the white facings back into wear and kept these until 1888. The new pattern helmet which replaced the shako had brass or gilt fittings with a spike on top, but in 1886 this was replaced by a ball-fitting. The black sheepskin for mounted officers had a white deckle-edge lining as may be seen in the Simkin plate (120c). A black undress sabretache with a gilt crown over 'VR' was worn up to the end of the century and was shown by Richard Simkin in his *Navy and Army Gazette* plate of 1897. This dress was worn up to the First World War and in 1918 the Army Service Corps was made Royal. Finally in 1965 reorganization saw it emerge as the Royal Corps of Transport.

The Royal Warrant, 1751

Extract from the Warrant dated 1 July 1751 'regulating the . . . Clothing, &c. and Rank or Number of Regiments of . . . Infantry'.

George R. – Our will and pleasure is, that the following regulations for the . . . clothing, &c. of our marching regiments of Foot . . . be duly observed and put in execution, at such times as these particulars are or shall be furnished . . .

No colonel to put his arms, crest, device, or livery, on any part of the appointments of the regiment under his command.

No part of the clothing or ornaments of the regiments to be altered after the following regulations are put in execution, but by us, or our Captain-General's permission . . .

Drummers' Clothing. The Drummers of all Royal Regiments are allow'd to wear the Royal Livery, viz. Red, lined, faced and lapelled on the Breast with Blue and laced with a Royal Lace. The Drummers of all the other Regts. are to be clothed with the Colour of the Facing of their Regts. lined, faced and Lapelled on the Breast with Red, and laced in such manner as the Colonel shall think fit for distinction sake, the Lace however being of the Colours of that on the Soldiers' Coats.

Grenadiers Caps. The front of the Grenadier caps is to be the same Colour as the Facings of the Regiment, with the King's Cypher embroidered, and Crown over it; the little Flaps to be Red with the White Horse & Motto over it, Nec Aspera Terrent; the back Part of the Cap to be Red, the turn-up to be the Colour of the Front with the Number of the Regiment in the middle Part behind. The Royal Regiment and the Six Old Corps differ from the foregoing Rule as specified hereafter . . .

1st Regiment or the Royal Regiment. In the centre of their Colours, the King's Cypher, within the Circle of St. Andrew and Crown over it, in the three Corners of the Second Colour, the Thistle and Crown . . . On the Grenadier Caps, the same device as in the Centre of the Colours, White Horse and the King's Motto over it, on the little Flap.

2d. Regiment or the Queen's Royal Regiment. In the Centre of each Colour the Queen's Cypher on a Red Ground, within the Garter, and Crown over it. In the three Corners of the Second Colour, the Lamb being the ancient Badge of the Regiment. On the Grenadier Caps the Queen's Cypher and Crown as in the Colours, White Horse & Motto Nec Aspera Terrent on the Flap . . .

3d. Regiment or the Buffs. In the centre of their colours, the Dragon being the ancient Badge, and the Rose and Crown in the Three Corners of their Second Colour. On the Grenadier Caps the Dragon, White Horse and King's Motto on the Flap.

4th Regiment or the King's Own Royal Regiment. In the centre of their Colours the King's Cypher on a Red Ground within the Garter, and Crown over it. In the three Corners of their Second Colour the Lyon of England being their ancient Badge. On the Grenadier Caps the King's Cypher as on the Colours and Crown over it (The White Horse and motto is given for these flaps and those of the following regiments).

5th Regiment. In the centre of their Colours, St. George Killing the Dragon, being their ancient Badge and in the three Corners of their Second Colour the Rose and Crown. On the Grenadier Caps, St. George Killing the Dragon . . .

6th Regiment. In the centre of their Colours, the Antelope being their ancient Badge and in the three Corners of their Second Colour, the Rose and Crown. On the Grenadier Caps, the Antelope . . .

7th Regiment or the Royal Fuzileers. In the centre of their Colours, the Rose within the Garter, and the Crown over it, the White Horse in the Corners of the Second Colour. On the Grenadier Caps, the Rose within the Garter and Crown . . .

8th Regiment or the King's Regiment. In the centre of their Colours the White Horse on a Red Ground within the Garter and Crown over it. In the three Corners of the Second Colour, the King's Cypher and Crown. On the Grenadier Caps, the White Horse . . .

18th Regiment or the Royal Irish. In the centre of their Colours, the Harp in a Blue Field, and the Crown over it, and in the three Corners of their Second Colour the Lyon of Nassau, King William the third's Arms. On the Grenadier Caps, the Harp and Crown . . .

21st Regiment or the Royal North British Fuzileers. In the centre of their Colours the Thistle within the Circle of St. Andrew, and Crown over it and in the three Corners of the Second Colour, the King's Cypher and Crown. On the Grenadier Caps, the Thistle . . .

23rd Regiment or the Royal Welch Fuzileers. In the centre of their Colours, the Device of the Prince of Wales, viz. three Feathers Issuing out of the Princes Coronet. In the three Corners of the Second Colour, the Badges of Edward the Black Prince, viz. Rising Sun, Red Dragon, and the three Feathers in the Coronet, Motto Ich Dien. On the Grenadier Caps the Feathers . . .

27th Regiment or the Inniskilling Regiment. Allowed to wear in the centre of their Colours a Castle with three Turretts, St. George's Colours flying in a Blue Field and the name Inniskilling over it. On the Grenadier Caps, the Castle & Name.

41st Regiment or the Invalids. In the centre of their Colours, the Rose and Thistle on a Red Ground within the Garter and Crown over it. In the three Corners of the Second Colour, the King's Cypher and Crown. On the Grenadier Caps the same device of the Rose and Thistle

conjoined within the Garter and Crown [these caps seem unusual for Invalids].
Highland Regiment. The grenadiers of the

Highland Regiment are allowed to wear Bear-Skin Fur Caps, with the King's Cypher in the Turn-up or Flap.

Appendix 2
The Royal Warrant, 1768

Extract from the Warrant dated 19 December 1768:

George R.
Our Will and Pleasure is, that the following Regulations for the colours, clothing, &c. of our marching regiments of foot, be duly observed and put in execution, at such times as the particulars are or shall be furnished.

No Colonel is to put his arms, crest, device, or livery, on any part of the appointments of the regiment under his command . . .

Uniforms of Officers. The number of each regiment to be on the buttons of the regiment of the officers and men. The coats are to be lapelled to the waist with the colour of the facing of the regiment and the colour not to be varied from what is particularly specified hereafter. They may be without embroidery or lace; but if the Colonel thinks fit, either gold or silver embroidered or laced buttonholes are permitted. To have cross pockets, and sleeves with round cuffs, and no slits: The lappels and cuffs to be of the same breadth as is ordered for the men. Epaulettes. The officers of grenadiers to wear an epaulette on each shoulder. Those of the battalion to wear one on the right shoulder. They are to be either of embroidery or lace, with gold or silver fringe.

Waistcoats. The waistcoats to be plain, without either embroidery or lace.

Swords and Sword-knots. The swords of each regiment are to be uniform, and the sword-knot of the whole to be crimson and gold in stripes. The hilts of the swords to be either gilt or silver, according to the colour of the buttons on the uniforms.

Hats. The hats to be laced either with gold or silver, as hereafter specified, and to be cocked uniformly.

Sashes and gorgets. The sashes to be of crimson silk, and worn round the waist. The King's arms to be engraved on the gorgets; also the number of the regiment. They are to be either gilt or silver, according to the colour of the buttons on the uniforms. The badges of those regiments which are entitled to any, are also to be engraved.

Caps, fuzils and pouches for grenadier officers. The officers of the grenadiers to wear black bear-skin caps; and to have fuzils, shoulder-belts and pouches. The shoulder-belts are to be

white or buff, according to the colour of their waistcoats.

Espontoons. The battalion officers to have espontoons.

Gaiters. The whole to have black linen gaiters, with black buttons, and small stiff tops, black garters and uniform buckles.

Drummers and fifers coats. The coats of the drummers and fifers of all the Royal regiments are to be red, faced and lapelled with blue, and laced with Royal lace. The waistcoats, breeches and linings of the coats, to be of the same colour as that which is ordered for their respective regiments. The coats of the drummers and fifers of those regiments which are faced with red, are to be white, faced, lapelled and lined with red; red waistcoats and breeches. Those of all other regiments are to be the colour of the facings of their regiments; faced and lapelled with red. The waistcoats, breeches and lining of those which have buff or white coats, are to be red. Those of all the others are to be of the same colour as that which is ordered for the men. To be laced in such manner as the Colonel shall think fit. The lace to be of the colour of that on the soldiers coats. The coats to have no hanging sleeves behind.

Drummers and fifers caps. The drummers and fifers to have black bear-skin caps. On the front, the King's Crest of silver plated metal on a black ground, with the trophies of colours and drums. The number of the regiment on the back part; also the badge, if entitled to any, as ordered for grenadiers.

Grenadiers caps. The caps of the grenadiers to be of black bear-skin. On the front the King's Crest of silver plated metal, on a black ground, with the motto, NEC ASPERA TERRENT. A grenade on the back part, with the number of the regiment on it. The Royal regiments and the six old corps are to have the crest and grenade and also the other particulars as hereafter specified. The badge of the Royal regiments is to be white and set on near the top of the back part of the cap. The height of the cap (without the bear-skin which reaches beyond the top) to be 12 inches.

Hats of the whole. The hats of the sergeants to be laced with silver. Those of the corporals and private men to have a white-tape binding. The breadth of the whole is to be an inch 1-4th; and no more to be on the back part of the brim, than what is necessary to sew it down. To have black cockades.

Caps for the officers and men of the regiment of fuzileers. The regiments of fuzileers are to have black bear-skin caps. They are to be made in the same manner as those which are ordered for the grenadiers, but not so high; and not to have the grenade on the back part.

Swords. All the sergeants of the regiment and the whole grenadier company, to have swords. The corporals and private men of the battalion companies (except the regiment of Royal Highlanders) to have no swords. All the drummers and fifers to have a short sword with a scimitar blade.

Gaiters. The sergeants, corporals, drummers, fifers and private men to have black gaiters of the same sort as is ordered for officers; also black garters and uniform buckles.

Pioneers. Each pioneer to have an axe, a saw and an apron; a cap with a leather crown and a black bear-skin front, on which is to be the King's crest in white, on a red ground; also an axe and a saw. The number of the regiment to be on the back part of the cap.

The specially permitted devices and badges on the grenadier caps were similar to those in 1751. For the 1st or Royal Regiment, the cap had the King's Crest with the King's Cypher within the Circle of St Andrew and the Crown above. For the 2nd or Queen's Royal Regiment, the King's Cypher and Crown as well as the King's Crest. For the 3rd or Buffs, the King's Crest and the Dragon. For the 4th or the King's Own Royal Regiment, the King's Crest and the King's Cypher and Crown. For the 5th Regiment, the King's Crest and St George killing the Dragon. For the 6th, the King's Crest and the Antelope. For the 7th or Royal Fuzileers the King's Crest and the Rose within the Garter and the Crown above. For the 8th or King's Regiment, the King's Crest and the White Horse. For the 18th or Royal Irish, the King's Crest and the Harp and Crown. For the 21st or Royal North British Fuzileers, the King's Crest and the Thistle. For the 23rd or Royal Welch Fuzileers, the King's Crest and the 'Feathers' of the Prince of Wales. For the 27th or Inniskilling Regiment, the King's Crest and the Castle of Inniskilling with the name. For the 41st or Invalids, the King's Crest and the Rose and Thistle. For the 42nd or Royal Highlanders, the King's Crest and St Andrew while the 60th or Royal Americans had the King's Crest with the King's Cypher and Crown.

Appendix 3

Regiments and their facings before and after 1881

	Title pre-1881	Facings	Title post-1881	Facings
1st	(The Royal Scots)	blue	1st & 2nd Bns. The Royal Scots (Lothian) Regiment	blue
2nd	(Queen's Royal)	blue	1st & 2nd Bns. The Queen's (Royal West Surrey Regiment)	blue
3rd	(East Kent, The Buffs)	buff	1st & 2nd Bns. The Buffs (East Kent Regiment)	white
4th	(King's Own Royal)	blue	1st & 2nd Bns. The King's Own (Royal Lancaster Regiment)	blue
5th	(Northumberland Fusiliers)	bright green	1st & 2nd Bns. The Northumberland Fusiliers	white
6th	(Royal 1st Warwickshire)	blue	1st & 2nd Bns. The Royal Warwickshire Regiment	blue
7th	(Royal Fusiliers)	blue	1st & 2nd Bns. The Royal Fusiliers (City of London Regiment)	blue
8th	(The King's)	blue	1st & 2nd Bns. The King's (Liverpool Regiment)	blue
9th	(East Norfolk)	yellow	1st & 2nd Bns. The Norfolk Regiment	white
10th	(North Lincoln)	yellow	1st & 2nd Bns. The Lincoln Regiment	white
11th	(North Devonshire)	lincoln green	1st & 2nd Bns. The Devonshire Regiment	white
12th	(East Suffolk)	yellow	1st & 2nd Bns. The Suffolk Regiment	white
13th	(1st Somersetshire) (Prince Albert's Light Infantry)	blue	1st & 2nd Bns. The Prince Albert's (Somerset Light Infantry)	blue
14th	(Buckinghamshire) (Prince of Wales's Own)	buff	1st & 2nd Bns. The Prince of Wales's Own (West Yorkshire Regiment)	white
15th	(York, East Riding)	yellow	1st & 2nd Bns. The East Yorkshire Regiment	white
16th	(Bedfordshire)	yellow	1st & 2nd Bns. The Bedfordshire Regiment	white
17th	(Leicestershire)	white	1st & 2nd Bns. The Leicestershire Regiment	white

Title pre-1881	*Facings*	*Title post-1881*	*Facings*
18th (The Royal Irish)	blue	1st & 2nd Bns. The Royal Irish Regiment	blue
19th (1st Yorks, North Riding) (Princess of Wales's Own)	grass green	1st & 2nd Bns. The Princess of Wales's Own (Yorkshire Regiment)	white
20th (East Devonshire)	yellow	1st & 2nd Bns. The Lancashire Fusiliers	white
21st (Royal Scots Fusiliers)	blue	1st & 2nd Bns. The Royal Scots Fusiliers	blue
22nd (Cheshire)	buff	1st & 2nd Bns. The Cheshire Regiment	white
23rd (Royal Welsh Fusiliers)	blue	1st & 2nd Bns. The Royal Welsh Fusiliers	blue
24th (2nd Warwickshire)	grass green	1st & 2nd Bns. The South Wales Borderers	white
25th (King's Own Borderers)	blue	1st & 2nd Bns. The King's Own Borderers	blue
26th (Cameronian)	yellow	1st Bn. The Cameronians (Scottish Rifles)	dark green
27th (Inniskilling)	buff	1st Bn. The Royal Inniskilling Fusiliers	blue
28th (North Gloucestershire)	yellow	1st Bn. The Gloucestershire Regiment	white
29th (Worcestershire)	yellow	1st Bn. The Worcestershire Regiment	white
30th (Cambridgeshire)	yellow	1st Bn. The East Lancashire Regiment	white
31st (Huntingdonshire)	buff	1st Bn. The East Surrey Regiment	white
32nd (Cornwall) (Light Infantry)	white	1st Bn. The Duke of Cornwall's Light Infantry	white
33rd (Duke of Wellington's Regiment)	scarlet	1st Bn. The Duke of Wellington's (West Riding Regiment)	white
34th (Cumberland)	yellow	1st Bn. The Border Regiment	white
35th (Royal Sussex)	blue	1st Bn. The Royal Sussex Regiment	blue
36th (Herefordshire)	grass green	2nd Bn. The Worcestershire Regiment	white
37th (North Hampshire)	yellow	1st Bn. The Hampshire Regiment	white
38th (1st Staffordshire)	yellow	1st Bn. The South Staffordshire Regiment	white
39th (Dorsetshire)	grass green	1st Bn. The Dorsetshire Regiment	white
40th (2nd Somersetshire)	buff	1st Bn. The Prince of Wales's Volunteers (South Lancashire Regiment)	white
41st (The Welsh)	white	1st Bn. The Welsh Regiment	white
42nd (Royal Highland, the Black Watch)	blue	1st Bn. The Black Watch (Royal Highlanders)	blue
43rd (Monmouthshire Light Infantry)	white	1st Bn. The Oxfordshire Light Infantry	white
44th (East Essex)	yellow	1st Bn. The Essex Regiment	white
45th (Nottinghamshire) (Sherwood Foresters)	lincoln green	1st Bn. The Sherwood Foresters (Derbyshire Regiment)	white
46th (South Devonshire)	yellow	2nd Bn. The Duke of Cornwall's Light Infantry	white
47th (Lancashire)	white	1st Bn. The Loyal North Lancashire Regiment	white
48th (Northamptonshire)	buff	1st Bn. The Northamptonshire Regiment	white
49th (Hertfordshire) (Princess Charlotte of Wales's)	lincoln green	1st Bn. The Princess Charlotte of Wales's (Berkshire Regiment)	blue
50th (Queen's Own)	blue	1st Bn. The Queen's Own (Kent Regiment)	blue
51st (2nd Yorkshire, West Riding, King's Own Light Infantry)	blue	1st Bn. The King's Own (Light Infantry) (South Yorkshire)	blue
52nd (Oxfordshire) (Light Infantry)	buff	2nd Bn. The Oxfordshire Light Infantry	white
53rd (Shropshire)	scarlet	1st Bn. The King's (Shropshire Light Infantry)	blue
54th (West Norfolk)	grass green	2nd Bn. The Dorset Regiment	white
55th (Westmoreland)	lincoln green	2nd Bn. The Border Regiment	white
56th (West Essex)	purple	2nd Bn. The Essex Regiment	white
57th (West Middlesex)	yellow	1st Bn. The Duke of Cambridge's Own (Middlesex Regiment)	white
58th (Rutlandshire)	black	2nd Bn. The Northamptonshire Regiment	white
59th (2nd Nottinghamshire)	white	2nd Bn. The East Lancashire Regiment	white
60th (King's Royal Rifle Corps)	scarlet	The King's Royal Rifle Corps	scarlet
61st (South Gloucestershire)	buff	2nd Bn. The Gloucestershire Regiment	white
62nd (Wiltshire)	buff	1st Bn. The Duke of Edinburgh's (Wiltshire Regiment)	white
63rd (West Suffolk)	lincoln green	1st Bn. The Manchester Regiment	white
64th (2nd Staffordshire)	black	1st Bn. The Prince of Wales's (North Staffordshire Regiment)	white
65th (2nd Yorkshire, North Riding)	white	1st Bn. The York & Lancashire Regiment	white
66th (Berkshire)	grass green	2nd Bn. The Princess Charlotte of Wales's (Berkshire Regiment)	blue
67th (South Hampshire)	yellow	2nd Bn. The Hampshire Regiment	white
68th (Durham) (Light Infantry)	dark green	1st Bn. The Durham Light Infantry	white
69th (South Lincolnshire)	lincoln green	2nd Bn. The Welsh Regiment	white
70th (Surrey)	black	2nd Bn. The East Surrey Regiment	white
71st (Highland) (Light Infantry)	buff	1st Bn. The Highland Light Infantry	yellow
72nd (Duke of Albany's Own Highlanders)	yellow	1st Bn. Seaforth Highlanders (Ross-shire Buffs, the Duke of Albany's)	yellow
73rd (Perthshire)	dark green	2nd Bn. The Black Watch (Royal Highlanders)	blue
74th (Highlanders)	white	2nd Bn. The Highland Light Infantry	yellow
75th (Stirlingshire)	yellow	1st Bn. The Gordon Highlanders	yellow

Title pre-1881	Facings	Title post-1881	Facings
76th	scarlet	2nd Bn. The Duke of Wellington's (West Riding Regiment)	white
77th (East Middlesex)	yellow	2nd Bn. The Duke of Cambridge's Own (Middlesex Regiment)	white
78th (Highlanders) (Ross-shire Buffs)	buff	2nd Bn. The Seaforth Highlanders (Ross-shire Buffs, The Duke of Albany's)	yellow
79th (Queen's Own Cameron Highlanders)	blue	The Queen's Own Cameron Highlanders	blue
80th (Staffordshire Volunteers)	yellow	2nd Bn. The South Staffordshire Regiment	white
81st (Loyal Lincoln Volunteers)	buff	2nd Bn. The Loyal North Lancashire Regiment	white
82nd (Prince of Wales's Volunteers)	yellow	2nd Bn. The Prince of Wales's Volunteers (South Lancashire Regiment)	white
83rd (County of Dublin)	yellow	1st Bn. The Royal Irish Rifles	dark green
84th (York and Lancaster)	yellow	2nd Bn. The York and Lancaster Regiment	white
85th (Bucks Volunteers) (King's Light Infantry)	blue	2nd Bn. The King's (Shropshire Light Infantry)	blue
86th (Royal County Down)	blue	2nd Bn. The Royal Irish Rifles	dark green
87th (Royal Irish Fusiliers)	blue	1st Bn. The Princess Victoria's (Royal Irish Fusiliers)	blue
88th (Connaught Rangers)	yellow	1st Bn. The Connaught Rangers	green
89th (Princess Victoria's)	black	2nd Bn. The Princess Victoria's (Royal Irish Fusiliers)	blue
90th (Perthshire Volunteers) (Light Infantry)	buff	2nd Bn. The Cameronians (Scottish Rifles)	dark green
91st (Princess Louise's Argyllshire Highlanders)	yellow	1st Bn. Princess Louise's (Sutherland and Argyll Highlanders)	yellow
92nd (Gordon Highlanders)	yellow	2nd Bn. The Gordon Highlanders	yellow
93rd (Sutherland Highlanders)	yellow	2nd Bn. The Princess Louise's (Sutherland and Argyll Highlanders)	yellow
94th	lincoln green	2nd Bn. The Connaught Rangers	green
95th (Derbyshire)	yellow	2nd Bn. The Sherwood Foresters (Derbyshire Regiment)	white
96th	yellow	2nd Bn. The Manchester Regiment	white
97th (Earl of Ulster's)	sky blue	2nd Bn. The Queen's Own (Royal West Kent Regiment)	blue
98th (Prince of Wales's)	white	2nd Bn. The Prince of Wales's (North Staffordshire Regiment)	white
99th (Duke of Edinburgh's)	yellow	2nd Bn. The Duke of Edinburgh's (Wiltshire Regiment)	white
100th (or Prince of Wales's Canadian)	blue	1st Bn. The Prince of Wales's Leinster Regiment (Royal Canadians)	blue
101st (Royal Bengal Fusiliers)	blue	1st Bn. The Royal Munster Fusiliers	blue
102nd (Royal Madras Fusiliers)	blue	1st Bn. The Dublin Fusiliers	blue
103rd (Royal Bombay Fusiliers)	blue	2nd Bn. The Royal Dublin Fusiliers	blue
104th (Bengal Fusiliers)	dark blue	2nd Bn. The Royal Munster Fusiliers	blue
105th (Madras Light Infantry)	buff	2nd Bn. The King's Own (Yorkshire Light Infantry)	blue
106th (Bombay Light Infantry)	white	2nd Bn. The Durham Light Infantry	white
107th (Bengal Infantry)	white	2nd Bn. The Royal Sussex Regiment	blue
108th (Madras Infantry)	pale yellow	2nd Bn. The Royal Inniskilling Fusiliers	blue
109th (Bombay Infantry)	white	2nd Bn. The Prince of Wales's Leinster Regiment (Royal Canadians)	blue
Rifle Brigade (The Prince Consort's Own)	black	The Rifle Brigade (The Prince Consort's Own)	black

Glossary

aiguillette a plaited cord with hanging needles, aiglets or points of various designs worn on the chest by staff officers, originally intended to clear touch-hole of pistol.

Albert chaco a cylindrical head-dress of the time of Prince Albert worn *c*. 1844 to the Crimean War.

anklet protections to go around the lower leg of leather or canvas.

apron usually of leather, for drummers or pioneers to protect garment.

Austrian knot an elaborate knot of cord or braid worn in the cuffs.

badge a mark of distinction covering many patterns, either of royal origin or regimental device. Also to mark trade, occupation or rank.

ball-tuft a ball of wool or cotton worn on a shako in varying colours to denote units, company or special distinction.

balmoral a Scottish bonnet usually of blue.

bandolier a shoulder-belt to hold ammunition.

bastion-shaped the pointed loop around a buttonhole which also swelled before reaching the sharp end.

beard not normally an Army distinction but permitted for pioneers and bagpipers.

bearskin the fur caps worn by Foot Guards, grenadiers and sometimes by fusiliers.

bell the open piece of metal to hold the tassel on a sporran.

bell-shaped the shape that a wide-topped shako took after 1816.

belted plaid the early plaid which was held in place by a belt in the middle.

belt-plate the metal plate which fastened a waist- or shoulder-belt.

bicorn/bicorne a hat with two corners or points, a cocked hat.

black-cock feather worn by Scottish regiments in the head-dress.

bombardier a junior non-commissioned officer in the artillery.

bonnet a Scottish cap of thick cloth or woollen, of various styles.

booting the strengthening on the cuffs and inner sides of overalls usually of leather.

boxed epaulette an epaulette of which the bullion or fringe has been fixed instead of hanging freely.

boss a circular cord ornament worn on head-dress. Also an ear-boss on head-dress.

braid woven material to strengthen brim of hat, or for buttonholes and elsewhere on coats. In metal wire for officers (also called lace).

breeches nether-garments which finished at the knees worn until replaced by trousers or overalls.

broadsword a sword with a broad blade and an enclosed hilt carried by Highlanders (not a claymore, which had a cross hilt).

brodrick an undress cap introduced in 1902 for other ranks, getting its nickname from Sir John Brodrick, Secretary of State for War.

bullion gold and silver wire or ribbon made into a hollow spiral. Used on officers' epaulettes and other parts of uniform.

busby name given to fur caps after maker, W. Busby of the Strand, London.

button for other ranks, made of brass, pewter or composition; for officers, of silver or gold.

cap a head covering without a brim but could have a peak, of many materials and fashions.

cap-lines lines or cords tied or fastened to a cap and the body to prevent loss if fallen from the head.

cartridge box a container attached to a belt to hold ammunition.

chaco a shako, but so-named later in Victorian times.

chin-scales the metal scales on the strap of a head-dress to go under the chin.

chin-strap a strap of leather, etc., sometimes with chain links.

clothing in military parlance, normally refers to other ranks' uniforms as opposed to 'dress' of officers.

coat an upper garment of many sizes and fashions usually with material below the waist.

coatee an upper garment which has the skirts cut away in front leaving tails behind or a simple back.

cocked hat a hat which has the brim turned up in one or more places.

cord round cord of various colours and material for head-dress and body garments.

crows-foot cord or braid made in three loops as decoration on garments.

cuff originally the turned-back sleeve, but later facing sewn on lower sleeve in distinctive shape.

cypher initials or letters in cursive fashion linked together to make a special device.

device a design or figure often with a military connection but not always.

dicing   a pattern made of small squares, as in the case of the band on Highland head-dress.

doublet   originally a civilian garment but popular among Scots having special skirts or flaps.

dress   in the military usage applies mainly to officers and can cover full dress, mess dress and State dress.

Dress Regulations   special regulations or books issued to cover the dress of officers.

embroidery   special needlework in silk or in metal thread on officers' garments.

Enniskillin   this is officially Inniskilling in military titles.

ensign   the most junior infantry commissioned officer who carried the ensign or regimental colour.

epaulette   from the French meaning 'shoulder', an ornamental strap usually with fringe, bullion and/or embroidered devices.

equipment   with regards to the soldier this relates to the personal items like belts, pouches, etc. carried by him.

eyes   braid, cord or embroidery made in small circles were known as eyes.

facings   coats could be lined with a plain material to make them better fitting, but a stronger material could be used as a facing and being a different colour made a regimental distinction.

fatigue dress   the dress worn during menial duties could be fatigue or undress.

feather   a single feather could be worn in the head-dress as in the Highland regiments but later more than one feather was used. See hackle.

feathering   when material was sewn between the seams, this was the term used.

Feathers   the feathers or plumes used in the crest of the Prince of Wales were often just known as the Feathers.

festoon   an elaborately plaited cord with tassels on a shako.

field officer   in a regiment the major, lieutenant-colonel and colonel were so named as the others were company officers.

flank company   on either side of the battalion companies could be grenadier or light companies.

flap   a piece of material to keep the cuff in position but also refers to the patches on the back of coat or tunic.

flash   the ends of the ribbon to keep the queue in order were retained by the Royal Welsh Fusiliers as an ornament on the back of the collar.

fleur-de-lys   this emblem from the French coat-of-arms is part of the drummers' lace of the Foot Guards. The Manchester Regiment also wore it as a badge.

fly-plaid   this type of plaid was attached to the left shoulder to hang freely.

forage cap   a small undress cap to be worn on non-ceremonial occasions.

fringe   this thin twisted material in metal hung from junior officers' epaulettes. Also used by drummers in various colours.

frock   a body garment for non-ceremonial occasions in various materials and shapes.

gaiters   needed in early days to protect hose, later worn with overalls or to the knee with breeches.

gaiter-trousers   tight-fitting trousers which finished with buttons on the lower leg.

gauntlet-cuff   cuff on Scottish doublet which was open at the back.

gauntlets   gloves with high upper parts worn by pioneers and some musicians.

glengarry   Scottish woollen bonnet folded with red toorie and ribbons.

gorget   the first piece of armour to be put on and the last to be removed when a cuirass was worn in ancient days; became the mark of an officer.

gorget-patch   cloth pieces on collar where gorget ribbons had been fastened, denoting high rank or special duties.

hackle   short feathers attached to a stem, cut or 'hacked' to shape.

halbert/halberd   a long staved weapon with a metal head having a broad cutting edge on one side and a hook on the other, carried by sergeants of infantry up to 1790.

hanging-sleeve   the hanging sleeves of the ancient doublet were continued on musicians to emphasize peaceful intentions.

hat   a head-covering with a brim all round of leather, felt or other material.

Highland dress   the Black Watch in 1739 brought the plaid and Scots bonnet into the British Army with other Highland articles.

holes   these referred to the buttonholes in military garments.

hummel   the 'hummel' or humble bonnet was Scottish and gradually changed shape.

jacket   from 'jack', a small coat worn by light infantry and on service.

jam-pot cuff   a simple round cuff without decoration.

Kilmarnock   a town in Scotland where bonnets were made for the British Army. The name was given first to a simple bonnet, and later to a full-dress version.

kilt   a pleated garment made of tartan and from a waistband.

knapsack   a bag or sack to carry items needed by a soldier in the field.

knee-apron   aprons worn by side-drummers on the left leg.

knot could be a simple design like the Austrian knot on the sleeve, but also a thick twisted cord of metal threads on officers' shoulders.

lace a term for military braid often with a pattern, for officers in gold or silver thread, for men and drummers in coloured threads or plain colours on the body garments.

lambskin used as horse furniture but also in busbies of riflemen.

lapel/lappel turned-back material on front of coat, somewhat like revers.

levée an evening function at which special uniforms were worn.

lining the material inside a garment to make ease of wear and as a protection.

loop in military use covered many special features, like the braid around a buttonhole, the arrangement of cords on the chest or cuffs and the ribbons of a gorget which 'looped' over collar buttons.

Lowlander in the British Army, meaning a soldier from the Lowlands of Scotland, as opposed to the Highlands.

marine a soldier who served at sea on ships and part of the Army until 1748.

match twisted material which was ignited to detonate gunpowder.

matross an artillery man ranking lower than a gunner.

musician a soldier playing a musical instrument to make melody, not for signals or calls.

number in regiments the number indicated the rank or precedence and appeared in badges and insignia.

olivets thread-covered shapes or moulds worn instead of buttons.

overalls originally intended to go over breeches and to reach to the ankle but later became garments in their own right, like trousers.

Oxford mixture a dark grey mixture of cloth, usually for trousers.

pantaloon originally a nether-garment of breeches and stockings combined, but later called pants and at one time applied to breeches worn by horse-riders.

pelisse an upper jacket to be worn in bad weather, often slung from the left shoulder.

pioneer soldier who undertook labouring tasks and wore traditional dress.

piping the coloured edging or stripes on garments or caps.

plastron broad piece of material on chest, from Italian '*piastra*', a breast-plate.

plate a piece of metal to fasten a belt or as ornament on head-dress.

plume a feather or hair on head-dress, but also under throat of horse.

pompon French for the tuft on a head-dress.

popinjay a parrot or woodpecker, of which the green colour was a facing colour.

pot the simple metal helmet worn by pikemen.

pugri/pagri/puggaree cloth or a scarf wound round the head or a tropical head-dress.

purse the sporran of highlanders.

puttees/putties cloth worn around the legs to cover the top of the boots to prevent dust or mud entering the footwear.

queue the bound back hair of a soldier.

quillons the cross-bars on a sword.

racoon a skin used at one time for fusilier caps.

Regency shako shako worn during the Regency of George, later George IV.

reversed facings term referring to coat where the facings are the main colour.

rose may be the pattern of lace or the ornament on side of helmet.

Royal Regiment regiment which has a royal commander or colonel.

Russia braid a narrow braid used in tracing and embroidery.

sabretache an ornamental pouch hanging near the sword, originally worn because no pockets were possible in the tight breeches.

sash when worn by officers and sergeants was in the national colour worn over the shoulder or around the waist.

scarf worn by drum-majors of the Foot Guard in State clothing. Had been worn by officers in seventeenth century.

schako/tschako spelling for shako before taken into British Army.

seal or sealed pattern an article approved by the Board of Ordnance and sealed with wax.

sealskin worn by riflemen for their full-dress caps.

serpent wooden wind instrument with many curves like a serpent.

service dress dress worn on service and in action, non-ceremonial.

shako/chaco a head-dress from the Magyar *czak*, indicating a peak.

shalloon a cloth used for lining, originally used in Châlon France.

shamrock pattern of lace for Irish regiments.

shawl worn by Irish pipers.

sheepskin or lambskins, worn by mounted officer over saddlery.

shoulder-cords gold cords worn by officers after 1880 to carry rank badges.

shoulder-knot worn in the early eighteenth century to keep the sword-belt in place.

shoulder-plaid after the plaid was divided into the kilt, the upper part hung from the shoulder.

skean dhu small knife carried by Highlanders in the hose.

sphinx/sphynx for fighting in Egypt many regiments were granted the badge of the sphinx which indicated that service.

spontoon/espontoon a long staved weapon with a metal spike-head carried by officers up to about 1775. The sergeant's halbert was replaced in 1791 by a spontoon and carried until 1830.

sporran the Scottish purse worn on the kilt.

stock worn around the neck of a soldier of leather or cloth, replaced in the nineteenth century by a black cloth tab.

strapping the extra material added to cavalry nether-wear to give strength.

sword-knot a strip of leather or material attached to the hilt of a sword, the loop of which went over the wrist to prevent loss.

tails the long portions of a coat or coatee at the back.

tam-o-shanter broad-topped Scottish bonnet with toorie.

target the shape of lace on front of shako after Waterloo.

Tarleton name given to the light dragoon head-dress, also worn by light infantry.

tartan a type of weave, not necessarily in Scottish colourings.

tassels ornaments used on cords of head-dress and on sporrans.

thistle a pattern used to indicate Scottish regiments, also in badges.

throat-plume a hair plume hung underneath a horse-neck in regimental colours.

ticking a striped cotton or linen material used for lining or trousers in warm climates.

time-beater applied to the coloured men attached to bands, not regimental drummers.

toorie/tourie the short ends (or bobble) on the top of a Scottish bonnet.

Tower indicates the Tower of London, the arsenal or storehouse of the British Army.

trews the Scottish name for trousers; if in tartan, sometimes cut on bias.

tricorn/tricorne a three-cornered hat.

trophy originally the spoils of war but later a design showing militant articles.

trousers loose nether-garments reaching to the ankles.

tuft may be ball of head-dress, thick fringe on some shoulder-straps, or the rosettes of gorget ribbons.

tunic a body garment with skirts all round, replacing the tailed coatee.

turn-backs the front skirts of the coat or the front opening on chest.

under-garments worn under coat like waistcoat and breeches.

undress clothing for fatigues and informal occasions.

uniform dress of both officer and men in the Army.

velvet material occasionally used for officers' facings or trimmings.

waist-belt to support weapons, later as distinction.

Waterloo shako retrospectively so-named, worn 1812–15.

white metal could be silver or other metal.

wings ornaments on shoulders for flank companies.

yellow metal could be gold or other yellow-coloured metal.

Bibliography

Prime Sources

A Representation of the Cloathing of His Majesty's Household and of all the Forces upon the Establishment of Great Britain and Ireland, 1742

Oil-paintings by David Morier of the British Army, *c.* 1750, in the Royal Collection, Windsor

Royal warrants, General and Army Orders, clothing regulations and letters in the Public Records Office and the old War Office Library

Uniforms of Infantry according to the King's Regulations of 19 December 1768

Printed Dress Regulations (of Officers) from 1822 to 1934

Charles Hamilton Smith, drawings and prints from 1800 to 1815

Various tailors' books: W. Jones and Co., Herbert, etc., *c.* 1808–*c.* 1850

Various lace-makers' books: Webb, Bullmore and Patrick, etc., *c.* 1815–1843

Army Lists from 1740 to present day

Secondary Sources

Campbell, D. A., *Dress of the Royal Artillery*, London, 1971

Cannon, R., *Many Official Regimental Histories, 1837–c. 1850*

Chichester, H. and Burgess-Short, G., *The Records & Badges of every Regiment & Corps in the British Army*, London, 1900

Connolly, T. W. J., *History of the Royal Sappers and Miners*, London, 1855

Hamilton, F. W., *History of the Grenadier Guards*, London, 1874

Macdonald, R. J., *History of the Dress of the Royal Regiment of Artillery*, London, 1899

MacKinnon, D., *The Origin and Services of the Coldstream Guards*, London, 1833

Massé, C. H., *The Predecessors of the Royal Army Service Corps 1757–1888*, Aldershot, 1948

Maurice, F., *History of the Scots Guards 1642–1914*, London, 1934

Parkyn, H. G., *Shoulder-belt Plates & Buttons*, Aldershot, 1956

Porter, W., *History of the Corps of Royal Engineers*, London and New York, 1889

Walton, C., *History of the British Standing Army AD 1661–1700*, London, 1874

Journals of the Society for Army Historical Research, 1921 to present day

Army Museums Ogilby Trust, *Index to British Military Costume Prints 1500, 1914*, London, 1972

Many regimental histories and records of infantry, including such works as A. N. E. Browne's *Notes on the Dress of the 71st Regiment*, have been consulted for organization, changes, etc., but most uniform details have been taken from primary sources in the Public Records Office, the War Office Library, the Royal United Services Institute, the Victoria and Albert Museum, the National Army Museum and regimental museums, collected over some fifty years.

My thanks and appreciation are given to the staff of these establishments who have helped me so much in the past.

Index

Note: Items of dress that are mentioned frequently throughout the text are not listed, nor are pages with plates, for which page 7 should be consulted